Children, Health and Well-being

Sociology of Health and Illness Monograph Series

Edited by Professor Ian Rees Jones
Cardiff School of Social Sciences
WISERD
46 Park Place
Cardiff
CF10 3BB
Wales, UK

Current titles

Children, Health and Well-being: Policy Debates and Lived Experience
edited by *Geraldine Brady, Pam Lowe and Sonja Olin Lauritzen*

From Health Behaviours to Health Practices: Critical Perspectives
edited by *Simon Cohn*

Pandemics and Emerging Infectious Diseases: The Sociological Agenda
edited by *Robert Dingwall, Lily M Hoffman and Karen Staniland*

The Sociology of Medical Screening: Critical Perspectives, New Directions (2012)
edited by *Natalie Armstrong and Helen Eborall*

Body Work in Health and Social Care: Critical Themes, New Agendas (2011)
edited by *Julia Twigg, Carol Wolkowitz, Rachel Lara Cohen and Sarah Nettleton*

Technogenarians: Studying Health and Illness Through an Ageing, Science, and Technology Lens (2010)
edited by *Kelly Joyce and Meika Loe*

Communication in Healthcare Settings: Policy, Participation and New Technologies (2009)
edited by *Alison Pilnick, Jon Hindmarsh and Virginia Teas Gill*

Pharmaceuticals and Society: Critical Discourses and Debates (2009)
edited by *Simon J. Williams, Jonathan Gabe and Peter Davis*

Ethnicity, Health and Health Care: Understanding Diversity, Tackling Disadvantage (2008)
edited by *Waqar I. U. Ahmad and Hannah Bradby*

The View From Here: Bioethics and the Social Sciences (2007)
edited by *Raymond de Vries, Leigh Turner, Kristina Orfali and Charles Bosk*

The Social Organisation of Healthcare Work (2006)
edited by *Davina Allen and Alison Pilnick*

Social Movements in Health (2005)
edited by *Phil Brown and Stephen Zavestoski*

Health and the Media (2004)
edited by *Clive Seale*

Partners in Health, Partners in Crime: Exploring the boundaries of criminology and sociology of health and illness (2003)
edited by *Stefan Timmermans and Jonathan Gabe*

Rationing: Constructed Realities and Professional Practices (2002)
edited by *David Hughes and Donald Light*

Rethinking the Sociology of Mental Health (2000)
edited by *Joan Busfield*

Sociological Perspectives on the New Genetics (1999)
edited by *Peter Conrad and Jonathan Gabe*

The Sociology of Health Inequalities (1998)
edited by *Mel Bartley, David Blane and George Davey Smith*

The Sociology of Medical Science (1997)
edited by *Mary Ann Elston*

Health and the Sociology of Emotion (1996)
edited by *Veronica James and Jonathan Gabe*

Medicine, Health and Risk (1995)
edited by *Jonathan Gabe*

Children, Health and Well-being
Policy Debates and Lived Experience

Edited by

Geraldine Brady, Pam Lowe and Sonja Olin Lauritzen

Library of Congress Cataloging-in-Publication data is available for this book.

ISBN 9781119069515 (paperback)

A catalogue record for this book is available from the British Library.

Set in 9.5/11.5pt TimesNewRomanMTStd by Aptara Inc., New Delhi, India
Printed and bound in Malaysia by Vivar Printing Sdn Bhd

1   2015

Contents

Notes on contributors

Geraldine Brady Centre for Communities and Social Justice, Coventry University, UK

Pam Lowe School of Languages and Social Sciences, Aston University, UK

Sonja Olin Lauritzen Department of Education, Stockholm University, Sweden

Disa Bergnehr Department of Child Studies, Linköping University, Sweden

Karin Zetterqvist Nelson Department of Child Studies, Linköping University, Sweden

Ellie Lee SSPSSR Cornwallis Building, University of Kent, UK

Jan Macvarish CHSS, University of Kent, UK

Gillian M. Martin Department of Sociology, University of Malta, Malta

Stephanie A. Alexander School of Public Health, l'Université de Montréal, Canada

Caroline Fusco Faculty of Kinesiology and Physical Education, University of Toronto, Canada

Katherine L. Frohlich Institut de recherche en santé publique de l'Université de Montréal, University of Montréal, Canada

Terese Wilhelmsen Norwegian Centre for Child Research, Norwegian University of Science and Technology, Norway

Randi Dyblie Nilsen Norwegian Centre for Child Research, Norwegian University of Science and Technology, Norway

Lise Mogensen Medical Education Unit, School of Medicine, University of Western Sydney, Australia

Jan Mason School of Social Sciences and Psychology, University of Western Sydney, Australia

Sarah Bernays London School of Hygiene and Tropical Medicine, UK

Janet Seeley London School of Hygiene and Tropical Medicine, UK and MRC/UVRI Uganda Research Unit on AIDS, Uganda

Tim Rhodes London School of Hygiene and Tropical Medicine, UK

viii   Notes on contributors

Zivai Mupambireyi   Centre for Sexual Health and HIV/AIDS Research, Zimbabwe and University College, London, UK

Marie-Louise Stjerna   Södertörn University, School of Culture and Education, Sweden

Laura Jenkins   University of Sheffield, UK

Berry Mayall   Social Science Research Unit, UCL Institute of Education, University of London, UK

1

Connecting a sociology of childhood perspective with the study of child health, illness and wellbeing: introduction
Geraldine Brady, Pam Lowe and Sonja Olin Lauritzen

The health and wellbeing of children and young people has been studied from a range of different perspectives in social science and the health sciences as a whole. Much of the research to date has been for or on children and has focused on promoting health, detecting illness and its causes or investigating the social determinants of health. While these make vital contributions to making the world better for children and young people, we would argue there is also a need for research with children, research from a child perspective, to fully understand the meaning and impact of health and illness in children's lives. Furthermore, there is a need to explore the social and cultural contexts of child health that frame the lived experiences of children and their parents. More specifically, there is a need to interrogate the explicit as well as the implicit perceptions of childhood and the child in health policy, perceptions that are reproduced in various health and social practices. The purpose of this issue is to contribute to a further understanding of these issues by bridging developments in the sociology of childhood and the sociology of health and illness.

In the last decades we have seen a growing interest across disciplines in research on children's own experiences and understandings of health and illness. It can be argued that this increasing interest has been stimulated by developments in the sociology of childhood. Through the 1990s a body of work emerged which criticised dominant notions of child development where children were largely depicted as immature and passive objects of socialisation (Burman 1994, Halldén 1991, James and Prout 1997, Qvortrup 1994).

Scholars of the sociology of childhood problematised these notions of the child by theorising the ways in which childhood is socially constructed and understandings of the child vary across different sociocultural contexts. Importantly, the focus was shifted from seeing children as immature becomings on their way to adulthood to a focus on children as beings and as competent actors with a social agency of their own, not only influenced by but also influencing their social worlds (James et al. 1998, James and Prout 1997, Qvortrup 1994). Moreover, by understanding children as a specific social group, attention could be directed at children's rights and the structures that enabled and restricted control over their lives (Alanen and Mayall 2001).

Since these early years, the theoretical positions and central concepts in the sociology of childhood (and its place in sociology) have been, and are, debated (see, for example, Alanen 2014, James 2010, Moran-Ellis 2010). At the same time, empirical studies of children and childhoods have been burgeoning in sociology and in other disciplines. Although a full account of these developments and disciplinary differences falls outside the scope of this

Children, Health and Well-being: Policy Debates and Lived Experience, First Edition. Edited by Geraldine Brady, Pam Lowe and Sonja Olin Lauritzen. Chapters © 2015 The Authors. Book Compilation © 2015 Foundation for the Sociology of Health & Illness/Blackwell Publishing Ltd.

issue, here we want to draw attention to some of the central concepts and theoretical points of departure in this tradition that we find of particular interest for studies of child health and wellbeing.

Firstly, seeing children as a social (minority) group draws our attention to the ways this group is placed and perceived in the structures of societies. Children as a social group need to be understood in relation to other social groups. Importantly, work on children as positioned in intergenerational relations has added to understanding of the dynamics in relations between children, parents and adult society (Mayall 1996, 1998). This involves power relations and the ways children (as a group) are listened to and taken account of in different social settings, such as in healthcare settings and at school, but also prevailing discourses and images of the child in social and health policy and health promotion interventions addressing children and young people.

Secondly, understanding children as social agents and as co-constructors of their social worlds is fundamental to studying their experiences and ways of dealing with health and wellbeing in everyday life. Child agency is a core issue in the sociology of childhood, but it has also been debated in this tradition in recent years. Agency is not to be seen as just something positive, or a personal competence, but as a more complex and multidimensional concept (Valentine 2011). Children's agency is bounded by and in intergenerational relations as well as in wider socioeconomic contexts and bodily, social and material resources. This raises questions about whose actions should impact on whom (Tisdall and Punch 2012). Power and participation are situated and changeable, which calls for attention to how children's agency is perceived, facilitated and restrained in specific settings.

Thirdly, in recent years, there has been a turn towards seeing children as beings (not just becomings). However, it is also argued that all humans are becomings; subjects who develop and change as they experience the world and in relation to different social contexts (Lee 2001, 2005, Prout 2005, Uprichard 2008). Further, there is an issue with diversity and variation in children's lives. There is no typical child. Children are of different ages, gender, ethnicity, socioeconomic circumstances and capacity. They live in different national and cultural contexts and attend different educational institutions. Thus, they are subject to different structures and discourses on children and childhoods (Prout 2005). Increasingly, conceptualisations of the child that homogenise and decontextualise children and their lives are being viewed as problematic (see, for example, Singal and Muthukrishna, 2014).

We argue that there is a need to reflect more broadly on learning from the sociology of childhood in research on child health. This tradition is now well established and there is much evidence to indicate that children are competent social actors, yet we are in agreement with Tisdall and Punch when they state that:

> Focusing on children and young people's perspectives, agency and participation is no longer sufficient; greater emphasis is needed on the intricacies, complexities, tensions, ambiguities and ambivalences of children and young people's lives across both Majority and Minority World contexts. (2012: 22)

These issues also raise questions about research methodology. The risk of homogenising and decontextualising children also applies to the context of research on children's lives. If it is important to do research with children, how do we locate children at the centre of knowledge production? How can we access children's perspectives and lived experience? One avenue suggested is to use a range of methods to take account of diversity between children (see, for example, Christensen and James 2000) or to involve children as actors in research as a way to overcome the power imbalance between the child and the researcher (Alderson 2000,

Mason and Hood 2011) which, however, might create new methodological problems (Harden *et al.* 2000). On the other hand, whether research with children is necessarily different from research with adults is also being questioned. 'If children are competent social actors, why are special "child-friendly methods" needed to communicate with them?' (Punch 2002: 321). These, and other methodological issues are part and parcel of research with children and need to be addressed to obtain a child's perspective on health and wellbeing.

So, what are the child health issues and concerns in contemporary society? Children are diagnosed with an increasing range of conditions and are subject to more and more elaborate child health and welfare interventions, reflecting a medical perspective on the changing panorama of illness and health risks in the 21st century. We see today a growing concern with mental health (for example, the autistic spectrum), as well as emerging contested illnesses (attention deficit hyperactivity disorder [ADHD]), life-style related conditions (obesity and allergies) or 'new' infectious diseases (HIV/AIDS). However, we would argue that in trying to bridge the sociology of childhood with that of health and illness, it is important to look beyond what is discussed as child health issues and take account of issues currently debated in the sociology of health and illness more generally. Health behaviour approaches have almost universally been adopted by those involved in healthcare research, with little critical attention paid to the conceptualization of health behaviour (Cohn, 2014). The assumption that there are easily identifiable and observable forms of health behaviour can be difficult to challenge, not least because the way in which health behaviours are seen as the outcome of individual choices has become established as the norm. This model also draws on ideas about agency, particularly in relation to choice and personal responsibility, often devoid of the social, economic and political context in which such agency is being enacted. In addition, a focus on health risks and surveillance medicine, as well as on lay understandings and patient perspectives, are relevant in the study of child health. However, research on these health issues, similarly to the old issues of chronic or life threatening illness, have largely been limited to the taken-for-granted adult person (Williams 2000). Expanding research to other phases of the life-course to include childhood is important not only to understand the meaning of child health and children's experiences but also to add important knowledge at a more general level to the understandings of health and illness.

Themes of this issue

As outlined above, in this issue we focus on the ways that socially and culturally constructed understandings and conceptualisations of childhood impact on issues of health and wellbeing and on the ways in which children exercise agency and competence in dealing with health and illness. A further consideration is how agency is bounded in intergenerational relations; while the focus of this issue is on children, the role of parents as mediators and facilitators in the healthcare division of labour (Stacey 1988, Mayall 1996) cannot be underestimated. Further, health, we argue, can be understood only by locating children as embodied beings (Bendelow 2009) in different social and cultural contexts. To advance our understandings of child health, it is necessary to situate child health issues in wider social, economic, cultural and national contexts as well as in the variety of public and social policies that will impact on dominant ways of understanding childhood and on children's lives and opportunities.

Children's daily lives play out across the social contexts which structure their lives. The settings of school and home largely organise children's lives, while their movement between such settings straddles the public and private domains. Messages about health are communicated to children both explicitly and implicitly so that they begin to learn social norms around health and, sometimes, change their behaviour in response to such messages. Mayall has argued that 'child health is not a neutral, factual concept; notions of child health are constructed out of essentially political considerations' (Mayall 1996:22). It may be assumed that children are relatively passive and conforming when faced with illness or diagnoses, yet children do exercise choices. Children have an active role in the management of health risks, their conditions and interactions with healthcare services. Moreover, they develop a repertoire of strategies to cope and sometimes to resist adult defined agendas (Bluebond-Langner 1978, 1996). Adults can be unaware of the ways in which children are interpreting information on health and making it meaningful to their lives. Previous health research has shown that even chronologically young children are competent reporters of their illness experiences (Alderson 1993) and that children can understand complex information if it is presented in appropriate ways (Alderson and Goodey 1996).

Since Mayall's 1998 article in this journal calling for a sociology of child health, research published in this area has increased but is sometimes disparately located. In this issue, the aim is to contribute to the development of a sociology of child health by bringing together current research that draws on the sociology of childhood and to address three cross-cutting themes that we have identified as being important in the study of child health and wellbeing:

Theme 1: situating children within health policy, which sets out the significance and pervasive influence of health policy in shaping the lives of children and their families.

Theme 2: practices of children's health and wellbeing, which focuses on health policy in action by looking at interactions between professionals, parents and children.

Theme 3: children as health actors, with a specific focus on the lived experiences of children and young people themselves.

Taken together, these three themes can offer examples of differing contexts and encourage reflection on current and culturally specific ways of knowing and understanding children's health.

Theme 1: situating children within health policy
The health of the child is seen as a signifier for the current and future health of the nation, placing their bodies at the intersection of ideas about social order. Armstrong's (1995) influential work on surveillance medicine clarified how this new 20th century medical paradigm became particularly concerned with the child and child development, over time and into the future. Children are thus a critical object of state policy, where the main focus is on children as future citizens (Mayall 1998), (which raises questions as to whether the future-focus of policy is always in the best interests of children in the here and now). The health policy focus is on risks and includes a preoccupation with children's body size, development and behaviour. These developments are reflected in an increase in preventive medicine and various programmes for health promotion as well as early detection and intervention in groups of people considered to be at risk, to a large extent directed at children and their parents. While surveillance of child health is not new, it is important to understanding the ways in which children are categorised as healthy or ill, normal or deviant; categorisations that contribute to shaping the embodied lives of children and young people. For example, research on medicalisation as well as psychiatrisation of child development and behaviour (Le Francois and Coppock 2014), followed by pharmaceuticalisation (Williams *et al.* 2011) has raised

the question of how categories of child deviance are constructed in the p: surveillance and also how diagnosis can function as a tool to categorise in 2009).

Health promotion information aimed at parents often raises awareness (of protective factors – it is professed that knowing about risks can help parents to consider the best ways of supporting and optimising the wellbeing of children. The risk is usually described as potentially increasing the likelihood of a child or young person developing phys- ical, mental or social difficulties. One main issue with this kind of approach is that many of the factors that put children at risk are not amenable to change by families as they are struc- tural factors such as poverty, stigmatisation and the poor provision of education and welfare. Not being in a position to minimise such risks, coupled with the emphasis on their long-term consequences for children, can leave parents feeling inadequate and also contributes to the depoliticisation and individualisation of social problems (Conrad 1976, Zola 1972).

Against this backdrop, and in a world of health and social inequalities, a critical engage- ment with the ways in which health policy and practice impacts on children is required. It is also important to analyse the ideas and images of children and childhood present in policy documents and health interventions. Such ideas and images are typically taken for granted, but in-depth analyses of child health policy documents and programmes tell us something about the prevailing understandings of the child in our societies. It also reveals the ways in which deviance from perceived norms becomes a matter for concern and intervention. The ways in which child health and normality are reflected in health policy and practice thus have implications for children and young people as well as their parents and carers.

Theme 2: practices of children's health and wellbeing
In a sociological approach to health, health care is recognised as part of a social process, carried out in the public domain by paid professionals and privately by unpaid, lay carers (Stacey 1988). Health may also be understood variously; for example, professional beliefs may differ from lay beliefs, adult beliefs may differ from children's beliefs and all are vari- ously influenced by a range of factors. Understandings of child health are thus to be seen as relational and constructed in communication between different actors in everyday life. Also, ideas about child health and how children should be treated vary across social and cultural contexts both in and between different societies, not least between the global North and South, which stresses the importance of seeing children's health and wellbeing as con- textually embedded (Singal and Muthukrishna 2014).

As we cannot assume a linear relationship between policy and practice, it is important to consider how health policy becomes translated into practice in healthcare encounters at different levels: in surveillance and intervention programmes directed at children and young people (or those considered to be at risk) – initiated and carried out by the social and health services – and at the level of the clinical encounter initiated by parents (or others) to deal with the health and illness of the individual child.

Sociology of health and illness research has shed light on the impact of surveillance medicine and has demonstrated how messages of normality and deviance are communicated explicitly as well as implicitly when carried out in health practice (Olin Lauritzen and Sachs 2001). But we still need to know more about the content of these messages. What are the ideas about childhood and the child as well as ideas about normality and deviance inherent in surveillance and intervention and communicated to children and parents? Also, the chang- ing panorama of what is considered a deviance from normal development and behaviour in children needs to be addressed, as well as the fact that the surveillance and monitoring of

…dren's minds and bodies is carried out from an adult perspective and children are not always asked about their views or included in decision-making about their care.

At the level of clinical encounters between professionals, parents and children in various healthcare settings, the different voices of these parties can be identified and intergenerational aspects and power relations of the interaction can be laid bare and examined. Early work by Strong (1979) and Silverman (1987) explored the details of how the degree of 'medical doubt' concerning the health of the child patient created different formats of the clinical encounter. This has been followed by studies of how professional and moral understandings and disciplinary frameworks, as well as the structural organisation of healthcare, shape healthcare encounters and the power relations in these encounters (White 2002).

Detailed micro analyses have shed further light on the dynamics of the interaction and power relations between health professionals, parents and children – including the ways in which children contribute to or are excluded in these processes (Aronsson and Rundström 1988, Clemente 2009). Dimond (2014) argues that research on the triadic relationship between children, parents and healthcare professionals in clinical settings is much needed to help to enhance understanding. From what is known about the role of adults in health encounters they often dismiss or reframe children's own bodily sensations and experiences (Carter 2002) to fit existing frameworks of understanding. When it comes to children's voices and agency in healthcare interaction, important contributions have been made, for instance, on children's consent to treatment (Alderson 1993, Alderson and Goodey 1996) but more knowledge is needed to explore children's experiences and capacities. Importantly, patterns of interaction and power dynamics in health practices need to be explored further from a child perspective and across different sociocultural contexts.

Theme 3 – Children as health actors
The third theme of this issue focuses specifically on children's own experiences of health and illness, of living with a condition and on children's active participation in the management of their bodies and minds. Exploring the lived experience of children brings to the fore their role as healthcare actors. We acknowledge that in the field of child health, the views of children, as service users, are beginning to be sought, often through consultation or evaluation. However, perhaps unsurprisingly, the social and political context of lay/professional, adult/child interaction and embedded social relations and structures are often not explicated thoroughly enough to provide a deeper understanding of the experience of children. Consequently, the data gained from such exercises can be superficial. Crucially, we cannot fully understand the impact and meaning of health and illness in children's lives without bringing in children's experiences, understandings, competence and agency in dealing with these issues (Mayall 1996, 1998). Examples that show this is possible include studies that have accessed the views of children over a range of areas such as in relation to doctor–patient consultations (Rindstedt 2014), the design of children's health services and spaces (Birch *et al.* 2007) and treatment preferences and their impact (Coad 2010). It is clear that by using a range of different methodological approaches research can show how children's concerns often differ from adult-centred ones.

One important issue in the lives of children and young people is the social implication and impact of receiving a medical diagnosis. This can have both negative and positive effects on children's identity and embodied lives, both from their own perspective and the way that they are seen by others. Earlier research in this field has indicated that children's competence and understanding in dealing with a medical diagnosis is often underestimated (Berntsson *et al.* 2007, Brady 2005). This may particularly be the case where definitions are contested or there are debates over prevention or treatment. Questions are raised about children's own priorities, concerns and agendas and how they can be in conflict with those of adults (Brady 2014, Williams *et al.* 2007).

Children's and young people's experiences and understandings of health, illness and medical interventions are interesting per se. Moreover, children's understandings also have implications for how they act to promote health, how they deal with illness and manage risks to their health in everyday life. On the one hand, 'Children use their resourcefulness to stretch adult-imposed boundaries to limits more acceptable to themselves' (Punch 2001: 34), a fact that is especially evident in research into children's management of risks and of medication. On the other hand, children's dealing with health and illness has to be understood relationally: being healthy or ill, competent or not, takes place, so to say, in relation to others and in the complexity of local contexts. There is also a spatial dimension to consideration of children's health in that a number of sites of health practices, including early year childcare settings, school (the classroom and playground), the family home and wider public space are of importance.

Introduction to the collection

The following chapters, all anchored in a sociology of childhood perspective, include contributions from a range of disciplines, countries and sociocultural contexts as well as different methodological approaches. They address different cases of health policy and practice as well as children's (and parent's) experiences of a range of conditions and ways of 'doing health.'

The first chapters address the ways in which children are positioned in health policy. In their chapter, Bergnéhr and Zetterqvist Nelson take mental–health-promoting interventions to explore the ways in which children are situated in health policy; how young people are viewed, understood, thought about and positioned. While this research analyses the Nordic context, such public health interventions are increasingly being introduced to children and young people across the world. Two themes thread through the analysis – that the child is largely assumed to be passive and formed by adults and that ideas about health and wellbeing are often highly individualised and decontextualised. These themes appear throughout the book. The study draws attention to school as a site of health promotion and maintenance and argues for a need to know more about children's experiences of such (mental) health interventions, which are largely normalised and seen as part of school life in some countries.

In the next chapter, Lowe, Lee and MacVarish focus on images of children and parents in health policy documents, more specifically on 'brain claims' in English health and welfare policies from 1998 to 2012. The authors describe how determinist ideas about brain development, drawing on quasi-neuro-scientific discourses, are becoming prevalent in understandings of children and child development. They discuss this development as a drive in policy that amounts to understanding children's development and growth in increasingly narrow terms. Although focused on England in this instance, it is argued that such brain claims are impacting on policy and practice across the western, neoliberal world. Taken together, these two chapters demonstrate how a detailed analysis of health policy documents and programmes can reveal implicit ideas about the child; ideas that will impact on practice and are translated in communication with parents and children.

The chapters that follow focus precisely on such practices, and on the complex dynamics in the translation and communication of notions of the child as well as the divides between health, illness or deviance from the norm. Research undertaken by Martin focuses on public health messages of concern and panic about childhood obesity and explores how the issues of obesity and additional weight are understood by children and their mothers in Malta. By ethnographically studying the children in a primary school setting she is able to identify the subtle ways in which children understand and depict their own bodies (as fat or not), as well as highlighting interesting differences between the bodily accounts given by younger children (5-year olds) and those somewhat older (10-year olds). She argues that the younger children are buffered by robust protective strategies in their group, while children in the older group perceive themselves to be different and are indeed so labelled; they develop private coping strategies to manage the levels of exclusion often felt. In doing this, Martin draws attention to the ways children's bodies are both biologically and socially constructed.

Also in this collection, Alexander, Fusco and Frohlich begin by acknowledging increasing public health concerns about childhood obesity. In Canada, public health institutions are emphasising active play as a way of combatting obesity. The chapter highlights the contrast between public health discourses and children's own diverse, lived experiences of playing. They show how some children adopted the understanding of active play, while others highlighted the importance of other more sedentary activities. They argue that there may be unintentional consequences in limiting understandings of play to an active mode. This chapter again highlights the need to properly understand children's lives before interventions are planned and executed. Both of these studies relating to obesity highlight the ways in which messages on one of the major public health issues in the Western world are communicated, taken up and understood by children and their parents.

The following chapter, by Wilhelmsen and Dyblie-Nilsen also explores the practices of children's health and wellbeing. In this case the focus is on how normal child development is communicated to parents in an early years setting, in a Norwegian day-care centre. The chapter addresses the processes and tools used to assess and define children's behaviour as either normal or deviant. The chapter shows the complexity of parents' experiences of pathways towards a diagnosis of a 'non-normal' condition, such as ADHD, and a 'special-needs' designation. Parents have their everyday understanding of their child, which may agree or disagree with the professional perspective. In their study they also show how forms and charts used to map behaviour serve to provide a visual representation of deviance and difference and are regarded as evidence, legitimating the forms of power at work in the social construction of knowledge.

The following three contributions address the understandings and experiences of children and young people who are living with different conditions. Mogensen and Mason consider the label of autism and the meaning of this diagnosis to a group of five young people in Australia. The young people were able to choose how they communicated with the researchers, who used participatory research methods, and were able to share their understandings of autism and its impact on their sense of self and identity. More specifically, the authors show how the young people integrated their understandings of the autism diagnosis with their sense of self, and the different positive or negative meanings the diagnosis could take on in this process. Also, these young people clearly desired to be in control of the ways in which they dealt with their diagnosis, and Mogensen and Mason suggest that ways of minimising stigma and marginalisation associated with a diagnosis of autism need to be considered at a policy level.

Bernays, Seeley, Rhodes and Mupambireyi also explore children as health actors, in this case the illness narratives of children living with HIV and accessing antiretroviral treatment (ART). They note that in previous research into HIV, adult views have been the focus, acting as proxy representations of the experience of children. The narratives told by the children themselves reveal a complex picture of illness stories, resistance to being defined as ill, and what the authors identify as protest talk – where children strive to come to terms with the ambiguities of being regarded as sick while feeling and looking well.

Their narratives illuminate the challenge involved in achieving a sense of normalcy. Importantly, this chapter highlights the social challenges which accompany long-term adherence to treatment (in this case ART), a theme that is also relevant to other chapters in this monograph.

Stjerna's paper on the management of food allergy, a potentially life threatening condition, brings to the fore debates about risks to children's health. A study of young Swedish people with a food allergy highlights how the everyday management of this condition is contending with health risks as well as social risks, the risk of a severe bodily reaction as well as of being seen as different by their peers or others when trying to avoid 'dangerous' food or using medication. Not only is risk involved here but also issue of trust and responsibility. This chapter sheds light on the relational elements of the agency of the young people in the management of their condition, in the ways they are dependent on contexts, environments and the behaviour of other people.

Researchers are adopting various methods and methodologies in order to understand the perspectives of children. Jenkins discusses a micro-analysis of children as health actors, drawing on a study that focuses on the interaction that takes place between children and their parents in the family home. Analysis of video recordings of English family mealtimes reveals the ways in which children express bodily sensations, which are often redefined or denied by parents. Using conversation analysis to drill down into the interactions the chapter draws attention to the agency of children. In investigating the rights of children to report on their own embodied experience it adds to our understanding of the enactment of power dynamics in families and raises questions about the ways in which, from an early age, children's own experiences are denied or shaped by more dominant adult understandings which make claims to meaning.

The final chapter is a fitting contribution from Mayall, who originally called for a sociology of child health in 1998. Building on her previous theoretical and empirical research on the status of childhood, she discusses developments in the sociology of childhood and reflects on possible avenues for future research. She makes explicit the minority status of children and positions children in intergenerational relations by drawing attention to bodily relations between adults and children, particularly focusing on ideas about the body that structure children's experiences of their bodies and emotions. This chapter focuses on health and wellbeing, rather than illness or sickness, and points out that 'Wellbeing is associated with being a valued and respected person.'

Spanning the three key themes, the chapters in this collection contribute to a critical analysis of child health policy and notions of child health and normality, as well as to our understandings of the active contributions children make to deal with health and illness in their own lives. Through analysing the relationship between concepts of child health and illness – as they are represented in health policy, discourse and dominant understandings – and children's actual lived experiences, a sociological lens is afforded that helps to illuminate the complexities of structure and agency as well as the interaction between biological and social processes.

These chapters show how a focus on childhood health can be an appropriate vehicle to appreciate the ways children uniquely experience their childhood while being part of the structural category of a generation. In exploring the life-worlds of a range of children, these research accounts show that there is little that is universal about 'the child' and it is more appropriate to refer to a variety of childhoods, which draws our attention to the importance of not uncritically adopting Western values in research and health policy globally. These predominantly empirical contributions, carried out in different sociocultural contexts, are much needed to contribute to a more substantial volume of research on child health from a sociology of childhood perspective and to generate further developments at a theoretical level.

To conclude, the chapters presented here suggest theoretical and empirical research potential for a sociology of children's health and illness. The collection thus goes some way to seriously beginning to address the migration of the sociology of child health from the margins into the mainstream of sociology of health and illness. In the endeavour to promote the social study of child health, it is, of course, also important to take account of contributions from neighbouring fields such as childhood geographies, child disability studies, studies of children's play and others that we have not been able to include in this issue. Finally, we hope that this issue will encourage productive debate among a wide audience, including academics as well as policymakers, healthcare professionals and people who are involved with children, and young people and their parents in everyday life.

References

Alanen, L. (2014) Editorial: theorizing childhood, *Childhood*, 21, 1, 3–6.

Alanen, L. and Mayall, B. (2001) *Conceptualising Child Adult Relations.* London: Routledge and Falmer.

Alderson, P. (1993) *Children's Consent to Surgery*. Buckingham: Open University Press.

Alderson, P. (2000) Children as researchers: the effects of participation rights on research methodology. In Christensen, P. and James, A. (eds) *Research with Children: Perspectives and Practice.* London: Falmer Press.

Alderson, P. and Goodey, C. (1996) Research with disabled children: how useful is child-centred ethics? *Children & Society*, 10, 2, 106–116.

Armstrong, D. (1995) The rise of surveillance medicine, *Sociology of Health & Illness*, 17, 3, 393–404.

Aronsson, K. and Rundström, B. (1988) Child discourse and parental control in paediatric consultations, *Text and Talk*, 8, 3, 159–89.

Bendelow, G. (2009) *Health, Emotion and the Body*. London: Polity Press.

Berntsson, L., Berg, M., Brydolf, M. and Hellstrom, A.L. (2007) Adolescents' experiences of well-being when living with a long term illness or disability, *Scandinavian Journal of Caring Sciences*, 21, 4, 419–25.

Birch, J., Curtis, P. and James, A. (2007) Sense and sensibilities: in search of the child friendly hospital, *Built Environment*, 33, 4, 2, 405–16.

Bluebond-Langner, M. (1978) *The Private Worlds of Dying Children.* Princeton: Princeton University Press.

Bluebond-Langner, M. (1996) *In the Shadow of Illness. Parents and siblings of the chronically ill child.* Princeton: Princeton University Press.

Brady, G. (2005) ADHD, diagnosis and identity. In Newnes, C. and Radcliffe, N. (eds) *Making and Breaking Children's Lives*. Ross-on-Wye: PCCS Books.

Brady, G. (2014) Children and ADHD: seeking control within the constraints of diagnosis, *Children & Society*, 28, 3, 218–30.

Burman, E. (1994) *Deconstructing Developmental Psychology.* London: Routledge.

Carter, B. (2002) Chronic pain in childhood and the medical encounter: professional ventriloquism and hidden voices, *Qualitative Health Research*, 12, 1, 28–41.

Clemente, I. (2009) Progressivity and participation: children's management of parental assistance in paediatric chronic pain encounters, *Sociology of Health & Illness*, 31, 6, 872–8.

Coad, J. (2010) *The Impact of Cancer on a Child's World: the Views of Children Aged 7–13 Living with and Beyond Cancer*. London: CLIC Sargent.

Cohn, S. (2014) From health behaviours to health practices: critical perspectives, *Sociology of Health & Illness*, 36, 2, 1–6.

Conrad, P. (1976) *Identifying Hyperactive Children: the Medicalisation of Deviant Behaviour*. Lexington: Lexington books.

Christensen, P. and James, A. (eds) (2000) *Research with Children: Perspectives and Practice*. London: Falmer Press.

Dimond, R. (2014) Negotiating identity at the intersection of paediatric and genetic medicine: the parent as facilitator, narrator and patient, *Sociology of Health & Illness*, 36, 1, 1–14.

Halldén, G. (1991) The child as a project and the child as being: parents' ideas as frame of reference, *Childhood and Society*, 5, 4, 334–46.

Harden, J., Scott, S., Backett-Milburn, K. and Jackson, S. (2000) 'Can't talk, won't talk?' Methodological issues in researching children, *Sociological Research Online*, 5, 2. Available at www.socresonline.org.uk/5/2/harden.html (accessed 25 January 2015).

James, A. (2010) Competition or integration? The next step in childhood studies? *Childhood*, 17, 4, 485–499.

James, A. and Prout, A. (1997) *Constructing and Reconstructing Childhood*. London: Falmer.

James, A., Jenks, C. and Prout, A. (1998) *Theorising Childhood*. Cambridge: Polity Press.

Jutel, A. (2009) Sociology of diagnosis: a preliminary review, *Sociology of Health & Illness*, 31, 2, 278–99.

Le Francois, B. and Coppock, V. (2014) Psychiatrised children and their rights: starting the conversation, *Children and Society*, 28, 3, 165–256.

Lee, N. (2001) *Childhood and Society: Growing Up in an Age of Uncertainty*. Buckingham: Open University Press.

Lee, N. (2005) *Childhood and Human Value: Development, Separation and Separability*. Maidenhead: Open University.

Mason, J. and Hood, S. (2011) Exploring issues of children as actors in social research, *Children and Youth Service Review*, 33, 4, 490–5.

Mayall, B. (1996) *Children, Health and the Social Order*. Buckingham: Open University Press.

Mayall, B. (1998) Towards a sociology of child health, *Sociology of Health & Illness*, 20, 3, 269–88.

Moran-Ellis, J. (2010) Reflections on the sociology of childhood in the UK, *Current Sociology*, 58, 2, 186–205.

Olin Lauritzen, S. and Sachs, L. (2001) Normality, risk and the future: implicit communication of threat in health surveillance, *Sociology of Health & Illness*, 23, 4, 497–516.

Prout, A. (2005) *The Future of Childhood*. London: Routledge Falmer.

Punch, S. (2001) Negotiating autonomy: childhoods in rural Bolivia. In Alanen, L. and Mayall, B. (eds) *Conceptualising Child-Adult Relations*. London: Routledge.

Punch, S. (2002) Research with children: the same or different from research with adults, *Childhood*, 9, 3, 321–40.

Qvortrup, J. (1994) Childhood matters: an introduction. In Qvortrup, J., Bardy, M., Sgritta, G. and Wintersberger, H. (eds) *Childhood Matters: Social Theory, Practice and Politics*. Avebury: Ashgate.

Rindstedt, C. (2014) Children's strategies to handle cancer: a video ethnography of imaginal coping, *Child: Care, Health and Development*, 40, 4, 580–6.

Silverman, D. (1987) *Communication and Medical Practice. Social Relations in the Clinic*. London: Sage.

Singal, N. and Muthukrishna, N. (2014) Education, childhood and disability in countries in the South – re-positioning the debates, *Childhood*, 21, 3, 293–307.

Stacey, M. (1988) *The Sociology of Health and Healing: a Textbook*. London: Routledge.

Strong, P. (1979) *The Ceremonial Order of the Clinic. Parents, Doctors and Medical Bureaucracies*. London: Routledge and Kegan Paul.

Tisdall, K. and Punch, S. (2012) Not so new? Looking critically at childhood studies, *Children's Geographies*, 10, 3, 249–64.

Uprichard, E. (2008) Children as 'being and becomings': children, childhood and temporality, *Children & Society*, 22, 4, 303–13.

Valentine, K. (2011) Accounting for agency, *Children & Society*, 25, 5, 347–58.

White, S. (2002) Accomplishing 'the case' in paediatrics and child health: medicine and morality in inter-professional talk, *Sociology of Health & Illness*, 24, 4, 409–35.

Williams, S. (2000) Chronic illness as biographical disruption or biographical disruption as chronic illness?: reflections on a core concept. *Sociology of Health & Illness*, 22, 1, 40–67.

Williams, S., Lowe, P. and Griffiths, F. (2007) Embodying and embedding children's sleep: some sociological comments and observations, *Sociological Research Online*, 12, 5. Available at www.socresonline.org.uk/12/5/6.html (accessed 25 January 2015).

Williams, S., Martin, P. and Gabe, J. (2011) The Pharmaceuticalisation of Society: a framework for analysis, *Sociology of Health & Illness*, 33, 5, 710–25.

Zola, I. K. (1972) Medicine as an institute of social control, *Sociological Review*, 20, 4, 487–503.

2

Where is the child? A discursive exploration of the positioning of children in research on mental–health-promoting interventions
Disa Bergnehr and Karin Zetterqvist Nelson

Introduction

Children's health and wellbeing are on the political agenda in many nations. Concerns are being raised about the increasing number of stress-related symptoms and health problems they experience. It has been suggested that universal health-promoting services are essential in the work to reverse such trends (for example, Marmot 2010, World Health Organization [WHO] 2005), and schools have been identified as appropriate settings for initiatives aimed at children (WHO 1997). Consequently, during recent decades a vast range of interventions offered through schools have been developed, implemented and evaluated (Watson *et al.* 2012). These interventions take different forms. For instance, they may consist of scheduled, teacher-led group activities once or twice a week for a term or longer – sometimes referred to as programmes or health education – or of individual health dialogues or counselling sessions about eating habits, physical training and nutrition, provided by the school health personnel. Some interventions focus on physical aspects and others on improving children's mental health, while broader approaches address both physical and mental health issues (Aggleton Dennison and Warwick 2010, Samdal and Rowling 2013, Vince Whitman and Aldinger 2009).

According to the WHO, one important criterion for the effectiveness of health interventions is participation and empowerment:

> [P]articipation is essential to sustain efforts. People have to be at the centre of health promotion action and decision-making processes for them to be effective…. Health promotion is carried out by and with people, not on or to people. (WHO n.d.)

The WHO's emphasis on the importance of including service users in the decision-making process corresponds with national and global policies proposing that children, like adults, should be consulted in matters that concern them, including their health and education (Todd 2012, UNICEF 1989).

It has been increasingly recognised that acknowledging children's opinions and experiences is central to the development of health interventions and improved health (Fattore, Mason, and Watson 2012, Graham and Fitzgerald 2011, Mason and Hood 2011), but how this idea is applied varies (Evans and Spicer 2008). Health-promoting research has proposed two approaches to children's participation – token participation and genuine participation.

Children, Health and Well-being: Policy Debates and Lived Experience, First Edition. Edited by Geraldine Brady, Pam Lowe and Sonja Olin Lauritzen. Chapters © 2015 The Authors. Book Compilation © 2015 Foundation for the Sociology of Health & Illness/Blackwell Publishing Ltd.

Token participation means that children take part in the intervention in the sense that their individual behaviour and health outcomes are defined and measured by adults. Genuine participation, on the other hand, actively involves children in choosing health-promoting activities, acknowledges their opinions and regards individual health outcomes as dependent on contextual and interrelational factors (Simovska 2007). However, such an approach to genuine participation has been critically examined and contested by Holland *et al.* (2010), who argue that it rests on a notion of power as something one has or does not have. Drawing on a relational view of power and Foucauldian theory, they stress the significance of seeing participation in relation to the specific context and situation, and asking questions about *how* children's and young people's participation is enacted rather than *how much* they participated (Holland *et al.* 2010).

The focus in the present chapter is mental–health-promoting interventions for children and young people in compulsory schooling. Such interventions are offered to all or large groups of children, the general aim being to improve their mental health and social relations, for instance through training in social skills, coping strategies and self-reflection (Kvist Lindholm and Zetterqvist Nelson 2014, Watson *et al.* 2012, Wickström 2013). The children are expected to acquire a range of abilities by partaking in the interventions and moulding themselves accordingly (Watson *et al.* 2012). The activities are often part of the regular schedule, and as such are part of the children's everyday school life. Consequently, interventions are more or less mandatory. As such, it would be natural to enable children to express their opinions and experiences about the interventions per se. Previous research on children and health, drawing on sociology of childhood, has shown that children at various ages are fully capable of reflecting on and evaluating various health-care interventions (for example, Bluebond-Langner 1980, 1996, Coppock 2007, Kvist Lindholm and Zetterqvist Nelson 2014, Mayall 1996, Singh 2013, Wickström 2013). Within this theoretical framework children are conceptualised as interdependent co-constructers of their social worlds, whose agency is facilitated and restrained by intergenerational power relations as well as by political context, age, gender, socioeconomic status, bodily resources, individual strategies and so on (for example, James and Prout 1997, Qvortrup 1994). The present article sets out to explore how children are conceptualised in research articles on universal mental health interventions.

Conceptualising children's health and agency

Inspired by the sociology of childhood, children's views and experiences are included to an increasing extent in the development of indicator research used to measure children's wellbeing. Although still marginal, this epistemological approach 'not only acknowledges children's agency, but also attends to structural issues as they influence children's contributions' (Mason and Hood 2011: 492). Such research regards children's perspectives as being of equal importance to those of the adult researchers (Lieggio *et al.* 2010). However, there are ontological obstacles to incorporating children as collaborators and acknowledging children's agency (Mason and Hood 2011, Todd 2012, Watson 2012, Wyness Harrison and Buchanan 2004). During the past 50 years, children have been predominantly conceptualised through the mainstream concepts of child development and socialisation. In the traditions of psychology and sociology, children have primarily been depicted as passive and formed by adults; their participatory rights are restricted vis-à-vis adults due to their 'immaturity', that is, their age (Burman 1995). This dominant notion of children was challenged by the new sociology of childhood in the 1990s (James and Prout 1997, Qvortrup 1994).

However, theorising within this field has continued and other issues have been illuminated. For instance, the stress on children as beings, originally launched as a critical alternative to seeing them as mere becomings, has been called into question by pointing out that adults and children are alike – as humans we are all social subjects who continuously develop and change in relation to the material and social context and the experiences we obtain from these (Lee 2001, 2005, Prout 2005). Children, as well as adults, are both *being* and *becoming,* simultaneously interdependent and vulnerable as competent active agents (see also Gallacher and Gallagher 2008, Uprichard 2008). Furthermore, agency as a theoretical concept has been critically scrutinised by those who argue against notions of agency as something inherently good and positive and desired by all children and young people (Tisdall and Punch 2012: 256). Valentine suggests the recognition of agency as a 'complex, multidimensional and ambivalent' concept (Valentine 2011: 348); that one should avoid seeing agency as a personal competence and instead illuminate differences and hierarchies among individuals.

Our theoretical and analytical departure corresponds with sociology of childhood scholars who look upon health, wellbeing and agency as 'relational and embedded' (Watson *et al.* 2012: 223); as formed in relationships with others and dynamically contingent on the social, economic, political and material context (Mayall 1996). By our actions and existence, we influence and take part in shaping our life, others' lives and society, but the dynamics of power structure social relations in the continuous process of (re)defining who should have a say and whose actions should impact on whom (Tisdall and Punch 2012, Valentine 2011). All in all, power and participation are situated and changeable, which calls for attention to how children's (and adults') agency is perceived, facilitated and restrained in specific settings.

The study

The present study explores the discursive positioning of children in research articles on mental-health-promoting interventions through schools, the central research questions being: are children – the service users – positioned as active or passive agents? Are children's health and wellbeing contextualised, and if so how? How is the child perceived; that is, how are age, gender, socioeconomic status, family structure, dis/ability, and so on accounted for?

The choice to use research articles as data was influenced by earlier explorations of how cultural representations and constructions of subjects and knowledge are produced in scientific texts (Bitsch and Stemerding 2013, Burman 1994, Latour 1993, Martin 1991, Oswell 2013). Research publications are valuable in that they tell us about dominant and less dominant conceptualisations of a certain phenomenon or subject in the context of research. The language of science is regarded as reflecting as well as producing the truths that influence subjectivities, power relations and praxis. In addition, the status of scientific reports is high (Latour 1993, Martin 1991). Politicians, civil servants and practitioners are expected to take decisions based on research knowledge. Health care, education and the social services have particularly strong ties to evidence-based practice; that is, to ideas and suggestions about what works that are produced through research (Krejsler 2013). Consequently, it is of great relevance to investigate the conceptualisations of children and children's health found in texts that have high societal status and are likely to have an influence on praxis.

Data and sample procedure

The sample consists of 10 original research articles from eight journals. The texts explore interventions that cover social skills, self-esteem, coping, bullying and stress or general health promotion or education aimed at children and young people in compulsory education. The articles originate from Denmark ($n = 1$), Finland ($n = 3$), Norway ($n = 1$) and Sweden ($n = 5$). The Appendix contains additional information on each article – the research design, data, informants and type of intervention.

As there is an extensive body of research on mental–health-promoting interventions through schools, conducting a thorough textual discourse analysis required selective sampling. The following criteria for including articles in the sample were: (i) those produced in the Nordic countries, in order to limit the sample (additionally, this geographical area has a tradition of universal health policies and a political emphasis on children's right to participation); (ii) those peer-reviewed in international journals, since such publications are commonly regarded as being proof of high-quality research that is as such translatable and applicable; (iii) those written in English, the dominant language of publication in the Western world; and (iv) those published between January 2008 and March 2013, since a 5-year period would provide recent publications on mental health initiatives and limit the sample to a manageable number.

Articles were searched for in the following databases: the Cumulative Index of Nursing and Allied Health Literature, SCOPUS (multidisciplinary database), ERIC (education) and ASSIA (social science abstracts). The procedure was carefully undertaken with the assistance of a librarian in an effort to detect and cover all published research articles that fulfilled the criteria. There may be articles that did not surface, owing to their being registered in other databases or because their keywords did not match the search terms. A couple of articles were excluded from the sample since university colleagues of ours had authored them.

The articles are regarded as texts co-produced within the peer-review system. A number (1–10) refers to each research article in the results section, instead of the conventional way of citing (that is, author, year of publication). See Appendix 1 for clarification.

Analytical procedure
The analytical procedure was carried out in a dialogical manner, in which the analyses were continuously compared and discussed between the authors. The ways the child and children were positioned within the texts and throughout the sample were analysed by close scrutiny of the discourse. Discourse 'refers to socially organised frameworks of meaning that define categories and specify domains of what can be said and done' (Burman 1994: 2) in speech and texts. The discourse 'constructs the topic … It also influences how ideas are put into practice and used to regulate the conduct of others' (Hall 2001: 72). Typically, a topic – an idea, a phenomenon or a subject – can be positioned in several ways, affirmed, rejected or ignored, causing implicit or explicit struggles over which positioning should dominate (Foucault 1978, Weedon 1987). As an example; children may be positioned both as passive and active in the sample overall as well as within a specific text, but close scrutiny can detect the predominance or marginalisation of certain positions.

Through the analytical process, recurrent themes emerged in how the child and children were positioned in the texts' syntax and wording. The results section is outlined on the basis of these themes, which we have chosen to categorise and name as: the informing child, forming the child, the contextualised child, and the decontextualised child.

Results

The informing child
Of the 10 research articles, eight include children as informants. Of these, the controlled trials (articles 4, 5, 6, 7 and 8) measure the impact of the intervention on the child's behaviour and

wellbeing. This is accomplished using questionnaires in which children report on a number of items pre-intervention and post-intervention, and in some cases, during the intervention. The programme or intervention is in focus in these texts. The following quote signifies how the objective of the research can be framed:

> A health promotion programme comprising massage and mental training was implemented for a single academic year in one school … in order to strengthen and maintain wellbeing…. A questionnaire was developed and tested, resulting in 23 items distributed across the following six areas: self-reliance; leisure time; being an outsider; general and home satisfaction; school satisfaction; and school environment. (Article 4: 25)

It goes without saying that the questionnaires play an important role in the methodological design of the trial studies. Children's self-reports become the device through which the effect of the intervention is measured, rather than a technique through which their opinions and perceptions of their social wellbeing and mental health are gathered. By completing the questionnaire, the children inform the researcher of their health status. The main interest in these studies concerns the intervention outcomes, measuring the effect in relation to various theoretical definitions of mental health. The children are positioned as informants and participants, in accordance with Simovska's (2007) term 'token participation'.

One article that, similar to the articles describing controlled trials, aims to investigate intervention outcomes explores the school nurse health dialogue. The data are from a panel survey containing a number of questions directed at children. The questionnaire is designed to 'study adolescents' perceived health and health behaviours in their social context' (Article 1: 43). The text correlates the children's self-reported health dialogue outcomes with reports on the quality of their relationships with their father and mother as well as with the family structure. In this regard, health is related to contextual factors. As informants, the children are positioned similarly to the articles presenting the controlled trials – they provide information about their health status, but they do not participate as informants on, for instance, their opinions about the intervention as such. In addition, the notion of the child as being formed by adults is evident, for instance when the purpose of the health dialogue (that is, the intervention) is presented as follows: 'The aim of the visits is to monitor students' health and to support them in making healthy choices' (Article 1: 43).

In two of the texts examining the same intervention (articles 2 and 3), the children are depicted as providing information in a different manner to that depicted in most of the other articles. They are referred to as important actors with an impact on intervention processes and outcomes, and whose opinions are solicited and considered. The following quotes exemplify how the children are discursively constructed in these texts:

> The aim was to analyse if young students could be substantive participants in a health-promoting school project. The specific aims were to analyse the changes the students proposed in their school environment, how these changes were prioritised by a school health committee and to discuss the students' proposals and the changes from a health and gender perspective. (Article 3: 489)

> A qualitative methodology was chosen as a means of acquiring deeper understanding of pupils' perspectives on their school experience. (Article 2: 57)

In the texts, children are positioned as agents fully capable of providing information about their views on how health and wellbeing can be improved, and about their experiences in relation to intervention activities. The articles discursively render children's experiences of great value and illuminate their agency. Besides these articles, children's perceptions of the intervention per se receive little or no attention in the texts – either in the presentation of the study design, the data collection or the discussions and conclusions.

Two articles (articles 9 and 10) do not include children as informants, although children are subjected to the intervention. However, in these particular research texts, the children's actions and opinions of the intervention are brought up:

> The pupils actively participated in workshops by asking questions, solving problems and participating in conversations. Only a couple of School A pupils revealed their frustration with the group work and needed extra guidance from the researcher. The attendance to pupils' participatory workshops was high, as only a few pupils were absent during the workshops. (Article 10: 280)

Another example is: 'Pupils tested the activities, such as health education lessons, and gave valuable feedback to teachers and the researcher' (Article 9: 4). The quotes position the children as active agents whose opinions and experiences are taken into account in the evaluation and outlining of the intervention. Nevertheless, the observations of their actions do not result in further discussion of their role in the outcome of the intervention; for instance, the extract quoted above is not followed by any discussion as to why some children were frustrated with or avoided the activities. Moreover, one of the articles (Article 10) refers to the interviews being conducted with teachers and 'families' on their experiences of the intervention. 'The family' is in actuality parents (that is, one parent from each family). Accordingly, the children were not given the opportunity to share their experiences of the intervention activities, although the recurrent wording of the article tends to indicate that this may have been the case. There appears to be a taken-for-granted assumption (in this particular text) that parents' perceptions represent the child's experiences of an intervention. Many childhood scholars refute such a premise. They argue that it would be a mistake to assume that children experience a phenomenon, an event, or for that matter, life, in a similar manner to their parent(s), or that parent(s) are fully aware of and thus able to replicate the child's ideas (for example, Mayall 1994).

Participation in a health-promotion intervention at school requires some kind of agency, and the initiatives evaluated in the sample certainly appear to encourage, to a large extent, active participation and dialogue. But the question remains: why is this only explicitly elucidated, alluded to and explored in a limited number of the articles?

Forming the child

In most cases, the parts presenting the research questions, design and methodology are imbued with the perception of the child as a passive recipient of intervention activities. The following quote exemplifies this:

> The aim of this study is to evaluate the effects of a school-based drama program on social relationships in the class room and bullying and victimisation of school-age children. A further aim was to determine whether the program intensity influenced the outcome in terms of improved social relationships and decreased bullying experiences. (Article 6: 7)

In the above quotation, as in the overall text, the effects of the programme are of central concern, while the children are positioned as passive. Similar discursive constructions are also frequent throughout the sample: the focus is on the interventions' effects on the children, while discussions of the children's effects on the interventions are mostly absent. The success or failure of the intervention (that is, the measured effects) is not discussed in relation to the agency of the recipients.

Although the children are positioned as passive in relation to intervention activities, an underlying assumption contradicts such a conceptualisation, as great competence is concurrently attributed to children – they are expected to develop their social skills and abilities by partaking in the intervention. One could suggest this implies a traditional notion of socialisation permeates the research (see Burman 1994). Another example is taken from a study of a social emotional learning programme (SET):

> SET focuses on helping to develop the following five functions of the students: self-awareness, managing one's emotions, empathy, motivation and social competence .... The following themes recur in the tasks: social problem solution, handling strong emotions, appreciating similarities and differences, clarification of values, conflict management, interpretation of pictures and narratives, making more of what makes one feel good, resisting peer pressure and being able to say 'No', knowing what one is feeling, recognising people and situations, cooperation, listening to and relaying messages, setting goals and working to attain them, giving and receiving positive feedback and stress management. (Article 7: 136)

The paragraph illuminates once more the centrality of intervention effects. In addition, the above quotation exemplifies how ambitious the aspirations are on what the children should embrace and learn; that is, what the intervention should engender. Furthermore, the article positions the child as passive and moulded by adult, expert knowledge. The exclusive attention to self-reported health effects disregards the children's experiences of and influence on the intervention per se.

Several of the interventions evaluated in the sample are referred to in the texts as beneficial to children, since they improve and internalise a number of valuable social skills. It could be argued that these skills (for example, conflict management, coping with stress and self-awareness) are never-ending challenges that come with being human. This is a potent argument for justifying the intervention, as the research articles discursively do. However, too much emphasis on the individuals' potential to change their own and others' behaviour and wellbeing risks ignoring the influence of societal and social factors (Mayall 1996, Watson et al. 2012). The following section is dedicated to the exploration of how 'the child' – that is, the heterogeneous group of children – is depicted in the sample, and how contextual factors are acknowledged in the texts.

The (de)contextualised child

As stated previously, our analytical departure is that health and wellbeing are influenced by and experienced through social relations, personal attributes, and contextual factors (Mayall 1996, Watson et al. 2012). In the sample, the sociodemographic characteristics of the children in focus are commonly presented, albeit to varying extents. One of the articles (Article 5) provides comprehensive details on the children taking part in the randomised controlled trial: their mean age, the number of boys and girls, family structure, national origin and parents' educational level. Moreover, the sociodemographics of the communities where the schools are located and the children reside are explicated. Gender and socioeconomic status are controlled for in the analysis of intervention outcomes. Furthermore, this particular article is unique in the sample in that it discursively positions the children's self-reports on health outcomes as equivalent to those of the parents and teachers. Additionally, in syntax, the children are overall actively positioned. Throughout the results section, differences and similarities between the children, parents and teachers are juxtaposed. By doing this, parallel with referring to potential differences due to gender and family background, the text depicts children as a group consisting of individuals with varying experiences as well as a group that may regard matters differently from adults. The article is a good example of a text in which the measured results are explored by accounting for children as a heterogeneous rather than homogenous category, and in which they are actively positioned.

Another text (Article 4) refers to gender, age, family background and physical activity as being controlled for at baseline. However, only gender is controlled for and illuminated in the pre-test and post-test comparison. Thus, the article fails to discuss the possible influence of age and socioeconomic status on intervention effects, inevitably depicting children's health as independent of such variables. This is similar to other texts, in which subgroups based on children's age are referred to in the analysis but aspects such as gender, family structure and socioeconomic status are not discussed (Article 7). In another article (Article 8), gender, class and school are controlled for, but the children's family background is not presented. The children in these texts are positioned as passive recipients of the intervention provided. This discursive way of positioning children renders the conceptualisation of children's mental health as being primarily contingent on individual skills rather than contextual factors.

One of the research articles briefly elucidates the relational nature of wellbeing by framing the children and teachers as collaborative partners who benefit equally from the intervention. The intervention – a drama programme – is presented as follows:

> By entering fictional world created in the drama, the students and teachers can move on safely into it. In this drama-learning process, the student creates new relationships of meaning through transformative process. The student and teacher gain new perspectives about themselves, each other, and on reality. (Article 6: 6)

The above quote illustrates how both children and adults (the students and teachers) are referred to somewhat equally, and how relational aspects of wellbeing can be pointed out. However, in the text at stake, when the results are discussed, the child–adult collaboration or the relational aspect on wellbeing is not elaborated, and nor are contextual or sociodemographic factors.

The notion that health and public health interventions are conditional on collaborative work between children and adults as well as on social (peer) relations and structural conditions permeates a couple of the articles (articles 2 and 3). In these, age, socioeconomic status and family structure are presented, albeit in a general manner. In one (Article 2), gender is a central analytical factor and the influence of age on the children's participation in focus group interviews is briefly reflected upon. Neither gender nor age is central to the analyses in the other text (Article 3), but their possible impact on intervention outcomes and the children's experiences of the intervention is discussed. The research is based on the children's written proposals on how to change the school environment so as to improve their wellbeing. A detected weakness, as reported, is

> that it was not possible to discern the individual consequences for the students of the intervention, nor was information available on student proposals in relation to their socio-economic background or gender. (Article 3: 506)

Here, the embedded and relational nature of children's wellbeing is pointed out, as is the importance of recognising the individual child. Thus, by indicating the limitations of the study, significant issues surrounding children as participants and children's health are illuminated.

The two texts involving parents (Article 9) and parents and teachers (Article 10) as informants (and no children) evaluate an intervention aiming to develop children's health education by strengthening home–school collaboration. Besides the children's age, no other background characteristics of the adult participants or the children at whom the intervention is aimed are provided. Additionally, mothers and fathers are grouped together as 'parents' (Article 9). The texts repeatedly emphasise that the home–school partnership is essential to successful health promotion, but the children are predominantly positioned as passive and decontextualised. The discourse equates the home–school relation with parent–teacher collaboration, thus excluding the children.

It is worth noting that disability is not discussed as a factor that could influence the child's health and wellbeing, participation, and experiences of a certain intervention either in the objectives or analyses, or in the discussions or conclusions in the research articles. It is also worth considering the overall lack of reflection on the school setting as such. The texts implicitly or explicitly assume that schools are appropriate for mental health promotion. This has been questioned, however (for example, Bergnehr 2015a, Bergnehr 2015b, St Leger 2004, Watson *et al.* 2012).

Concluding discussion

The results of the present study show that children are discursively positioned within the texts in varying ways. A recurring depiction is the child as formed by adults that dominates at the expense of acknowledging children as social actors. These instances concur with a discursive construction of health as individualised and decontextualised. Most of the texts do not reflect global ambitions to consider children's experiences and objectives, or WHO's suggestion to carry out health promotion by and with people, rather than on or to people (WHO n.d.), or sociology of childhood perspectives on health and wellbeing as contextualised and relational. But there are exceptions, from research articles presenting quantitative designs as well as from texts analysing qualitative data. In the discourse of these texts, children are contextualised and 'the child' is illuminated; health is discursively construed as culturally and socially related. In addition, the quantitative research design (Article 5) positions children as active agents whose reports are equal in value to those of the adults, and which provides a nuanced discussion of the results. This is in contrast to other articles based on quantitative data, in which children's reports are mainly presented as intervention outcomes. The qualitative studies (articles 2 and 3) utilise children as informants whose experiences of the intervention per se are of value, and as agents whose actions have an influence on intervention activities and outcomes. Previous research has shown that it is possible to involve children's experiences and opinions in the construction of questionnaires as well as when evaluating health interventions with qualitative methods (Fattore, Mason and Watson 2012, Liegghio, Nelson, and Evans 2010, Mason and Hood 2011). Consequently, we propose that these strategies be further developed and applied in health research.

The present study investigates how children are positioned in recent peer-reviewed articles evaluating mental–health-promoting interventions. Peer review is referred to as a system that guarantees high-quality research. At present, intervention effectiveness and outcomes are prominent topics for investigation (Krejsler 2013). This accords with the demands that health research be translatable to practitioners. Therefore, it may be difficult to acquire funding for or acknowledgment of research other than effectiveness studies or process evaluations. However, even if this were the case, we have shown in our analysis that it does not preclude raising questions about children as agents and informants, the contextual impact on outcomes and health, and the school as an appropriate or unsuitable setting for health promotion.

Children co-construct their lives in the context of their relations to adults and peers; their agency is enabled and restrained by the societal and material context in which they live and, therefore, their health and wellbeing are relational and contextually embedded (Watson *et al*. 2012). The understanding of these relational and embedded processes, and that children's experiences of and views on interventions could actually improve the activities is imperative for successful research on health promotion. Children – like adult service users – should be given the possibility to decide upon, evaluate and influence potential changes to health-care services (Fattore, Mason, and Watson 2012, Graham and Fitzgerald 2011, WHO n.d.). We propose that future studies pay more attention to children's experiences of universal health interventions. The results of the present study suggest that a child-centred and service-user approach should be increasingly applied when public health interventions aimed at children are designed, implemented and evaluated. In such cases, health-promotion research could benefit from engaging with sociology of childhood perspectives.

Throughout this chapter, we have applied the concepts of children and the child rather than, for instance, students or pupils or teenagers. This in itself could risk homogenising and decontextualising children. Indeed, the children referred to in the sample are of different ages, come from different national contexts, attend different schools, and so on. Some of the interventions the texts discuss are directed at primary school, others at adolescents; the intervention activities differ in content and duration. Nevertheless, these aspects do not appear to have an influence on the discourse when comparing the research articles. For instance, texts referring to interventions offered to adolescents do not discuss children's experiences of, or motives to engage or not engage in the intervention, to any greater extent than do those involving children in primary school. Age as such, we propose, needs further attention in discussions on children's participation and agency with regard to health-promoting interventions (see Tisdall and Punch 2012, Valentine 2011).

In addition, we suggest a more vibrant discussion on the part of the school system in the structuring of children's agency. It has been proposed that children's lives have been increasingly regulated, standardised and adult-controlled, particularly through prolonged mandatory schooling (Prout 2005). Through the schools, children's mobility, activities and core subject knowledge are in part controlled. It could be argued that when introducing mental–health-promoting interventions in compulsory school settings, national and local governments take another step further to regulate children by utilising instruments that aim to direct how a child lives, feels, behaves and handles emotions. This calls for critical and child-oriented research on mental–health-promoting interventions in school settings.

Acknowledgements

We would like to thank the anonymous reviewers and the editors for their constructive and helpful comments during the review process.

References

Aggleton, P., Dennison, C. and Warwick, I. (2010) *Promoting Health and Wellbeing through Schools*. London and New York: Routledge.

Bergnehr, D. (2015a) Advancing home-school relations through parent support? Ethnography and Education, doi: 10.1080/17457823.2014.985240.

Bergnehr, D. (2015b) Föräldrastöd genom skolan: Diskursiva tillämpningar av nationell politik inom en svensk kommun [Parent support through the schools: The discursive recontextualisation of national policies in a Swedish local authority]. Nordic Studies in Education, 35, 1, 70–83.

Bitsch, L. and Stemerding, D. (2013) The innovation journey of genomics and asthma research, *Sociology of Health & Illness*, 35, 8, 1164–80.

Bluebond-Langner, M. (1980) *The Private Worlds of Dying Children.* Princeton: Princeton University Press.

Bluebond-Langner, M. (1996) *In the Shadow of Illness.* Princeton: Princeton University Press.

Borup, I.K. and Holstein, B.E. (2011) Family relations and the outcome of health promotion dialogues with school nurses in Denmark, *Vård i Norden*, 31, 1, 43–6.

Burman, E. (1994) *Deconstructing Developmental Psychology.* London and New York: Routledge.

Coppock, V. (2007) It's good to talk! A multidimensional qualitative study of the effectiveness of emotional literacy work in schools, *Children & Society*, 21, 6, 405–19.

Evans, R. and Spicer, N. (2008) Is participation prevention? A blurring of discourses in children's preventive initiatives in the UK, *Childhood*, 15, 1, 50–73.

Fattore, T., Mason, J. and Watson, E. (2012) Locating the child centrally as subject in research: towards a child interpretation of wellbeing, *Child Indicators Research*, 5, 3, 423–35.

Foucault, M. (1978) *The History of Sexuality, Vol. 1, An Introduction.* London: Penguin.

Gallacher, L. and Gallagher, M. (2008) Methodological immaturity in childhood research? Thinking through 'participatory methods', *Childhood*, 15, 4, 499–516.

Gillander Gådin, K., Weiner, G. and Ahlgren, C. (2009) Young students as participants in school health promotion: an intervention study in a Swedish elementary school, *International Journal of Circumpolar Health*, 68, 5, 498–507.

Gillander Gådin, K., Weiner, G. and Ahlgren, C. (2013) School health promotion to increase empowerment, gender equality and pupil participation: a focus group study of a Swedish elementary school initiative, *Scandinavian Journal of Educational Research*, 57, 1, 54–70.

Graham, A. and Fitzgerald, R. (2011) Supporting children's social and emotional wellbeing: does 'having a say' matter?, *Children & Society*, 25, 6, 447–57.

Hall, S. (2001) Foucault: power, knowledge and discourse. In Wetherell, M., Taylor, S. and Yates, S.J. (eds) *Discourse Theory and Practice – A Reader*. London, Thousand Oaks and New Delhi: Sage.

Haraldsson, K.S., Lindgren, E.-C.M., Fridlund, B.G.A., Baigi, A.M.A.E., *et al.* (2008) Evaluation of a school-based health promotion programme for adolescents aged 12–15 years with focus on wellbeing related to stress, *Public Health*, 122, 1, 25–33.

Holen, S., Waaktaar, T., Lervåg, A. and Ystgaard, M. (2012) The effectiveness of a universal school-based programme on coping and mental health: a randomised, controlled study of Zippy's Friends, *Educational Psychology*, 32, 5, 657–77.

Holland, S., Renold, E., Ross, N.J. and Hillman, A. (2010) Power, agency and participatory agendas: a critical exploration of young people's engagement in participate qualitative research, *Childhood*, 17, 3, 360–75.

James, A. and Prout, A. (1997) *Constructing and Reconstructing Childhood.* London: Falmer.

Joronen, K., Konu, A., Rankin, S.H. and Åstedt-Kurki, P. (2011) An evaluation of a drama program to enhance social relationships and anti-bullying at elementary school: a controlled study, *Health Promotion International*, 27, 1, 5–12.

Kimber, B., Sandell, R. and Bremberg, S. (2008a) Social and emotional training in Swedish classrooms for the promotion of mental health: results from an effectiveness study in Sweden, *Health Promotion International*, 23, 2, 134–43.

Kimber, B., Sandell, R. and Bremberg, S. (2008b) Social and emotional training in Swedish schools for the promotion of mental health: an effectiveness study of 5 years of intervention, *Health Education Research*, 23, 6, 931–40.

Krejsler, J.B. (2013) What works in education and social welfare? A mapping of the evidence discourse and reflections upon consequences for professionals, *Scandinavian Journal of Educational Research*, 57, 1, 16–32.

Kvist Lindholm, S. and Zetterqvist Nelson, K. (2014) 'Apparently I've got low self-esteem': schoolgirls' perspectives on a school-based public health intervention, *Children & Society*, doi:10.1111/chso.12083.

Latour, B. (1993) *We Have Never Been Modern.* Cambridge: Harvard University Press.

Lee, N. (2001) *Childhood and Society: Growing Up in an Age of Uncertainty.* Maidenhead: Open University Press.

Lee, N. (2005) *Childhood and Human Value: Development, Separation and Separability*. Maidenhead: Open University Press.

Liegghio, M., Nelson, G. and Evans, S.D. (2010) Partnering with children diagnosed with mental health issues: contributions of a sociology of childhood perspective to participatory action research, *American Journal of Community Psychology*, 46, 1-2, 84–99.

Marmot, M. (2010) *Fair Society – Healthy Lives: the Marmot Review.* UCL Institute of Health Equity. Available at http://www.instituteofhealthequity.org/projects/fair-society-healthy-lives-the-marmot-review(accessed 4 September 2014).

Martin, E. (1991) The egg and the sperm: how science has constructed a romance based on stereotypical male-female roles, *Signs*, 16, 3, 485–501.

Mason, J. and Hood, S. (2011) Exploring issues of children as actors in social research, *Children and Youth Service Review*, 33, 4, 490–5.

Mayall, B. (1994) *Children's Childhoods: Observed and Experienced.* London and Washington: Falmer Press.

Mayall, B. (1996) *Children, Health and the Social Order*. Buckingham and Philadelphia: Open University Press.

Oswell, D. (2013) *The Agency of Children: From Family to Global Human Rights.* Cambridge: Cambridge University Press.

Prout, A. (2005) *The Future of Childhood*. London and New York: RoutledgeFalmer.

Qvortrup, J. (1994) *Childhood Matters: Social Theory, Practice and Politics*. Aldershot: Avebury.

St Leger, L. (2004) What's the place of schools in promoting health? Are we too optimistic?, *Health Promotion International*, 19, 4, 405–08.

Samdal, O. and Rowling, L. (2013) *The Implementation of Health Promoting Schools: Exploring the Theories of What, Why and How*. London and New York: Routledge.

Simovska, V. (2007) The changing meanings of participation in school-based health education and health promotion: the participants' voice, *Health Education Research*, 22, 6, 864–78.

Singh, I. (2013) Brain talk: power and negotiation in children's discourse about self, brain and behaviour, *Sociology of Health & Illness*, 35, 6, 813–27.

Sormunen, M., Saaranen, T., Tossavainen, K. and Turunen, H. (2012) Process evaluation of an elementary school health learning intervention in Finland, *Health Education*, 112, 3, 272–91.

Sormunen, M., Tossavainen, K. and Turunen, H. (2013) Finnish parental involvement ethos, health support, health education knowledge and participation: results from a 2-year school health intervention, *Health Education Research*, 28, 2, 179–91.

Tisdall, K. and Punch, S. (2012) Not so new? Looking critically at childhood studies, *Children's Geographies*, 10, 3, 249–63.

Todd, L. (2012) Critical dialogue, critical methodology: bridging the research gap to young people's participation in evaluating children's services, *Children's Geographies*, 10, 2, 187–200.

UNICEF (1989) Convention on the Rights of the Child. Available at http://www.unicef.org.uk/ UNICEFs-Work/UN-Convention/ (accessed 11 September 2014).

Uprichard, E. (2008) Children as 'being and becomings': children, childhood and temporality, *Children & Society*, 22, 4, 303–13.

Valentine, K. (2011) Accounting for agency, *Children & Society*, 25, 5, 347–58.

Vince Whitman, C. and Aldinger, C.E. (2009) *Case Studies in Global School Health Promotion: From Research to Practice*. New York: Springer.

Watson, D., Emery, C., Bayliss, P., Boushel, M., and McInnes, K. (2012) *Children's Social and Emotional Wellbeing in Schools: A Critical Perspective*. Bristol: Policy Press.

Weedon, C. (1987) *Feminist Practice and Poststructuralist Theory*. Oxford: Basil Blackwell.

8

Wickström, A. (2013) From individual to relational strategies: Transforming a manual-based psycho-educational course at school, *Childhood*, 20, 2, 215–28.

World Health Organization (WHO) (n.d.) Jakarta Declaration on Leading Health Promotion into the 21st Century. Available at http://www.who.int/healthpromotion/conferences/previous/jakarta/declaration/en/ (accessed 10 June 2013).

WHO (1997) *Promoting Health Through Schools*. Geneva: WHO.

WHO (2005) *The Bangkok Charter for Health Promotion in a Globalized World*. Bangkok: WHO.

Wyness, M., Harrison, L. and Buchanan, I. (2004) Childhood, politics and ambiguity: towards an agenda for children's political inclusion, *Sociology*, 38, 1, 81–99.

Appendix A

Table A1   *Sample*

Article	Design and data	Sample and informants	Intervention
1. Borup and Holstein (2011)	Panel survey. Self-reported questionnaire.	55 schools. 5205 children 11–15 yrs.	Health promotion dialogues with school nurse.
2. Gillander *et al.* (2013)	Process study. Focus group interviews.	1 school. 6 focus groups with children 7–12 yrs.	Project promoting active participation, gender equality and empowerment.
3. Gillander *et al.* (2009)	Textual analyses. Written proposals and protocols.	1 school. 41 documents composed by children aged 7–12 years and staff.	Group discussions on health-promoting factors.
4. Haraldsson *et al.* (2008)	Controlled study. Self-reported questionnaires pre- and post-intervention.	1 intervention and 1 control school. 440 children aged 12–15 years.	Programme (1 year duration) promoting well-being and preventing stress through massage and mental training.
5. Holen *et al.* (2012)	Randomized controlled study. Self-reported questionnaire. Parent and teacher questionnaire.	35 schools. 1483 children aged 7–8 years, parents and teachers.	24 weekly lessons to promote coping strategies and mental health.
6. Joronen *et al.* (2011)	Quasi-experimental longitudinal controlled study. Self-reported questionnaire pre- and post-intervention.	1 intervention and 1 control school. 134 children aged 10–12 years.	Programme to promote social wellbeing. Class room drama sessions and follow-up activities at home.
7. Kimber *et al.* (2008a)	Quasi-experimental longitudinal controlled study. Self-reported questionnaire; baseline and subsequent assessments.	2 intervention and 2 control schools, 41 classes. Children aged 7–14 years.	Programme offering social and emotional training 1–2 times a week during consecutive years.

(continued)

Table A1   *(continued)*

Article	Design and data	Sample and informants	Intervention
8. Kimber *et al.* (2008b)	Effectiveness study, quasi-experimental and longitudinal control study. Self-reported questionnaires each year.	2 intervention and 2 control schools. Children aged 12–16 years.	Programme offering social and emotional training 1–2 times a week during consecutive years.
9. Sormunen *et al.* (2013)	Quasi-experimental control study; participatory action research. Parent questionnaire pre- and post-intervention.	2 intervention and 2 control schools. 184 parents.	2-year intervention to increase home-school partnership for children's health learning. Grade 4–6 children.
10. Sormunen *et al.* (2012)	Process evaluation. Documents; interviews.	Interviews with 2 teachers and 3 parents.	2-year intervention to increase home-school partnership for children's health learning.

3

Biologising parenting: neuroscience discourse, English social and public health policy and understandings of the child

Pam Lowe, Ellie Lee and Jan Macvarish

Introduction

In recent years, claims about children's developing brains have become central to the formation of child health and welfare policies in England. Moreover, this has included a strong shift towards the construction of parenting as a key determinant of brain development and thus the child's future. While these policies assert that they are based on neuro-scientific discoveries, their relationship to neuroscience has been debated (see for example Wilson 2002). This trend is part of the broader shift to 'neuroculture' in which interpretations of the brain are reconstructing existing understandings of mind/body, nature/culture, and identity/development (Vidal 2009, Williams *et al.* 2012). Within child health and welfare policies, we will argue that 'neuroculture' has led to a particular portrayal of children and childhood, one that is marked by a lack of acknowledgment of child personhood. In addition, within the resulting parental determinism, the emphasis on intervention produces a specific idea of children 'at risk' thus justifying a culture of surveillance and monitoring in relation to family life.

This chapter arises from a wider study of the emergence of 'neuroculture' in parenting policies.[1] The study was not a critique of neuroscience itself, but sought to investigate through documentary analysis the ways in which ideas about children's brain development were shaping the policy context. Within this we considered the construction of the child within policy discourse, in particular, the significance attributed to parental actions in developing the child's brain for good or bad. This chapter will describe how the child[2] is represented within these claims and explore their implications for children and their parents more generally. We will argue that despite policy claims that the child is at the centre of policy thinking and that 'every child matters', the research has shown that by focusing on the brain, a highly reductionist and limiting construction of the child is produced which has implications for the design of health and welfare services.

The rise of 'neurocultural' claims

As many authors have documented, while neuroscience and brain-imaging techniques have future potential to assist in the development of scientific insights, many of the current claims about neuroscience in popular arenas are not based on evidence (see for example, Racine *et al.*

Children, Health and Well-being: Policy Debates and Lived Experience, First Edition. Edited by Geraldine Brady, Pam Lowe and Sonja Olin Lauritzen. Chapters © 2015 The Authors. Book Compilation © 2015 Foundation for the Sociology of Health & Illness/Blackwell Publishing Ltd.

2010, O'Connor *et al.* 2012, Satel and Lilienfeld 2013). As Rose and Abi-Rached 2013 argue (2013) while policymakers may look to neuroscience for answers to issues such as enhancing child development or reducing anti-social behaviour, to date it has few answers. Moreover, the areas of policy now using brain development to give weight to their claims are often those with a longer history of similar interventions. Rose and Abi-Rached (2013: 162) suggest that while the neuroscientific arguments may be being used to give policy initiatives 'a sheen of objectivity', they are also an important indicator of a shift of broader understandings about the brain.

An important element is that often in wider discourses the limits of neuroscience are frequently overlooked. As Roskies (2006) argues, neuroscience can show the mechanisms for behaviour, but it does not show that the brain determines behaviour. Fine et al (2013) maintain that over simplified and rigid brain-to-behaviour narratives fail to account for the interplay of social and environmental factors. Yet as Satel and Lilienfeld (2013: 15) suggest, within some neuro-discourses, the mind and the brain are coming to be seen as identical rather than interrelated:

> Brain-based explanations … for social behaviours that elude crucial psychological, social, and cultural levels of analysis fall into the trap of neurocentrism … The brain enables the mind and thus the person. But neuroscience cannot yet, if ever, explain how this happens.

In other words, while neuroscience has the capacity to bring new understandings about brain functioning and aid the development of understandings of brain conditions such as dementia, it cannot be used to explain humanity more broadly (Tallis 2012).

'Neurocultural' claims and children's brains

In relation to children, much of the focus within brain-based understandings constructs the early years as a time of unique neural vulnerability, when without the correct environmental influences, normal development will be disrupted and may never be recovered (Thornton 2011). Bruer (1999) has argued that these claims have arisen from three particular ideas associated with brain development in the first three years that have been misconstrued. The first idea is that the developmental synaptogenesis (rapid increase in synapse density) that takes place is uniquely significant. Bruer (1999) argues that the early years are not the only time for developmental synaptogenesis and more synapses do not necessarily mean more brain functioning. The second idea is the early years are a time-sensitive period for development. Although it is the case that a few areas are time-sensitive (for example, deprivation of vision during early years will affect development), Bruer (1999) points out that time-sensitive skills or behaviours are exceptions and it is an exaggeration to see the early years as a general time-sensitive period. The final area is the notion of enriched environments. Bruer (1999) argues that while very extreme neglect can negatively impact on a child's brain development, this is not the same as saying that brain development can be enhanced by enriching environments in the early years.[3]

The notion that the brains of neglected children are at risk is worth considering further. While it is the case that very extreme circumstances can lead to altered brain development (Behan *et al.* 2008), the issue is complex. The issue of deprivation and neglect has been extensively explored following the discovery of children raised in Romanian Orphanages in the 1990s where large numbers of malnourished children were found confined to cots within institutions with minimum adult contact and little to no sensory stimulation (Rutter *et al.* 1998). Many of these children were subsequently adopted into Western countries, and their progress has been tracked. Rutter and colleagues' (2010) research found that there could be good recovery even after this extreme early deprivation and that it was institutional deprivation, rather neglect itself, which was a key determinant of development issues. In addition, while the work of Perry (1997) is often used to justify brain-based approaches, he has always been clear that there is no automatic route between emotionally neglected children and adult violence.

Policy and the developing child

Yet despite the neuroscience understanding that the brain is actually notable for its 'plasticity' and it is adaptable rather than 'hard-wired' (see Pascual-Leone *et al.* 2005 for a discussion) this chapter will show that this has not stopped policymakers from adopting and incorporating deterministic 'brain claims' into English social and public health policy. In England, the claims began to be noticeable in the early 2000s, but since then there has been an expansion of the utilisations of them. The move to promote and adopt early intervention child health and welfare programmes (e.g. Allen and Duncan Smith 2008) is a notable example of this trend. These early intervention policies differ from previous social initiatives in that they are premised on the specific ideas arising from 'neuroculture' outlined above. They take as their starting point the notion that the 'early years' are the most important in a person's life because of an irreversible role in cognitive and emotional development and thus early intervention is justified and necessary (Macvarish *et al.* 2014).

In the earliest years of life, the 'environment' is usually understood to be the family or the mother, hence the intense focus on parenting and motherhood. Indeed as O'Connor and Joffe's (2013) study showed, the intra-uterine environment is increasingly named in media stories on brain and child-development. Media stories claim that what happens in the womb influences the future potential of a child in a range of areas from the risk of psychiatric disorders to sexual orientation (O'Connor and Joffe 2013). Hence early intervention policies are situated within a broader 'neurocultural' discourse that focuses on parenting as both a cause of and solution to the child's brain development. This deterministic view of child development fits into wider understandings of children's lives.

Turmel (2008) argues that the developmental model of childhood emerged at the turn of the twentieth century. He argues that it was the nineteenth century move for the categorisation and classification of children though observation and measurement which led to a development of the concept of the 'normal child' (Turmel 2008: 77). This concept is reflected in an understanding of child development as a series of universal stages which can be seen in the work of Piaget (Hill and Tisdall 1997, Turmel 2008). Turmel (2008) shows that while at first monitoring children was seen as a role for mothers, the site of observation shifted to experts with the founding of child-welfare clinics such as that opened by Pritchard in London in 1907. It is into this long history of child development concerns, parenting advice and child-welfare initiatives that the current policy initiatives need to be situated.

As Corsaro (2011) has outlined, there has been widespread criticism of the universal deterministic model of child development which fails to consider the ways in which children shape their own lives within the social and economic structures that they live in. Moreover even young children can be competent and articulate about their thoughts and feelings, providing they are asked in the right way (Alderson 2013). More recent developmental theories have often focused on the internalisation of adult skills and knowledge (James *et al.* 1998;

Corsaro, 2011), yet this understanding of children as social actors, albeit within a world usually shaped by adults, is rarely acknowledged. Consequently, it is not much of a leap between the notion that children are predestined to 'learn' the skills from adults to the idea that the brain itself needs to be 'wired' appropriately, and thus children's futures lives are predestined by early years brain development. We will argue that it is this notion of the brain rather than the mind that disembodies the child within health, welfare and parenting policies.

Wastell and White (2012) argue that this presumption of biological determinism and its associated medicalisation has had profound effects on child welfare, and led to a shift in emphasis to standardised targeted interventions to 'cure' the problem. Featherstone *et al.* (2013) have also raised concerns about the implications of this shift in policy and the links to changed understandings of child protection rather than family support. Both these papers draw attention to how the child is both biologised yet disembodied. The brain is thus becoming central to the identification of children 'at risk' and interventions targeted to manage this perceived biological lack. Moreover, as Hulbert (2004) has documented in the US, the brain is increasingly seen 'as the child' rather than being part of the child. Thus a normalised view of brain development based on a rigid understanding of child development leaves little room for children to be considered as autonomous individuals with the capacity to shape their own futures.

Moreover, understanding the architecture of the brain, tells us little about thoughts and feelings as mental activities do not, and probably never will, map easily onto brain regions (Satel and Lilienfeld 2013). If the brain is the sole or major determinant of responsibility for thoughts and actions, then any presumption of free-will could be seen to be illusionary (see Murphy and Brown, 2009 for a fuller discussion). Yet despite widespread critiques that a reductionist position is not warranted, the idea that brain development determines the mind, and thus future behaviour is increasingly central to child health and welfare policies. Indeed a key rationale for early intervention is that some parents are incapable of developing their children's brains 'properly' (Rose and Abi-Rached 2013). In other words, ideas of intergenerational transmission of 'good' and 'bad' behaviour through parenting is central to brain-based policy.

Methodology

This chapter is developed from a wider study concerned with the emergence and embedding of 'brain-based' claims in British policy concerned with 'parenting'. The object of the research was to understand the ways in which 'parenting' has been constructed as a policy problem, in particular, one which can be resolved through the adoption of 'scientific' approaches to its improvement. It was seeking to explore the adoption of concepts and vocabulary attributed to neuroscience as a particular focus in order to study what appeared to be an explicit 'scientisation' of the parent-child relationship.

The project sought to trace the adoption of claims using the authority of neuro-scientific evidence in policy-thinking from 1998 to 2012, through analysis of a purposive sample of 42 documents. These documents were selected by the research team in line with the criteria detailed below. We identified documents which were central to the formation of parenting policy across a number of domains. As well as those directly on parenting and early child development, the full sample included those looking at social exclusion, criminal justice and health and maternity services. Following an initial screening, 42 documents were chosen for full analysis based on the inclusion of key concepts (e.g. parenting, brains, attunement) and/or their influence on later policy. We thus sought to uncover a chronological account that mapped how brain discourses moved from being a 'backstage' discussion in early policies to a significant way of organising the relationship between health and early years practitioners, the parenting workforce and families.

Included in the sample were documents published by government departments including consultation and strategy documents (29), reports commissioned by government departments (7), as well as those emanating from advocacy groups (6) which have subsequently become key reference points in later policy. Full details of the sample can be found in Lee *et al*. (2013). All the documents were uploaded into NVivo (QSR International, Melbourne) and then thematically analysed, through close reading and coding of documents. These codes were then used to identify key themes. We also sought to identify the links between the different documents by tracing how understandings of the different concepts travelled through different documents over time. In addition we undertook some mapping of key terms (e.g. parenting, brain, cortisol) using the word count functions to get a sense of how the policy discourse was changing over time.

This chapter uses examples from our sample as representative of the broader trends we have found in the study. Quotations have been identified which illustrate how the two key areas: the eclipsing of the mind into the brain, and the brain rather than an embodied child, are deployed in parenting policies. This will illustrate the ways in which brain-determinism in parenting policies leads to a narrow conceptualisation of children and child health within which the child is simultaneously both central to the policy agenda, yet overlooked in terms of their personhood.

Mind-less brains

The idea of intergenerational disadvantage has a long history in English welfare policies, and a common theme among family welfare policies is the notion of 'breaking the cycle'. Cunningham (2005) has documented this history of interventions to 'save' children from incompetent or indifferent parents. What is new, however, is the idea that brain development is the key to achieving this (Rose and Abi-Rached 2013). For example, *Every Child Matters*[4] (Chief Secretary to the Treasury 2003) emphasised the role of parenting as a key site of potential intervention in children's lives, but made no mention of brain development. A year later, brain development is mentioned in *Support from the Start*[5] (Sutton *et al*. 2004). This report highlights a number of areas of risk factors for the development of behavioural issues in children and does mention the possibility of adverse brain development caused by stress (referencing the work of Perry). However, it argues that a combination of physiology and social factors could lead to aggressiveness (Sutton *et al*. 2004). Less than a decade later, the idea that brain development is a key determinate seems to be uncritically accepted in a wide range of reports. For example in *Healthy Lives, Healthy People*[6] (Department of Health 2010: 18) the role of neurons is central in this extract:

> At birth, babies have around a quarter of the brain neurons of an adult. By the age of 3, the young child has around twice the number of neurons of an adult – making the early years critical for the development of the brain, language, social, emotional and motor skills.

An important element is a new idea of the process of intergenerational transmission. At its heart, is the notion that dysfunctional families fail to develop their children's brains (probably because of their own brain-dysfunction). By intervening early enough in young children's

lives, the policy can ensure that the future children within these families have better opportunities for brain development and thus will be able to optimise their own children's lives in
future generations. Allen and Duncan Smith's (2008)[7] report is typical of this approach. It
focuses on children's brain development in the early years to justify a strategy of intervention:

> The Early Intervention objective is nothing less than to replace a vicious cycle with a
> virtuous circle; to help every child become a capable and responsible parent who in turn
> will raise better children who themselves will learn, attain and raise functional families
> of their own. (Allen and Duncan Smith 2008: 5).

This report claims that early intervention can reduce the 'flow' of people into the dysfunctional 'stock' (Allen and Duncan Smith 2008: 24). Although it does not overtly argue that we
need to limit the number of children born (except teenage pregnancy), it does seek to stop the
transmission of 'undesirable behaviours'. Within this report there are a remarkable number
of social issues that claimed to be potentially preventable should children's brains be built
properly. These include unemployment, criminality and drug-addiction (Allen and Duncan
Smith 2008: 12). Indeed the entire economic rationale for the policy is that it will reduce
future expenditure on welfare, health and criminal-justice services (Allen and Duncan Smith
2008: 15). Thus child brain development is a determinist feature of future behaviour, and parenting interventions are necessary as the (incompetent) parent's brains may not have developed sufficiently for them to be able to raise their children adequately without intervention.

What is interesting is the ways in which the mind, the thinking and feeling consciousness of
individuals, is both absent and present within policy documents. The emphasis on the brain
as central to the (good) functioning of the developing child, is portrayed as determined and
a matter of appropriate neuron-development. So for example in *Reaching Out: An Action
Plan on Social Exclusion*[8] it is stated that:

> It is also known from research just how important a child's early experiences are to the
> development of the brain. The child who is spoken to will develop speech and language
> neural systems, and the child who has motor practice and exploration opportunities will
> develop neural systems which allow walking, running and fine motor control. The child
> who is nurtured and loved will develop the neural networks which mediate empathy,
> compassion and the capacity to form healthy relationships (Cabinet Office 2006: 47).

In this extract we can see how the capacity of the mind to be thoughtful and have feelings
is reduced to particular neuron pathways, but it goes further than that. It uses an image
of very extreme neglect to justify the position. The idea that some children are never/rarely
spoken to and are tethered rather than being able to move is reminiscent of the conditions
of the Romanian orphanages which goes beyond issues of deprived households and social
exclusion.

The notion that empathy is a skill rooted in neurological development in early childhood
can also be found in other policy documents. For example in *The Child Health Promotion
Programme: Pregnancy and the First Five Years of Life* (Department of Health 2008)[9] the section entitled 'Promotion of social and emotional development' starts with the statement that:

> More is known today than ever about the neurological development of infants, and the
> impact of poor attachment and negative parenting on a child's physical, cognitive and
> socio-emotional development – not only in childhood, but also as a key determinant of
> adult health (Department of Health 2008: 23)

The section does not mention any other influence suggesting that neurological development is the sole or main cause. Later on the same page it highlights that successful parenting support includes:

> The ability to promote attachment, laying the foundations for a child's trust in the world, and its later capacity for empathy and responsiveness (Department of Health 2008: 23)

Taken together the statements in this report again suggest that the emotional intelligence of adults arises from brain development in early childhood. Clearly there are differences between children and groups of children in regards to emotional development. However the suggestion that these are reducible to brain development in early childhood ignores factors such as social and educational experiences (and resources) way beyond parent-child interactions. Indeed the meaning of 'empathy', 'compassion' and 'healthy relationships' are cultural and historical questions and the reduction of these to neural networks foregrounds brain-architecture at the expense of an understanding of the mind as thoughtful.

This policy premise that child brain development fixes the capacity to be empathetic and compassionate also seems to be undermined by the notion that parents can be trained to be ideal parents. If the brain development in childhood is deterministic, then it would seem reasonable to suggest that no amount of training could re-wire the adult brain. Yet a significant proportion of parenting policy is designed to ensure that inadequate parents learn to deliver appropriate emotional responses. For example Allen (2011: 17)[10] sets out the case for parenting interventions to develop the attunement of parents and young children. Attunement is deemed to be the ability to be able to respond to a child's emotional needs and without it children will lack empathy and have a propensity towards violence. The report emphasises that parenting interventions can assist to develop these skills, including an emphasis on non-violent parenting. Thus the propensity for violence seems to be both 'hard-wired' into children yet malleable in adults, a contradiction that is not easily explainable.

Yet what is clear in these brain-based policies is that the mind of the developing child is largely absent from the debates. Little consideration is given to the notion that children are thinking and feeling individuals who play a role in their own destinies. The ways that the brain comes to stand for the child will be developed further in the next section.

Brain as child

As Rose and Abi-Rached (2013) have outlined, while the idea that dysfunctional families 'hand on' their dysfunction through generations is not new, ideas from neuroscience have been used to argue that the brain is the mechanism of the transition. Typical of the explanatory frameworks is this version stated in *The Child Health Promotion Programme: Pregnancy and the First Five Years of Life*:

> A child's brain develops rapidly in the first two years of life, and is influenced by the emotional and physical environment as well as by genetic factors. Early interactions directly affect the way the brain is wired, and early relationships set the 'thermostat' for later control of the stress response. (Department of Health 2008: 9)

Again here we can see illustrated the emphasis on the first few years as the critical period in a child's life when the brain both develops and gets 'set'. The other indicator here that is noteworthy is the idea that a crucial component is the 'stress' response. This can be linked to the psychological notion that an insecure attachment between children and their primary care-givers will go on to have implications for other types of relationships. The idea of attachment as an essential part of child development arose from the work of Bowlby and others such as Ainsworth and despite the widespread evidence critiquing this understanding; it remains prominent in ideas about child development (Harris 2007, Wall 2010). A connection is made between the stress responses in childhood and later adult stress responses. The implication is that these children will be hyper-vigilant and thus have a tendency for antisocial behaviour leading to deviant adulthood. For example, in *The Foundation Years: Preventing Poor Children becoming Poor Adults*[11] it states:

> The development of a baby's brain is affected by the attachment to their parents and analysis of neglected children's brains has shown that their brain growth is significantly reduced. Where babies are often left to cry, their cortisol levels are increased and this can lead to a permanent increase in stress hormones later in life, which can impact on mental health. (Field 2010: 41)

The idea that brain-wiring is a crucial determinate of anti-social behaviour in later life is one of the ways in which the child's brain comes to stand in as the child. Thus, it is not the child as a person that needs to be cared for in their own right, but the brain that needs proper development. For example, *Early Intervention: Good Parents, Great Kids, Better Citizens* justifies early intervention because:

> Human infants arrive ready to be programmed by adults … Neuroscience can now explain why early conditions are so crucial: effectively, our brains are largely formed by what we experience in early life. (Allen and Duncan Smith 2008: 56–7)

It is only through the assumption that it is the brain rather than the child that is the key point of intervention that the focus on the 'right' form of parenting thus becomes a crucial determinate of child welfare. It is not necessary to reduce poverty or provide decent housing for example, as the only element that matters is the interaction between the parent and the child. Hence poverty for children is no longer measured in material terms, it is reduced to an attribute of parenting. After all, if the brain is the child, the needs and health of the body are no longer a necessary concern of the state, but just an outcome of (poor) parenting.

Parental determinism

Consequently, parents are repositioned as both a potential cause and solution to the 'problem' of the developing child, and the quality of parenting, rather than the child itself, come to be a major focus of state policy. Thus, while the child is nominally at the centre of early intervention policies, the focus remains on the child as a 'becoming' rather than a 'being' (Qvortrup, 1994). In other words, early intervention policies are based on the need to develop children as future citizens rather than an understanding of children as part of society today.

In this context, parenting can be understood as either 'optimising' or 'limiting' brain development in children. In terms of 'optimisation', 'neurocultural' ideas are deployed to underpin new insights into how we might enhance our child's brain capacity by loving and stimulating them in particular ways. In policy terms, the claims for this are about ensuring 'normal' development, but it is useful to remember that commercial claims of 'brain-training' toys and activities aimed at 'enhancing' child development are a constant background within wider culture (Nadesan 2002). The 'limiting' perspective has more pessimistic connotations, expressing anxieties about social disorder and alienated individuals but also constructing particular social groups (usually the poor) as neurologically disadvantaged and behaviourally problematic. In this invocation of brain science, the effects of inappropriate parenting are inscribed in the infant brain, bearing consequences not just for the child and its parents, but for society as a whole.

Hence within the policies, there is an increased emphasis on parent-training in order to potentially avoid these issues. Consequently parents are deemed to be a key determinate in the development of the child's brain, and thus the child itself. These ideas can be seen in the following extracts:

> The brain stem of a young child growing up in an atmosphere of unpredictable violence, such as families where routine domestic abuse takes place, is likely to become over reactive, by comparison with that of a child developing in a calm environment. If that unpredictable violence persists, the young child may learn to become hyper-vigilant to perceptions of threat; and this hyper-vigilance may undermine his capacity to concentrate on ordinary childhood activities, as well as making him over-prepared to respond impulsively and aggressively. (Sutton *et al.* 2004: 34)

> Although poor parenting practices can cause damage to children of all ages, the worst and deepest damage is done to children when their brains are being formed during their earliest months and years. The most serious damage takes place before birth and during the first 18 months of life when formation of the part of the brain governing emotional development has been identified to be taking place. (Allen 2011: 15)

These quotations illustrate the ways in which parenting is seen as a crucial determinate of brain development and thus determines the future potential of the child. However as Kagan (1998) has argued, the appeal of brain claims resides in the prior cultural tendency towards 'infant determinism' in which the early years are said to determine adult lives. Yaqub (2002) observes that the scientific vocabulary endows pre-existing commonsense ideas of infant determinism with renewed authority. As Wall (2010) and O'Connor *et al.* (2012) have shown, societal concern about the impact of early experiences on later development, developed with the popularisation of psychoanalysis and attachment theory in the early twentieth century. Ideas about brain development have now become an 'important reference point in child-rearing decisions' used to 'indicate the "correctness" of parenting practices' (O'Connor *et al.* 2012: 221).

Although the use of a neuro-vocabulary of synapses, neurons and cortisol might suggest that new scientific evidence demands a shake-up of existing ways of raising children, in fact, the recommendations using the authority of brain science are remarkably similar to existing ideas about what (and who) constitutes good parenting. This suggests that it is cultural norms, rather than scientific discovery, that are shaping the claims of good parenting within policy (Thompson and Nelson 2001, Wilson 2002).

Writing children off, holding parents to account

This chapter has set out three trends in policies related to the design and development of services for children and their families. Emerging from the adoption of neuroscientific ideas, the (potential) brain rather than the child has become the major site of intervention. As the brain has become more prominent, embodied children have increasingly disappeared from consideration. The ability of children to think, act or feel has been reduced to an outcome of their parent's behaviour towards them within the early years. The reduction of an understanding of children to a mind-less brain, stands in opposition to any recognition of children as social actors.

In her review of policy assumptions, Mayall (2006) argued that while there had been some changes in policymaking that recognised that children have a right to be heard, there were still underlying assumptions that the value of children was largely as future adults. She also argued that child protection is often prioritised over provision for children and children's participation is often tokenistic. This analysis has shown that in these policies this trend has continued. Understandings from the sociology of childhood, such as the social construction of childhoods and that children actively contribute to their own social development within co-constructed families (Corsaro 2011), do not appear in the documents. Moreover children's position as 'at risk' from poor parenting continues the theme of children as victims that Mayall (2006) previously identified.

In addition, the emphasis on parenting as the key determinate of child development has other important implications for children's health and welfare. It justifies increasingly harsh welfare regimes, as poverty need no longer be considered seriously, as the main concern is with current and potential transmission of social disorder. Good parenting is said to be able to provide 'resilience' to adverse circumstances, and thus investment in the provision of parenting classes can be prioritised over other issues such as an adequate income or housing. As Hulbert draws out, despite the intentions of many of the early US brain advocates that this way of understanding child development would increase public funding of programmes to help children, the consequences of the way brain science has been used in the US has seen profound fatalism and pessimism:

> If young brains subjected to deprived conditions, and to the inadequate parenting that often goes along with them, are irrevocably damaged – pickled in stress hormones, stripped of synapses – there is no time to waste, that is true. Yet such alarm, though it conveys urgency, can all too easily fuel defeatism. If children become neurologically unresilient at an early age, then only intrusive and intensive remedial efforts seem equal to the job. And if – or, let's face it, when – such intervention fails to materialise, the case for subsequent help is bound to seem weaker. (Hulbert 2004: 316)

The fact that this fatalism is not absolute – the child is negatively affected only if the parent fails to correctly nurture and stimulate the child – is significant. The idea that the years 0 to 3, or even minus 9 months to 3, represent a 'critical period' for development reduces any sense of a child's agency to a remarkably short time-frame, and it simultaneously demands of the parent the exercise of a huge amount of agency in doing the right thing for their child.

According to Nadesan (2002: 24), brain science, as popularised in the US, functions as a 'tool of social engineering for the poor' while also promising to 'engineer middle-class parents' anxiety by holding them accountable for each and every state of their infant's 'development'' (Nadesan 2002: 24). The project has found a similar trend in UK policy. Not only do brain claims shut down any discussion about different ways of raising children within policy understandings, they also promise to make parental love directly measurable in the behaviour of their offspring. The parent is therefore simultaneously disempowered by being denied the ability to make their own judgements about how best to raise their child while also having their love described as the architect of their child's brain, evident in the child's happiness and achievements and theoretically 'readable' through the technology of the brain scan. In this way, parents are held to account for an impossibly burdensome range of decisions by an apparently objective locus of authority – the brain.

Policies that seek to support families in crisis or ensure that children are protected are clearly important. Indeed if children and their parents enjoy or benefit from programmes developed from the new 'neurocultural' environment, this is clearly constructive. However, the deterministic accounts of brain-to-behaviour has other political consequences. It further erodes the line between children at risk and children who might become a risk to others (James and James 2008). In doing so, it justifies surveillance of (poor) families. Moreover, at the most extreme end of policy, Featherstone *et al.* (2013) have warned that in the name of protecting infant brains, state agencies are increasingly 'intervening early' in families deemed problematic to remove children from their birth parents into the custody of the state. In addition, it has been argued that such removals should be more rapidly converted into permanent adoptions by more suitable families to prevent permanent damage being inflicted on infant brains.

Conclusion

This chapter has sought to illustrate the ways in which the development of 'neurocultural' discourse has led to particular construction of the child within English health and social policy. It has documented the ways in which current policy discourse is increasingly focused on brains and parents rather than being concerned with children's embodied lives. The persistence of deterministic ideas indicates that the ideology of infant and parental determinism is prior to, and stronger than, any actual evidence emanating from the scientific domain. Within this policy framework, children as embodied social actors, have increasingly disappeared and have been replaced by the child as a mind-less brain, a potential victim of poor parenting. Thus while the policy rhetoric claims to be centred on the child, the focus on the brain leads to a limited understanding of children. As Hubert (2004: 316) states it reduces the infant child to a 'fate shaped by their parenthood'.

Clearly policy documents are different from both policy implementation and any actual impact on children and parent's lives. Nevertheless, they are an important indicator of trends in political understanding and can have implications for the resourcing of health and welfare services. Parents do provide a crucial component to children's lives, but the idea that children are just the outcome of parental actions is overly deterministic. It also ignores the important insights from the sociology of childhood that have clearly shown that children are active in the construction of their own and families lives. Moreover, rather than children being at the heart of child and family policy, brain-based claims refocuses the emphasis on parenting. The parenting/brain nexus configured in this policy discourse can be situated alongside health and welfare cuts without contradiction as it suggests that disadvantaged children need better trained parents rather than services.

Notes

1   The project Biologising Parenting: Neuroscience discourse and English social and public health policy was funded by the Faraday Institute within the 'Uses and Abuses of Biology' Grants Programme.
2   While children are not a homogenous group, within policies normative assumptions are often made. We use the term 'the child' to reflect the singular position often depicted.

3   For a detailed discussion of the rise of the Early Years Movement and the critiques on this position please see Macvarish *et al.* (2014).
4   Every Child Matters was published as a Green Paper which is a government consultation document.
5   Support from the Start was a research report for the Department of Education and Skills.
6   Healthy Lives, Healthy People: Our Strategy for Public Health in England was a White Paper, setting out government policy.
7   Early Intervention: Good Parents, Great Kids, Better Citizens was a report from the Centre for Social Justice (an independent think tank) but authored by two Members of Parliament.
8   Reaching Out was a government report setting out strategy for the Cabinet Office.
9   This document is best practice guidance from the Department of Health.
10   Early Intervention: The Next Steps was an independent report for government authored by an MP.
11   This was an independent report for the Prime Minister authored by an MP.

References

Alderson, P. (2013) *Childhoods Real and Imagined: Volume 1 An Introduction to Critical Realism and Childhood Studies.* Abingdon: Oxford.

Allen, G. (2011) *Early Intervention: the Next Steps. An Independent Report to Her Majesty's Government.* London: Cabinet Office.

Allen, G. and Duncan Smith, I. (2008) *Early Intervention: Good Parents, Great Kids, Better Citizens.* London: Centre for Social Justice and the Smith Institute.

Behan, M.E., Helder, E., Rothermel, R., Solomon, K. and Chugani, H.T. (2008) Incidence of specific absolute neurocognitive impairment in globally intact children with histories of early severe deprivation, *Child Neuropsychology*, 14, 5, 453–69.

Bruer, J. (1999) *The Myth of the First Three Years: A New Understanding of Early Brain Development.* New York: The Free Press.

Office, Cabinet (2006) *Reaching Out: An Action Plan on Social Exclusion.* London: Cabinet Office.

Corsaro, W.A. (2011) *The Sociology of Childhood*, 3rd edn. London: Sage.

Cunningham, H. (2005) *Children and Childhood in Western Society Since 1500.* Harlow: Pearson Educational.

Chief Secretary to the Treasury (2003) *Every Child Matters.* Cm5860 London: HMSO

Department of Health (2008) *The Child Health Promotion Programme Pregnancy and the First fIve Years of Life.* London: Central Office of Information.

Department of Health (2010) *Healthy Lives, Healthy People: Our Strategy for Public Health in England.* London: TSO.

Featherstone, B., Morris, K. and White, S. (2013) A Marriage Made in Hell: Early Intervention Meets Child Protection, *British Journal of Social Work*, 10, 1, 1–15.

Field, F. (2010) *The Foundation Years: Preventing Poor Children becoming Poor Adults: An Independent Report on Poverty and Life Chances.* London: Cabinet Office.

Fine, C., Jordan-Young, R., Kaiser, A. and Rippon, G. (2013) Plasticity, plasticity, plasticity … and the rigid problem of sex, *Trends in Cognitive Sciences*, 17, 11, 550–1.

Harris, J.R. (2007) *No Two Alike: Human Nature and Human Individuality.* New York: Norton.

Hill, M. and Tisdall, K. (1997) *Children and Society.* Harlow: Addison Wesley Longman.

Hulbert, A. (2004) *Raising America: Experts, Parents and a Century of Advice About Children.* New York: Vintage Books.

James, A. and James, A. (2008) Changing Childhood in the UK: Reconstructing Discourses of 'Risk' and 'Protection'. In James, A. and James, A. (eds) *European Childhoods: Cultures, Politics and Childhoods in Europe*. Basingstoke: Palgrave Macmillan.

James, A., Jenks, C. and Prout, A. (1998) *Theorizing Childhood*. Cambridge: Polity Press.

Kagan, J. (1998) *Three Seductive Ideas*. Cambridge, MA: Harvard University Press.

Lee, E., Macvarish, J. and Lowe, P (2013) The Uses and Abuses of Biology: Neuroscience, Parenting and Family Policy in Britain: A 'Key Findings' Report. Available at http://blogs.kent.ac.uk/parenting-culturestudies/research-themes/early-intervention/current-projects/. Date last accessed 27 November 2014.

Macvarish, J., Lee, E. and Lowe, P. (2014) The 'first three years' movement and the infant brain: A review of critiques, *Sociology Compass.*, 8, 6, 792–804.

Mayall, B. (2006) Values and Assumptions Underpinning Policy for Children and Young People in England, *Children's Geographies*, 4, 1, 9–17.

Murphy, N. and Brown, W. (2009) *Did My Neurons Make Me Do It? Philosophical and Neurobiological perspectives on Free Will*. Oxford: Oxford University Press.

Nadesan, M.H. (2002) Engineering the entrepreneurial infant: brain science, infant development toys, and governmentality, *Cultural Studies*, 16, 3, 401–32.

O' Connor, C. and Joffe, H. (2013) Media representations of early human development: protecting, feeding and loving the developing brain, *Social Science and Medicine*, 97, 3, 297–306.

O'Connor, C., Rees, G. and Joffe, H. (2012) Neuroscience in the Public Sphere, *Neuron*, 74, 2, 220–6.

Pascual-Leone, A., Amedi, A, Fregni, F. and Merabet, L. B. (2005) The plastic human brain cortex. *Annual Review of Neuroscience*, 28, 377–401.

Perry, B.D. (1997) Incubated in terror: neurodevelopmental factors in the 'cycle of violence'. In Osofsky, J. (ed) *Children, Youth and Violence: The Search for Solutions*. New York: Guilford Press.

Qvortrup, J. (1994) Introduction. In Qvortrup, J., Bardy, M., Sgritta, G. and Wintersberger, H. (eds) *Childhood Matters: Social Theory, Practice and Politics*. Aldershot: Avebury.

Racine, E., Waldman, S., Rosenberg, J. and Illes, J. (2010) Contemporary neuroscience in the media, *Social Science and Medicine*, 71, 4, 725–33.

Rose, N. and Abi-Rached, J.M. (2013) *Neuro: The New Brain Sciences and the Management of the Mind*. Princeton, NJ: Princeton University Press.

Roskies, A. (2006) Neuroscientific challenges to free will and responsibility, *Trends in Cognitive Sciences*, 10, 9, 419–23.

Rutter, M., Sonuga-Barke, E.J., Beckett, C., Castle, J., Kreppner, J., Kumsta, R., Schlotz, W., Stevens, S.E. and Bell, C.A. (2010) Deprivation-specific psychological patterns: effects of institutional deprivation, *Monographs of the Society for Research in Child Development*, 75.

Rutter, M. and the English and Romanian Adoptees (ERA) study team (1998) Developmental catch-up, and deficit, following adoption after severe global early privatio., *Journal of Child Psychology and Psychiatry*, 39, 4, 465–76.

Satel, S. and Lilienfeld, S.O. (2013) *Brainwashed: The Seductive Appeal of Mindless Neuroscience*. New York: Basic Books.

Sutton, C., Utting, D. and Farrington, D. (2004) Support from the start: working with young children and their families to reduce the risks of crime and anti-social behaviour. *Department for Education and Skills Brief No: RB524.*

Tallis, R. (2012) *Aping Mankind: Neuromania, Darwinitis and the Misrepresentation of Humanity*. Durham: Acumen Publishing.

Thompson, R.A. and Nelson, C.A. (2001) Developmental science and the media: early brain development, *American Psychologist*, 56, 1, 5–15.

Thornton, J.D. (2011) Neuroscience, affect, and the entrepreneurialization of motherhood, *Communication and Critical/Cultural Studies*, 8, 4, 399–424.

Turmel, A. (2008) *A Historical Sociology of Childhood: Developmental Thinking, Categorization and Graphic Visualisation*. Cambridge: Cambridge University Press.

Vidal, F. (2009) Brainhood, anthropological figure of modernity, *History of the Human Sciences*, 22, 1, 5–36.

40   Pam Lowe *et al.*

Wall, G. (2010) Mother's experiences with intensive parenting and brain development discourse, *Women's Studies International Forum*, 33, 3, 253–63.

Wastell, D. and White, S. (2012) Blinded by neuroscience: social policy, the family and the infant brain, *Families, Relationships and Societies*, 1, 3, 397–414.

Williams, S.J., Higgs, P. and Katz, S. (2012) Neuroculture, active ageing and the 'older brain': problems, promises and prospects, *Sociology of Health & Illness*, 34, 1, 64–78.

Wilson, H. (2002) Brain science, early Intervention and 'at risk' families: Implications for parents, professionals and social policy, *Social Policy & Society*, 1, 3, 191–202.

Yaqub, S. (2002) Poor children grow into poor adults: Harmful mechanisms or over-deterministic theory?, *Journal of International Development*, 14, 8, 1081–93.

4

Obesity in question: understandings of body shape, self and normalcy among children in Malta
Gillian M. Martin

Introduction

'Being fat' was well and truly medicalised when the World Health Organisation (2000) provided statistical evidence in a report aimed at preventing and managing what they termed 'the global epidemic'. Biomedical measurement techniques were standardised, morbidity predicted and the potential economic drain on national health funds flagged in the institutionalised fight against fat that followed. Despite intensive public health campaigns aimed at correcting individual lifestyle choices or countering structural obesogenic factors, biomedical research indicates that the trend for excess bodyweight persists in both developed and developing countries worldwide (de Onis *et al.* 2010).

Is all this simply manufactured fear and loathing – an obesity myth that takes centre-stage while 'more expansive and intimately connected problems associated with social injustice get hidden and suffocated by fat?' (Monaghan 2005: 308). Biomedical discourse on obesity clearly functions within a system of social surveillance and bio-power (Crossley 2004). These Foucauldian concepts are useful to highlight the political technology of the body and the strategic control of populations that ensues (Foucault 1991). With frequent reference to belligerent metaphors such as campaigns, fights and corrective regimes, the intensity of biomedical discourse is amplified and has pervasive effects on the ways that individuals, think and talk about being fat.

Where does this leave the individual? Rich and Evans (2005) offer a strong case for the need to rescue the marginalised individual from the powerful biomedical discourse on obesity which normalises one particular body shape by creating 'meanings that influence cultural understandings of health, the body and eating' (p. 344). Exposing the 'obesity myth' as a social construction brings the moral and ethical conditioning that is associated with it into question. Rich and Evans go on to claim that dominant anti-obesity medical discourse 'creates a "moral panic" about the state of an individual's or a nation's health and the choices they are to make to rectify it' (2005: 352). The biomedical literature, on the other hand, leads one to believe that it would be immoral *not* to panic about the progressive degradation in public health and wellbeing as a result of escalating rates of obesity (Lobstein *et al.* 2004). This chapter sets out to work within this juxtaposition of ontological perspectives. I hold that taking a radical social constructivist stance against the 'fat-is-bad' biomedical discourse would not do full justice to the lived reality of the child whose everyday interactions are framed within a dominant symbolic system capitalising the slim body shape.

Children, Health and Well-being: Policy Debates and Lived Experience, First Edition. Edited by Geraldine Brady, Pam Lowe and Sonja Olin Lauritzen. Chapters © 2015 The Authors. Book Compilation © 2015 Foundation for the Sociology of Health & Illness/Blackwell Publishing Ltd.

Theoretical perspectives and aims

This chapter argues within a critical realist perspective that acknowledges 'that there exists both an external world independently of human consciousness, and at the same time a dimension which includes our socially determined knowledge about reality' (Danemark *et al.* 2002: 5). The challenge here is to explore the intertwining of physical body shape (and its biomedical classification of weight status) with the sense of self and normalcy in children. I invite the reader to listen to the children. I set out to explore the child's own perspective on embodiment, examine the way this relates to the biomedical definitions, and highlight their emergent self/body image firmly rooted within a phenomenological understanding of meaning.

The child is conceived here as 'a person, a status, a course of action, a set of needs, rights or differences – in sum, as a social actor' (James *et al.* 1998: 207). This perspective hinges on the tenet that there is no 'essential child' but only those who are culturally located and socially constituted. This said, there is a danger of glossing over the fact that social action is almost always embodied action – of 'trading biological reductionism for social reductionism [where] the material body largely drops out of the picture' (Williams and Bendelow 2003: 135). My key emphasis here is to counter the problematic absent presence of the body by conceptualising it as 'a simultaneously biological and social phenomenon that is both shaped by but irreducible to contemporary social relations and structures' (Shilling 2003: 182). The challenge is to recognise the essential importance of the child's body as they explore and interact within their social environment and to acknowledge how their body is 'experienced, constructed and shifted by the interpretations and translations of adults, children, nature and technology' (James *et al.* 1998: 168).

The working concept of normalcy used here in relation to a child's body shape/weight has two facets – one biomedically defined and measured in terms of body mass index (BMI) and another, socially rooted and co-constructed in shared beliefs and values. This study was conducted with both perspectives in the frame, encouraging the participants to express their own understanding of what is normal or desirable, and then letting this lead the discussions in the field. During the analysis, however, these grounded concepts of normalcy were viewed in parallel with the biomedical definitions, in order to explore the ways a biomedical evaluation of body shape may impact on and feed back into the loop of reflexive embodiment during early childhood.

For conceptual clarity in the discussion that follows, I use the terms overweight/obese when referring to biomedical definitions of bodyweight, and chubby/fat when referring to lay descriptions of body shape. When analysing the child's perspective, the key to exploring normalcy is difference. The child's liminal perceptual experience of their own body or body-ekstasis (Vannini and Waskul 2006) developing as it does in continuous interaction with the other and incorporating the evaluative contrast with that other, is in essence an evaluation of difference (Vannini and Waskul 2006: 196). Any perception of discredited difference (Goffman 1990) may impact on the child's dynamic sense of self.

The working concept of self used here is embodied and rooted in relational dynamics. Though thoughts are certainly fundamental, a great number of these thoughts are about the body, or are influenced by how others interpret and interact with the body (Crossley 2001). To trace the interactional dynamics at the root of this process, I focus on the complex sedimentation of beliefs and values that constitute the child's self (Crossley 2006) the impact on the emotions and of the emotions in this process, and the consequent dynamic influence on body shape and health (James in Panter-Brick 1998).

The key aim is to explore understandings of body shape and how they impact on relational dynamics in the lived experiences of young children in Malta. The specific research questions are: (i) how do young children (irrespective of weight status) experience and understand their own body shape? and (ii) what are their experiences of being fat? How do relational dynamics impact on body shape and vice versa?

Methodology

The empirical coal-face for the data is the dynamic, relational dimension of social exchange in the lived experiences of young children in Malta, exploring the lasting impacts of these exchanges on the children's body/self, and vice versa. This is done by applying an inter-pretive methodology that acknowledges the socially rooted status of meaning, influenced by the individuals' own interpretation of the external world that exists independently of them.

Sample

This chapter draws on empirical data generated during an ethnographic study of children in Malta over a period of 12 months. Two primary schools were used as a sampling frame from which children in the entry class (Year 1, aged 5–6) and final class (Year 6, aged 10–11) were selected as a purposive sample ($n = 135$) in order to facilitate the comparison of data generated in these two milestone age groups. School A was an urban, mixed gender, government primary school (no fees and books provided free of charge). School B was a mixed gender church primary school (no school fees, but regular financial donations are expected) in a rural area, with students drawn from all over the island.

The children in the sample included the full classroom complement in each age group with the exception of two children whose parents did not offer consent. These children were allowed to participate in the class-based creative data-generating activities if they asked to; however their data were not recorded or collected. Observational data were gathered and analysed from children regardless of their weight status, as was the case with data generated through creative research participant-centred methods (described below).

A BMI census of the children in the sample was carried out using the International Obesity Task Force cut-off points (see Cole *et al.* 2000). This was done to facilitate critical engagement with biomedical discourse when analysing the qualitative data on body shape. There was one child in each age group who was underweight and children who were over-weight/obese made up 32 per cent of the overall sample: 19 per cent overweight and 13 per cent obese, which tallied well with the national statistics for that year (see Grech and Farrugia Sant'Angelo 2009).

The sample was chosen to tap into two key periods in the child's development – entry to formal schooling, and the period just before transition to secondary school. It was 'organi-cally extended' (Mason 2010) to include mothers, fathers and grandmothers once it became established in the field that these would be sources of rich data through in-depth qualitative interviews.

Context

Politically, Maltese territory includes two main populated islands – the larger, densely inhab-ited island of Malta and the much smaller and less structurally developed island of Gozo. Independent since 1964, and member of the EU since 2004, these islands share a common cultural matrix which features the Maltese language and Roman Catholicism at its core, rooted in the European cultural heritage resulting from a complex and varied colonial legacy. Most of the population is bilingual, with English as the official language used predominantly in education, commerce, the service industries, administration and academia. The 'studied arbitrariness' of two particular primary schools as my field location is best projected as part of the ethnographic process, one that sets out to offer a 'contingent window' (Candea 2007: 179) into the complexity of the social, cultural and physical relations within which young children in Malta develop.

Data collection
Framed within the new sociology of childhood (James *et al.* 1998, Mayall 2008) as described above, the agentic status of the child is central to my research design, which places children at the core of the research process as active collaborators. Two key qualitative methods used with the child participants were participant observation (approximately 500 hours over four school terms) and 'drawing with reflective commentary' task-based methods. Child-sourced data were triangulated with data drawn from in-depth creative interviews with the adults (parents, grandparents and teachers). Quantitative methods (short questionnaire, BMI census) were also used to gather ancillary data used descriptively in the analysis.

My key concern with the children was to use a participant-centred (Punch 2002) research tool that aimed at optimising ethical symmetry (Christenson and Prout 2002) by placing the child in a realistic position of power over the quality and details of the information they shared. For this purpose I adopted a visual, creative method which uses images rather than language as a primary focus to minimise the power imbalance inherent in the standard interview (Mitchell 2006), and offers the children tools through which they can communicate their own meanings and understandings (Bagnoli 2009). The children were invited to draw a picture of themselves and one of their best friend which they were then encouraged to comment on during informal individual follow-up sessions. This method shares a visual approach with the 'draw and write' technique (Pridmore and Bendelow 1995), designed to be non-threatening, fun and accessible to even very young children. It differs from this approach in the nature of the follow-up session after the drawing, which takes place individually as a casual conversation, recorded with permission, where the children use the drawing as 'illuminative artwork' (Rollins 2005) and are encouraged to talk about their self-portrait and also the one drawn by their best friend, if it is available. This offers a sensitive way of allowing the children to lead the way to 'cross over' from discussing the drawing to discussing their 'selves' and to talking reflexively about their real body if and when they felt comfortable to do so.

Participant observation took the form of daily immersion in the school routine. The use of the 'least adult role' (Mandell 1988) was used to blur the adult-child distinctions in the process of sharing tasks, fun and frustrations in the classroom and playground. The children accepted my regular participation in their classroom and recreation activities after my motivations and goals were simply described as wanting to learn about the ways they got on together. The consistent and routine sharing of everyday experiences was essential in establishing a trusting rapport with the children which led to enthusiastic engagement in task-based methods, and rich data collection during frank spontaneous conversations in both age groups.

The children were my key gatekeepers to the adults in the study. Semi-structured, creative interviews were conducted with mothers and grandmothers and some fathers, using visual elicitation methods. This allowed the participants to talk about body shape by responding spontaneously to the visuals, thus avoiding the issue of the influence of language choice and question framing. Conversations with participants were then led by *their* definitions of what is desirable and undesirable in relation to body shape and my choice of language reflected theirs.

Researcher impact

This research focuses on body shape – as a researcher interviewing and interacting with individuals who were predominantly very overweight, it is relevant to point out that my own weight status is and has always been slim. This said, my own personal experience of mothering two sons with dramatically different body shapes influenced this research in two important ways. The first concerns perspective and context: the difference in attitudes towards the overweight and the slim boy as they were growing up no doubt orientated my sociological antennae in the process of data gathering. The second was the impact on enhancing interview dynamics with parents and grandparents who were aware of the fact that body shape was my central interest. Using a photo of my own sons (with their permission) as a visual prompt during interviews immediately and consistently set the interviewee at ease and led to more fruitful and spontaneous interchanges.

Ethics

Institutional ethical clearance procedures were followed and particular attention was paid to the issue of informed consent (formally from parents or guardians and informally from the children), anonymity when presenting data, and confidentiality. The challenges of working with children within an institutional setting were constantly addressed, with particular attention given to offering a realistic option to abstain at every stage of the data gathering, emphasising this point especially when working with the 5-year olds. The key concern in relation to participant wellbeing was the danger of drawing attention to the overweight/obese children during data gathering and exposing them to potential teasing or bullying. This was minimised by focusing on the full class complement and using creative task-based techniques where all the children were encouraged to participate if they wanted to.

Analysis

Data gathered using the different techniques were converted to textual form (field notes and interview and conversation transcriptions). The interpretive reading of these data was centred on the participants' own descriptions with the aim of 'reading through or beyond the data' in its literal sense (Mason 2010: 149). Key themes related to the child's body shape were identified and used to lead the cross-sectional thematic analysis. Two of these descriptive categories: aesthetics and health were anticipated and influenced by the research questions, while that of happiness (taken here to mean self-fulfilment) was grounded in the data. Within each of these themes, exploration of the key conceptual categories of normalcy and self drove the analysis of how the child's body shape is related to what is considered beautiful and healthy (therefore normal) by the adults; or not different therefore normal by the children; how this is related to what makes the child and their significant others happy, and how this impacts on the child's sense of self. Transcript data from the two key methods of data generation (interviews with adult participants, and the children's reflections on their self-portraits) were analysed in parallel, with data from one source supplementing or calling into question the other. Participant observation data were particularly useful as a means of triangulation and of refining the orientation of in-depth interviews.

Findings

Mothers

The data clearly identify the mother as highly significant in the particular group of children in the study. Her input into the dynamic will lead the analysis here which will then go on to scrutinise the influence of peers and others in order to trace the impact of mothers and others on the child's developing sense of 'me'.

The significance of the mother was affirmed indirectly during my short interviews ($n = 55$) with the 5-year-olds when they were asked to give one word to describe themselves. 18 per cent of the group gave the word *sabieħ* or *sabieħa* (beautiful, gendered).[1] My next question to this response was 'how do you know?'. This question often surprised my 5-year-old collaborators who thought it was odd that I should ask. When pressed, they invariably responded: 'My mother told me!'.

When exploring the key themes of aesthetics, health and happiness in the data, there is a marked difference in the way mothers talk about chubby or fat babies/toddlers compared to when describing the chubby or fat older child. The very young are celebrated and valued, with interview data often demonstrating a subtext of symbolic capital and evidence of successful mothering. This contrasts with the apparently protective strategies used when discussing the older child. Interestingly, it was not simply what the mothers said that demonstrated this, but what was not said. The word that was blatantly missing in our interviews was 'fat'.

MM demonstrated this trait perfectly when she described that she was concerned about her younger son putting on weight:

> Look at my other son ... he eats a lot and I tell him 'be careful because you are going to start "getting big" (*terga' tikber*)'... because when he was in year 6 he 'became big' (*kiber*) ... then in Form 2 and Form 3 he lost some weight ... now he has stared to fill out again. (*jerga' jinfetah*)

What really concerned this mother was that her son was getting fat. Like most of the mothers interviewed, however, she expressed this concern without actually saying the word. One mother who used euphemisms in a similar way did so consciously and with a strategy of protection which she admits to abandoning when provoked to the extreme, leaving her with feelings of guilt:

MB: We don't use the word fat at home ... I hate it ... I hate using the word ... it is a very bad word ... I can offend you if I call you fat ... then sometimes, when I am angry ... please! [give me a break!]
GM: You say it?
MB: You're getting fat M! [raising voice]
GM: Then how do you feel when you say it?
MB: Very bad.

It is clear from the data that the overweight and obese children in both these age groups in the study are vigorously protected by their mothers. The protective strategy seems to have two sources of motivation – in some cases the mothers simply do not buy into the medical 'anti-fat' discourse, overriding scientific definitions of what is overweight by using the 'natural is normal' notion, offering a grounded example of resistance to medicine's 'micro-physics of power' (Foucault 1991) over the body. This was clearly demonstrated by one mother (LD) whose tall 5-year-old daughter has always been overweight:

> The doctor used to tell me that she was a bit overweight for her age ... but I used to go on the defensive because, after all ... I don't think you can calculate on a chart, how much a 5-year-old should weigh ... because when you look at children her age ... they are all short and weedy (*psiepes*), understand? While P is like a giant ... so I don't expect her to be the same weight that they say on the chart ... so I never really took it into consideration ... not at all.

Others acknowledge the fact that their child's weight may pose health problems in the future however, while the child is young, they do not believe that it is something the child should be held responsible for – they consider it to be a transient issue that will resolve as the child develops or 'matures'.

It is interesting to note that these protective strategies may implicitly perpetuate the fat-is-bad value system that the mother sets out to protect her child against, by buying into and therefore reinforcing, the biomedical and visual media's devaluation of the fat body shape. The issue that emerges clearly in the data, however, is that the biomedical political technology of the body and the media domination of the slim aesthetic set the dominant discourse on the issue of body shape/weight and health in the long term, with most mothers associating being fat in adolescence or adulthood with potential negative health issues and negative symbolic value. The key finding in this respect, however, is that the young chubby/fat child seems to be fairly well protected against negative implicit or explicit messages connected to their weight while still within the mother's domain of influence and while still functioning within the habitus of their primary group.

Mothers and others

This absence of negative sanctioning is attenuated by the positive attention that the rounded body shape in a young child seems to attract. Interview and observational data highlight the way that babies and very young children (those of preschool age) are positively valued and considered attractive if they look chubby. When the mothers interviewed responded to a photograph of approximately 10 month-old babies used as a visual elicitation tool, it was the chubby babies that were consistently described with positive language and selected as the most desirable. The visual aesthetic described by these mothers when talking about young children was frequently augmented by a physical element – the pleasure associated with hugging and squeezing the chubby baby or young child, as teaching assistant MM demonstrates:

MM: [picking up photo of chubby babies] … Now, isn't this one sweet?! [pointing to chubby baby, gentle laughter, making hugging arm movements].
GM: When you make these signs, they don't go onto my tape [laughter].
MM: Because you want to hug her … [she makes you] want to squeeze her [smiling].

Gender was not an issue when discussing babies or toddlers and body shape. This contrasted when focusing on older children,[2] where a clear gender bias was evident with many mothers and grandmothers admitting they had positive or neutral reactions towards overweight boys (who were often described as strong), while being disparaging about the way overweight girls looked. This preference was clearly linked to the influence of the media-dominated slim aesthetic with the most frequent remark being 'clothes won't look good on her'.

The exploration of the 10-year-old child's perspective resulted in data which corroborate the preferences expressed by the adults, with many of the overweight or obese children describing memories of the way they used to be praised and cuddled by their close relatives who specifically referred to their chubbiness as appealing. This, however, stands in contrast to their own expressed preferences of body shape. Here the children in both age groups held consistently and emphatically negative opinions about being fat. The interesting issue that became clear in this regard however, is that while the 10-year-old group had an accurate idea of their own medically defined weight status, and that of their classmates, the 5-year-olds almost consistently (with two exceptions) claimed that there were no fat children in their class. Yet there were at least five overweight or obese children in each of the classes in the study

These younger children seem to be clear about the view that fat = ugly but their day-to-day experiences and the stories that they tell about themselves and their classmates are intriguingly devoid of fat children. These data suggest that the positive attention (verbal and physical) from their adult significant others seems to influence their own body-ekstasis in such a way that the overweight 5-year-olds are not aware of their own fatness, nor that of the children around them. Borrowing from Leder (1990), if the body is its own blind spot and only becomes visible when it becomes dysfunctional, then, as long as the chubby body shape attracts praise and positive attention, the fat will remain absent, only appearing or, rather, 'dys-appearing' when the reflexive experience has negative affective value. This tends to happen as they grow out of their primary group and move on to the mass–media-influenced generalised other in the rough and tumble of the older children's playground.

During school recreation, the child's physical shape clearly had a significant influence on their interaction and status. This is one area, however, where the dynamic was markedly different when comparing the two age-groups in the study. The games that were predominant in the 5-year-old group were mainly based on role-play, where there usually is an adult role involved (mummy, policeman, teacher). It was not surprising to find that it was the taller children who claimed these roles. In both schools in the study, some of these tall children were also overweight or obese. Being overweight did not seem to impact on their peer status: height appears to be the key advantage and the 5-year-olds do not seem to value their fat-and-tall friends any less or more than their tall friends. In fact, being fat did not seem to be an issue at all in the younger group's playground.

The situation in the older group was very different. Here the children are certainly aware of their friends' weight and body shape and this does influence their group dynamics. One of the questions I asked the 10-year-olds is whether being overweight was an advantage or a disadvantage to a child their age. One response (BM, boy, aged 10, BMI normal) sums up the general feedback on this issue very well:

> Not everybody is the same … there are some who think that if you have friends [who are fat] … they will be stronger … you know when you fight … then they will be able to defend you … other times … some say … when you play, they won't be able to run as much as you.

This inability to perform well in the playground was frequently flagged as one of the main disadvantages by the overweight 10-year-old children interviewed. It was, in fact, the reason most quoted by both genders in this age group for wanting to lose weight. While being fat in the 5-year-olds' peer group seems to go by unnoticed during play, it is certainly an important issue in older children's playground. Although there is some evidence in the playground observations of this age group of a positive status attached to being chubby/fat,[3] the dominant dynamic is one of negative sanctions that range from the relatively benign exclusion during running games, to 'friendly' teasing, borne in good humour by the victim, right up to premeditated and repeated taunting that leave the overweight child traumatised. During my conversations with the 10-year olds there were frequent references to name-calling specifically related to being fat, especially on the football pitch or during after-school activities:

GM: When they call you these names … how does it make you feel?
JA: Nothing – I just don't speak to them.
GM: But … how does it make you feel?

JA: A bit sad.
GM: And what do you do?
JA: I don't speak to them.

The 10-year-olds seem to accept the verbal taunting about their body shape as part of their lot. They are very conscious of their fat body, and view sensitivity about the issue as a weakness they have to control. My conversation with RB, a 10-year-old girl (BMI: obese) adds more insight into the issue of personal coping strategies.

RB: The boy next to me calls me 'blob of fat' (*ċappa xaħam*), and it upsets me.
GM: Of course it upsets you … and what do you do when they call you this?
RB: Oh, I stay on my own [what else can I do? …] I try to change the situation, you know? … like once they called me this … you know … and to change the subject … I was drinking water … and I spilled it on me … to change the subject.

Like most of the children who admitted to being picked on about their weight, RB claimed that she did not tell her parents about the teasing. This was an issue I was able to confirm during interviews with the mothers where they invariably said that they didn't think there was a problem with teasing at the moment, but certainly worried about what would happen in secondary school. The 10-year-olds seem to have assumed ownership of their overweight body and admitting to being teased would simply highlight an issue they prefer to keep to themselves – away from the attention of others, significant others included.

Mothers, others and 'me'

This complex interplay of the self and others is the key sociological issue here. It is the process that underpins the child's developing sense of self where the reaction of others to the child's (overweight) body shape has important consequences (Crossley 2001, Mead 1967). The effect that this has on the child's concept of their own body/self or dynamic body-ekstasis is of major interest here. One mother, who has been overweight most of her life, brings the dynamic into focus:

RS: I believe that everybody starts out with [high] self-esteem … whether it is broken down or built up depends on the people around you.
GM: And is this process influenced by your body shape? … if [your self-esteem] is going to be broken down … is it because you are different?
RS: Because somebody else sees something different in you.

The data suggest that the children in the 5-year-old group have not yet noticed that others see them as 'different'. They have not been exposed to the negative labelling and the associated social sanctions that are linked to being overweight or obese in the adult world. Congruent with this lack of awareness of their own, or their friends' medically defined problematic weight status was the predominant tendency to claim that there were no fat children in their class.

When describing their own body shape all the 5-year-olds, with one exception, (who had a BMI: obese) said they were 'just right'. This contrasts sharply with the 10-year-old group where the children were acutely aware of differences in body shape, with only seven of the 27 overweight or obese children describing their body shape in positive terms.

This difference offers some insight into the dynamics that influence the child's evolving body-ekstasis. The overweight 5-year-olds operate in an environment where reaction to their body shape varies from the neutral indifference of classmates to the positive affective responses of significant others. When asked to rate their body shape they do so in the positive terms that are a reflection of these interactions.

The difference in the responses of the 10-year-olds is a clear indication of the labelling that occurs as the child ventures further from the protection of the immediate family group into the cut and thrust of the media-dominated, image-conscious peer group. Borrowing from Becker (1973) I suggest that as the child grows, they learn that fat people are outsiders in their image-conscious social environment. In contrast to the habitus of the very young child, where being overweight attenuated their symbolic capital, having a fat body is now clearly labelled as deviant. This undesired differentness has direct repercussions on the dynamics of social interaction of the child, especially with their peers. Goffman (1990) famously described the social consequences of these discrediting attributes as leading to stigma with the stigmatised individual reduced 'from a whole and usual person to a tainted, discounted one' (p. 12). Goffman's terminology might seem hyperbolic when applied to the lived experiences of the young children in this study, but the data do show how the overweight and obese children take on the stigmatised role when faced with taunting in the older children's playground devising coping techniques to disguise their distress, as described above.

The sociological implications of this go beyond the labelling process in the group and the stigma and social sanctions that result – it is the effects of these dynamics on the individual's sense of self that are of particular interest here. Based on the interpretation and internalisation of others' evaluations, the child habitually reflects on their emergent self-image while simultaneously symbolically communicating their own aesthetic evaluations of them. Clearly, the 5-year-olds in this study do not demonstrate this level of reflexivity – they simply see themselves through the eyes of their significant others and have not yet fully internalised the differences that define their bodies. The 10-year-olds, however, are functioning within a reflexive habitus where they habitually gather reflexive knowledge of their own emergent self/body. They are conscious of what others think of their bodies, and this goes towards defining how they view themselves and how they are in themselves.

The relationship between the bodily 'I' and bodily 'me' – the dynamic reflexivity that is at the basis of the individual's sense of self is one that the 10-year-olds in the study highlighted in the reflective commentary on their self-portraits. The children were asked to draw themselves in such a way that they would be recognisable. Emphasis was made to include any bodily features that were particular to them, so as to fix their identity. Interestingly, the 5-year-olds, whose drawing skills were a limiting factor in this exercise, diligently included details such as hair and eye colour, spectacles or freckles, but paid little attention to body shape (fig. 1).

The 10-year-olds, who were certainly capable of including body shape details, consistently drew slim figures when drawing themselves. While exploring this issue during their follow-up interviews, the overweight/obese children's response was invariably that they drew themselves 'as they would like people to see them' or 'as they wish to be'. RB, the 10-year-old girl, quoted above in her descriptions of verbal teasing, was particularly articulate in this respect. (fig. 2).

GM: Tell me about the drawing […] have you drawn it correctly?
RB: [Emphatic] No! [laughter] first of all … I never wear skirts … and … my tummy should be bigger [gentle laughter] and … lots of colours … in the clothes.

Figure 1   *FV, 5-years old, BMI normal: self-portrait*

Figure 2   *RB, 10-years old, BMI obese, self-portrait*

RB knows that she is not slim; however, like most of her overweight peers, she consciously drew herself as slim because that is the way the she would like to be seen. Reflexivity is clearly central to her sense of self – she has internalised others' aesthetic evaluation of her body and this informs her own comparative evaluation. Her body is fat, her friends and family know this, and she knows this. Her decision to draw herself as slim, – as she wishes that somebody would see her – not as she sees herself, opens a window onto the process of reflexivity that lies at the root of her embodiment. It highlights the dynamic interchange of cognition and perception that leads to her symbolically disowning her own true body shape.

Discussion and concluding remarks

This chapter set out to explore understandings of body shape and how they impact on relational dynamics in the lived experiences of young children in Malta. It explored the child's emergent self/body image through the shift in habitus from that of the protective and doting immediate family, through a period of hysteresis (Bourdieu 1977) with school entry, to the cut and thrust of interaction with peers in the older children's playground. The data were used to show how these interactions are useful indicators of what is considered desirable as a body shape of very young children, how this impacts on their lived experience of being fat and feeds back in to the loop of the child's reflexive embodiment. The rounded body shape was shown to shift from being the source of joy and symbolic capital in very young children to the cause of social, physical and aesthetic disadvantage in the 10-year-olds.

Normalising statements or commentary are not the purpose here. Rather than pitch the social construction of obesity against biomedical discourse and political technology of fat bodies, I have taken a bifocal lens to the lived experiences of children and argued from the view that the child's body is both a biological and socially constructed phenomenon. I let the children in the study lead the way by exploring their descriptions of what is normal (or, rather, not different) and desirable when it comes to body shape. Their descriptions were found to be directly influenced by the fluidity in the adults' aesthetic preferences and their understandings of what is a healthy body shape – both of which shift fundamentally as the child develops.

Data gathered from adult participants show how, though biomedicine sets the dominant discourse on the issue of body shape/weight and health in the long term, this is kept in abeyance when discussing very young babies and children. This is reflected in the contrasting lived experiences of the two age groups in the study. The overweight 10-year-olds, clearly aware of the aesthetic and functional disadvantages of their deviant body shape (which they symbolically disown), are in sharp contrast with the chubby and cute 5-year-olds who are still functioning within the habitus of their primary group.

While relational processes in the very young child's sphere of interaction tend to buffer potential negative sanctions related to being overweight (due to maternal protection) and may even promote the sedimentation of positive dispositions (due to the perceived symbolic capital of being a 'healthy, strong and happy' child), the 10-year-olds use private coping strategies to deal with the social sanctions that have become an accepted part of their routine interaction. These changes in the child's personal experience of being fat are fundamentally linked to the shifting concept of normalcy in the adult groups and its resulting impact on social dynamics, which then filter into the child's sphere of daily interactions.

Fatness is shown to be a fluid concept that adults and children co-construct in social interaction which inverts the associated symbolic value as the child grows. The goalposts are switched once the child leaves the primary group habitus, where the fat body shape was valued, and fat children protected. The lived experiences of the older children in the study show that being fat is closely tied to physical and social realities that they describe as undesirable, and that biomedical discourse sets out to correct. A robust understanding of the issue of childhood obesity would acknowledge the child's lived experience of being fat – the lifetime trajectory of the process of embodiment, and the physical legacy of relational dynamics in early childhood which may have a lasting impact on body shape and weight status.

Acknowledgements

This research was part-funded by a Malta Government Scholarship Scheme PhD scholarship. I am very grateful to Professor Nick Crossley at the University of Manchester for his advice and feedback. Thanks also go to the editors of this monograph and to the two anonymous reviewers for their constructive and detailed comments.

Notes

1   $N = 55$; nine children chose 'beautiful' of which four were boys and five girls.
2   The photos used as visual elicitations were of children aged approximately 10 years.
3   Predominantly in boys, and usually linked to tall stature, strength and some kind of sports-related skill, such as goalkeeper

References

Bagnoli, A. (2009) Beyond the standard interview: the use of graphic elicitation and arts-based methods, *Qualitative Research*, 9, 5, 547–70.
Becker, H.S. (1973) *Outsiders – Studies in the Sociology of Deviance*. New York: Free Press.
Bourdieu, P. (1977) *Outline of a Theory of Practice*. Cambridge: Cambridge University Press.
Candea, M. (2007) Arbitrary locations: in defence of the bounded field-site, *Journal of the Royal Anthropological Institute*, 13, 1, 167–84.
Christenson, P. and Prout, A. (2002) Working with ethical symmetry in social research with children, *Childhood*, 9, 4, 477–97.
Cole, T.J., Bellizzi, M.C., Flegal, K.M. and Dietz, W.H. (2000) Establishing a standard definition for child overweight and obesity worldwide: international survey, *British Medical Journal*, 320, 1240–3.
Crossley, N. (2001) *The Social Body*. London: Sage.
Crossley, N. (2004) Fat is a sociological issue: obesity rates in late modern, 'body conscious' societies, *Social Theory and Health*, 2, 222–53.
Crossley, N. (2006) *Reflexive Embodiment in Contemporary Society*. Maidenhead: Open University Press.
Danemark, B., Ekstrom, M., Jakobsen, L. and Karlsson, J.C. (2002) *Explaining Society: Critical Realism in the Social Sciences*. London and New York: Routledge.
de Onis, M., Blössner, M. and Borghi, E. (2010) Global prevalence and trends of overweight and obesity among preschool children, *American Journal of Clinical Nutrition*, 92, 5, 1257–64.
Foucault, M. (1991) *Discipline and Punish: The Birth of the Prison*. London: Penguin.
Goffman, E. (1990) *Stigma: Notes on the Management of Spoiled Identity*. London: Penguin.
Grech, V. and Farrugia Sant'Angelo, V. (2009) Body mass index estimation in a school-entry aged cohort in Malta, *International Journal of Pediatric Obesity*, 4, 2, 126–8.
James, A., Jenks, C. and Prout, A. (1998) *Theorizing Childhood*. Cambridge: Polity Press.
Leder, D. (1990) *The Absent Body*. Chicago: University of Chicago Press.

Lobstein, T., Baur, L. and Uauy, R. (2004) Obesity in children and young people: a crisis in public health, *Obesity Reviews*, 5, Suppl. 1, 4–85.

Mandell, N. (1988) The least-adult role in studying children, *Journal of Contemporary Ethnography*, 16, 4, 433–67.

Mason, J. (2010) *Qualitative Researching*, 2nd edn. London: Sage.

Mayall, B. (2008) *Towards a Sociology for Childhood*. Maidenhead: Open University Press.

Mead, G.H. (1967) *Mind Self and Society: from the Standpoint of a Social Behaviorist*. Chicago: University of Chicago Press.

Mitchell, L.M. (2006) Child-centered? Thinking critically about children's drawings as a visual research method, *Visual Anthropology Review*, 22, 1, 60–73.

Monaghan, L.F. (2005) Discussion piece: a critical take on the obesity debate, *Social Theory and Health*, 3, 4, 302–14.

Panter-Brick, C. (ed) (1998) *Biosocial Perspectives on Children*. Cambridge: Cambridge University Press.

Pridmore, P. and Bendelow, G. (1995) Images of health: exploring beliefs of children using the 'draw-and-write' technique, *Health Education Journal*, 54, 4, 473–88.

Punch, S. (2002) Research with children: the same or different from research with adults?, *Childhood*, 9, 3, 321–41.

Rich, E. and Evans, J. (2005) 'Fat ethics' – the obesity discourse and body politics, *Social Theory and Health*, 3, 4, 341–58.

Rollins, J.A. (2005) Tell me about it: drawing as a communication tool for children with cancer, *Journal of Pediatric Oncology Nursing*, 22, 4, 203–21.

Shilling, C. (2003) *The Body and Social Theory*, 2nd edn. London: Sage.

Vannini, P. and Waskul, D. (2006) Body ekstasis: socio-semiotic reflections on surpassing the dualism of body-image. In Waskul, D. and Vannini, P. (eds) *Body/Embodiment – Symbolic Interaction and the Sociology of the Body*. Aldershott: Ashgate.

Williams, S.J. and Bendelow, G.A. (2003) Constructionism and beyond. In Williams, S.J., Birke, L. and Bendelow, G.A. (eds) *Debating Biology: Sociological Reflections on Health, Medicine and Society*. London and New York: Routledge.

World Health Organisation (2000) *Obesity: Preventing and Managing the Global Epidemic*. Available at http://www.who.int/nutrition/publications/obesity/WHO_TRS_894/en/ (accessed 11 December 2014).

5

'You have to do 60 minutes of physical activity per day … I saw it on TV': Children's constructions of play in the context of Canadian public health discourse of playing for health

Stephanie A. Alexander, Caroline Fusco and Katherine L. Frohlich

Introduction

While it may appear banal to open an chapter with the often repeated claim about a global epidemic of childhood obesity (World Health Organisation [WHO] 2010), the actions taken in its name and the potential effects it has on children are far from banal. Indeed, public health institutions in many industrialised countries have been launching widespread calls to address childhood obesity, and efforts directed specifically at children have therefore been gaining widespread momentum (Shields 2006, WHO 2010). For instance in Canada, physical activity guidelines for children and youth have been developed in an attempt to provide evidence-based standards for physical activity to reduce childhood obesity rates (Tremblay *et al.* 2010). These guidelines state that 'children aged 5–11 years … should accumulate at least 60 minutes of physical activity daily' (Canadian Society for Exercise Physiology 2011).

Among the numerous interventions promoting physical activity for children, Canadian public health campaigns have recently taken a novel approach: they have begun to integrate children's play, specifically active play, as a critical component in childhood obesity prevention (Active Healthy Kids Canada [AHKC] 2012, ParticipACTION 2012). While gaining in popularity, we take issue with this new approach. Because public health institutions embody such powerful and authoritative forms of governmental regulation, their ways of constructing and resolving problems (that is, childhood obesity) often become politically and socially dominant (Bacchi 2009). When children's play is adopted for obesity prevention strategies, the emerging public health discourse may have a disproportionate influence in shaping children's play as a health practice. This, we argue, also runs the risk of reshaping play more generally, which itself may impact on the wellbeing of children.

One fruitful way to examine this emerging discourse (Foucault 1972) on play is by drawing on critical obesity scholarship (Rail 2012, Wright and Harwood 2009). A growing body of research has begun to critically examine obesity interventions that directly target youth for their possible unintended effects (such as disordered eating or the stigmatisation of overweight) (Beausoleil 2009, Gard 2011, Gard and Wright 2005, O'Dea 2005, Rail *et al.* 2010, Rich 2011, Wright and Harwood 2009). In this work some critical obesity scholars have theorised obesity discourses as 'biopedagogies' which include the normalising and regulating practices that provide knowledge about bodies and health, and that urge people to

Children, Health and Well-being: Policy Debates and Lived Experience, First Edition. Edited by Geraldine Brady, Pam Lowe and Sonja Olin Lauritzen. Chapters © 2015 The Authors. Book Compilation © 2015 Foundation for the Sociology of Health & Illness/Blackwell Publishing Ltd.

work on themselves in light of this knowledge (Rail 2012, Wright and Harwood 2009). This research has provided a valuable theoretical lens through which to critically explore anti-obesity efforts for what they teach the population about how they ought to live (Rail 2012, Wright and Harwood 2009).

Because children's play is becoming firmly enmeshed with obesity prevention efforts and its effects have not yet been examined, the current chapter draws on the concept of biopedagogies to critically examine how play is being taken up in Canadian public health. Furthermore, as biopedagogical practices are increasingly directed at children's play, this chapter places children's constructions of play in dialogue with the public health messages addressing play. This allows us to examine the public health discourse itself as well as the effects it may have on children's play.

Theoretical framework

Biopedagogies bring together Foucault's concept of biopower with the idea of pedagogy to form a 'pedagogy of bios', a practice that teaches people about how to live, eat and act (Harwood 2009: 15). Biopower (Foucault 2008) refers to the efforts on the part of the state to solidify itself through the expansion of governmental techniques to regulate and manage populations. Referring to Foucault's (1977) work, Burrows (2009) writes that the state, represented by government programmes, operates through 'a diffuse set of technologies to govern the actions of families, but also constitute families' understanding of themselves as viable, good and healthful' (p. 127). Governing technologies, which include documents and campaigns, produce normalising mechanisms that delineate appropriate body regulation practices (for example, weight) as well as the appropriate means of achieving these norms (Rail and Lafrance 2009). According to Harwood (2009) it is necessary to question obesity prevention practices to examine how we are '"taught", via biopedagogies, to be "healthy" (and good) citizens' (p. 17). Biopedagogies, then, is a useful theoretical concept for interrogating the public health interest in children's play as a regulatory strategy aimed at reducing children's risk of obesity.

The practice of linking play with physical activity and obesity prevention is potentially problematic for two related reasons. Firstly, as Wright (2009) suggests, biopedagogical practices govern children's bodies, which are sites 'where social meanings become embodied' (Wright 2009: 5). Thus, children may come to understand themselves in part through the social meanings attributed to their play activities; meanings increasingly informed by links between play and health, or alternatively between play, unhealthiness and risk. This, we argue, may unwittingly reshape the meanings and affective experiences that children attach to play. Secondly, in current Canadian public health discourses on play, children's perspectives are largely absent. This is an important omission, since children appear to have preferences for play that do not necessarily align with the kind of play promoted in public health (Alexander *et al.*, 2014).

In this chapter we place public health discourses in dialogue with children's constructions of play to put 'different registers of meaning into relation with each other' (Fullagar 2009: 110). This type of analysis 'unsettles the power–knowledge relations … the expert authority of policy and the assumed lack of expertise of individuals who, it is assumed, need to be 'better educated'.' (Fullagar 2009: 110). Specifically, the chapter examines how, when play is tied to obesity prevention efforts, the public health discourse on play may be establishing new norms for how children ought to play, and whether children are taking up these messages about play.

Methodology

Biopedagogical analysis
Harwood (2009) writes that the analysis of biopedagogies is informed by Rabinow and Rose's (2006) description of the three principal elements in the analysis of biopower. Firstly, the analysis questions the knowledge and the authorities (that is, pedagogues) who impart instructions, as well as the instructions (that is, truth discourses) that are being given; secondly, it questions the strategies for intervention 'in the name of life and health' (Rabinow and Rose 2006: 197), which ensure that individuals become 'objects to be worked on, to be pedagogized' (Harwood 2009: 24); and thirdly, it attends to modes of subjectification through which 'individuals are brought to work on themselves, under certain forms of authority, in relation to truth discourses, by means of practices of the self, in the name of their own life or health, that of their family or some other collectivity'. (Rabinow and Rose 2006: 197).

We thus begin our biopedagogical analysis with a questioning of the knowledge, the accepted 'truths' and the instructive practices around the problem of children's obesity (Bacchi 2009). We attend to the technologies of power (that is, strategies governing children's physical activity) as well as the technologies of the self (that is, techniques by which children come to regulate their own behaviour) (Arribas-Ayllon and Walkerdine 2008, Markula and Pringle 2006). Lastly, we examine subject positions (the repertoire of discourses about play that are available for children and families), as well as the modes of subjectification (the kinds of citizens the public health texts aim to produce) (Arribas-Ayllon and Walkerdine 2008, Bacchi 2009, Harwood 2009, Markula and Pringle 2006).

Data collection
We collected two sets of empirical data for this study: Canadian public health texts promoting active play to children and photo-elicited interviews about play from a group of Canadian children.

Public health texts.   We examined four Canadian organisations for texts relating to children's physical activity and play: (i) Health Canada; (ii) the Public Health Agency of Canada (PHAC), who set the public health agenda (for example, fighting child obesity) and fund health-related initiatives; (iii) AHKC and (iv) ParticipACTION, national organisations producing 'knowledge, insight and understanding' to increase physical activity among children (AHKC 2013).

Particularly relevant for this study was our analysis of the yearly "Physical Activity Report Card for Children and Youth"[1] (AHKC 2010, 2011 and 2012), which present the state of physical activity in Canada and the ParticipACTION campaigns and communications strategies (ParticipACTION 2011a, 2011b, 2011c, 2012, 2013a, 2013b), which educate Canadian families through adverts, worksheets and tips about how to engage in active play. All texts were publicly available online and written or published between 2007 and 2013.

Children's interviews.   Using snowball sampling, 25 English and French-speaking boys ($n = 10$) and girls ($n = 15$) aged 7 to 11 years living in Montréal, Canada were recruited. Four children were 7-years old, nine were 8-years old, seven were 9-years old, two were 10-years old and three were 11-years old. Of the 25 interviews conducted, 22 were in French and three in English. Five children spoke a language other than French or English at home (that is, Bengali, Armenian, Chinese, Spanish and Greek). The families were from diverse socioeconomic backgrounds.

Photographic, interview and observational material was collected over two sessions with the child at his/her family home. During the first session, which lasted approximately 2 hours, each child was lent a digital camera and asked to photograph anything that he/she considered part of his/her play. Detailed field notes were taken about the child's choice of what to photograph and about conversations had with the child. Each child selected six photographs, which were printed and brought to a second session. The second session was held approximately 2 weeks after the first, lasted approximately 1.5 hours and included a semi-structured, photo-elicited interview. The children were asked about play, physical activity, risk and pleasure and the six printed photographs were a basis on which to talk about play. The interviews were digitally recorded and transcribed verbatim. All children's names have been replaced with pseudonyms.

Coding.   All textual material was entered into the qualitative analysis software programme TAMS Analyzer for coding and analysis. Three themes emerged from our theoretical framework: 'imperatives of health'; 'cultural and political values' and 'technologies of power'. These were divided into several subthemes, which functioned as codes (examples include: play as physical activity, responsibility, self-governing play, subject categories, risk/safety, pleasure) (Alexander *et al.* 2014). Codes were developed and discussed between the authors. Textual material was coded and then further analysed through multiple readings of the material. Ethical approval for this study was received on 25 February 2011 from the University of Montréal's Health Research Ethics Committee and data were collected between April 2011 and March 2012.

Analysis

Our analysis begins with a problematisation of assumptions underlying the public health texts on childhood obesity. We then question the possible technologies of power that may be governing children's play in the name of obesity prevention and examine how these may produce particular subjects, practices and beliefs about ways to play. Drawing on children's interviews, we then examine whether children take up these messages and begin to regulate their own play activities.

Problem of obesity

According to Bacchi (2009), the assumption that governing practices are merely reacting to problems that already exist out there in the world must be challenged. She argues that the dominant conception of a problem, often constructed by governments and their agencies, is but one of many possible constructions (Bacchi 2009). One such problem in Canada is that of childhood obesity. For instance, one Canadian report suggests that 'obesity among young people has become a leading public health issue in Canada' resulting in numerous health risks, such as 'heart disease and type 2 diabetes … problems with the bones and joints, poor emotional health and well-being, and a reduced overall quality of life' (Public Health Agency of Canada 2008: 41). Furthermore, one of Health Canada's (2007) reports highlights the economic urgency of addressing the growing threat of childhood obesity:

> There are significant economic impacts related to obesity … It is estimated that physical inactivity costs the Canadian health care system at least $2.1 billion annually in direct health care costs, with an estimated annual economic burden to Canadian taxpayers at $5.3 billion. (Health Canada 2007: 97)

However, while the explicit problem of childhood obesity is clearly stated, this also carries an implicit representation of the causes of the problem (Bacchi 2009): children's inappropriate leisure choices. One physical activity organisation suggests:

An alarming modern-day trend has emerged – Canadian kids are coming home from school and are parking their bodies … hitting the couch after school has become the norm, with 73% of parents reporting that their children are engaged in very sedentary behaviours like watching TV, reading, or playing video and computer games after school. (AHKC 2011)

The modern trend of sedentary play and screen time thus represents the implicit problem, which is viewed as a major cause of childhood obesity. This implicit problem is also underscored by the solution formulated to address it: the promotion of active play. Because the government cannot directly regulate children's health behaviour, governmental and nongovernmental agencies (that is, AHKC and ParticipACTION) take on the role of urging children and families to engage in appropriate leisure choices (Fullagar 2009).

Active play promotion: biopedagogical practices and discursive effects
Active play (that is, physically active leisure activity) was first introduced as an indicator for children's physical activity in the 2008 Report Card, and by 2012 the Report Card was entirely dedicated to the promotion of active play. However, the central theme of the 2012 Report Card already evoked a swan song for active play. Entitled 'Is active play extinct?' the cover recalls an archaeology museum with a dinosaur skeleton looming over a display case that reads 'Ball: children's toy'. The Report Card states that '46% of kids aged 6–11 get 3 hours or less of active play … per week' (Active Health Kids Canada 2012: 12). They continue:

This is alarming news, as active play is a promising, accessible and cost-effective solution to help Canadian children and youth meet the Canadian Physical Activity Guidelines (p. 14).

Positioning active play as a thing of the past appears to be a way to justify its increased promotion. Active play is defined as including:

Essential qualities of play in general (i.e., fun, freely chosen, personally directed, spontaneous), but … active play involves physical activity at energy costs well above resting levels but often below 'exercise' levels. (Active Health Kids Canada 2012: 23)

Although active play is promoted as having the 'essential qualities of play', the main concern appears to be that children meet the guidelines of 60 minutes of physical activity per day.
In light of this, a new campaign entitled Bring Back Play! (ParticipACTION 2012) has been developed to 'encourage[s] parents to increase their children's physical activity levels by bringing back the kind of unstructured, active play that kept them healthy and happy when they were kids' (ParticipACTION 2012). Parents are also encouraged to be active themselves and to role model pleasurable physical activity:

Your kids are watching you, even when you're watching TV! … Make sure you live an active life. It's important that your child sees you running, walking and playing sports. Display a positive attitude that being active is fun and feels good. (ParticipACTION 2013a).

The campaign Think Again specifically targets mothers (ParticipACTION 2011a). It comprises a series of entertaining televised advertisements encouraging mothers to 'think again' about their children's physical activity. In one advertisement a mother exclaims: 'My Jamie plays soccer twice a week, that's plenty of activity!' after which a soccer ball enters from off-screen and hits her on the shoulder. It concludes with the message bold across the screen: 'Think again. Fact is, kids need at least 60 minutes of physical activity per day, every day' (ParticipACTION 2011a).

Printable workbooks with physical activity suggestions have also been created to teach children how to track and evaluate their physical activity levels. One workbook for children assigns a grade for different amounts of daily physical activity:

'A' – At least 60 minutes of moderate to vigorous physical activity (MVPA) daily for at least six days a week. More is even better. *Wow! You totally Rock!!!*

'B' – 60 minutes of MVPA daily for at least five days a week. You know it's fun to move around. *Why stop short!*

'C' – 60 minutes of MVPA daily for at least four days a week. *You are a halfway active sort of a kid.*

'D' – 60 minutes of MVPA daily for at least two days a week. So you know how to move … why not try something new?

'F' – Less than 60 minutes of MVPA daily. *Holy Cow! Do you realize that you've basically done nothing all week?* (ParticipACTION 2013b: 1)

This aligns with Burrows' (2009) argument that government campaigns function as biopedagogies that govern families and constitute their understandings of themselves as healthy citizens. Such campaigns encourage children to individualise physical activity messages and to begin to self-govern their leisure and adjust their 'ways of thinking, judging and acting upon themselves' (Rose 1999: xvi). Indeed, some children appeared to reconstruct such active play messages in their interviews. Arman, a 9-year-old boy, recalled word for word the televised Think Again campaign (ParticipACTION 2011a):

A: Ya … you should do 60 minutes of physical activity per day.
I: Where did you hear that?
A: I heard it on TV.
I: Do you try to do that?
A: Ya … but there are some things I don't understand in the advertisement. There's like a person who says 'Valérie plays soccer twice a week'. After that, there's like a ball that comes and hits her, and after that on the TV it says 'Think again'. But … I don't really understand why. Is she supposed to be better, or improve?
I: … what do you think they're saying?
A: Every day …. Two times per week, no. Everyday, yes.

Although he does not entirely understand the advertisement, Arman understands that children should be physically active and play sports every day and that Valérie, who only plays soccer twice per week, is perhaps 'supposed to be better, or improve'. However, his knowledge about being active every day was not always reflected in his own constructions of play.

While for Arman, play included being physically active (for example, acrobatics), most of the activities he characterised as play were not explicitly active. For instance, play for him included making ceramics, building model boats with his dad, playing the flute, doing magic tricks and playing on the computer. Arman's representations of play thus exhibit the multiplicity of discourses available in everyday life regarding play (Alldred and Burman 2005), even though the discourse about physical activity and play appears to be the most readily available.

Binati, an 8-year-old girl, says there are 'better and worse ways' to play. Indeed, Binati did not photograph a lot of toys nor did she discuss games or play explicitly. Her photographic representations of play included what she called 'pretty items' in her home, such as her mother's china, a chandelier in the living room and some plants and artificial flowers in the apartment stairwell. When asking her about playing, Binati talked about her exercise routine:

I: When you think of playing, what do you like doing best?
B: I like doing exercise.
I: What kind?
B: The kind like when you move your arms, move your feet, like this.
I: Is that something you do at school?
B: No, not at school, it's things I do at home. I don't do these at school.
I: What is that like for you?
B: I find it a little bit good.
I: OK, why do you do these exercises?
B: For making even better my body …
I: Do you sometimes just play?
B: You have to do exercise instead of play. It's not good.
I: You have to do exercise?
B: Yes, because me, I like it when my body is re-energised, it's much better and all.

Although Binati did not explicitly invoke public health discourses around active play, she nonetheless appeared to individualise wider discourses about physical activity and the body, reproducing ideas about what constitutes good or not good leisure activities.

Furthermore, unlike the public health texts promoting active play, many children pointed to the important role of affect involved in 'sedentary' forms of play, which appear to provide children with a sense of calm and relaxation. Florence, an 8-year-old girl, said that although she liked to play basketball and hockey, playing in calm, quiet ways felt good when she was sad or alone:

F: Sometimes I'm more sad. Say, you don't feel very good sometimes, well, you can just play, and this feels good … I read more, and I do what relaxes me … like knitting, and books … it feels good to do it when you are all alone.

Sebastien an 11-year-old boy discussed drawing as particularly relaxing. Although he spent a lot of time playing soccer, drawing was especially important to him:

S: Drawing is also when … I feel that I have to let my imagination out … What I like about drawing is that there are no limits, you can draw pretty much anything … and when I'm done my drawing, what I like is that, well, I'm relaxed. I drew something. I had fun.

Computer games, while often denigrated in public health texts, appeared to play a social role for some children. Sullivan a 9-year-old boy, who played a lot of hockey, also played computer games with his friends:

I: And computer games?
Sull: They're fun sometimes like when a friend comes over and we play on the computer, we play games. It's fun because you get to see the other, like your friend, like reacting, how they feel, that depends how you feel.

Given these responses, the public health position on sedentary play as unequivocally unhealthy must be questioned. Biddle *et al.* (2004) have challenged the notion of a 'couch kids' culture in modern western society' (p. 29), arguing that children's sedentary activities do not necessarily displace physical activities and do not have to be considered obstacles to physical activity.

Aligning with this argument, the children we interviewed constructed a diverse picture of play which was at once active and sedentary, and their sedentary activities did not foreclose them from also playing actively. The public health claims that sedentary play is unequivocally unhealthy neglect children's assertions about the enjoyment of playing in diverse ways and may obscure the benefits of sedentary play that children highlighted.

Negotiating tensions in public health knowledge: risk and play
Public health knowledge, though authoritative, is like much scientific knowledge: characterised by instability and contradiction, particularly with regard to what is labelled a health risk (Foucault 1980, Petersen and Lupton 1996). As outlined above, current public health interventions have created risk narratives around childhood obesity, which have extended to children's sedentary forms of play. However, within these interventions, active play itself embodies a set of risks for children, which further complicate the risk landscape of play.

In Canada a new initiative called Active and Safe After School has been launched with the aim of 'reducing injuries at playgrounds and other outdoor spaces, while encouraging our kids to lead an active, healthy lifestyle' (Public Health Agency of Canada 2012):

> While the Government of Canada encourages Canada's children and youth to become more active and live healthy lifestyles, it is also important to ensure their safety while being active. Through the Public Health Agency of Canada's Active and Safe initiative, the Government of Canada is investing $5 million over two years to ... reduce unintentional injuries among children and youth by improving the safety of outdoor play spaces (Public Health Agency of Canada 2012).

Implicitly then, this initiative to 'ensure safety while being active' suggests that while outdoor play is recommended, it is currently not entirely safe.

In line with such safety messages, many parents have increasingly voiced concerns about the risks of outdoor play (Boufous *et al.* 2004, O'Brien and Smith 2002, Veitch *et al.* 2006). Paradoxically then, within this public health discourse, parental anxieties are positioned as yet another obstacle to children's active play (McDermott 2007). For instance, the Report Card depicts parental concerns about safety in play as misguided:

> 58% of Canadian parents agree they are very concerned about keeping their children safe and feel they have to be 'over-protective of them in this world' ... Unfortunately, over-protective parenting, plus the lure of ever present technology, is driving kids into

highly controlled environments, where they have little opportunity to let loose, run around, build, explore ... Perhaps in a misguided bid to protect and direct them at all times, we have taken away our children's freedom to throw open the doors and go play. (AHKC 2012: 13)

Furthermore, while parents are asked to loosen one protective grip on play, they are also charged with producing new risks for children. The Report Card continues: 'The net result of our over-parenting behaviours is decreased physical activity, decreased fresh air and sunlight exposure, increased obesity and increased risk of harm from cyber-crime' (AHKC 2012: 24).

Given these messages, risks for children's play abound. While the risks of becoming obese are invoked to motivate children's active playing, various risks are also attributed to active play itself. Further compounding the risk landscape of play, parental over-protectiveness is construed not only as an obstacle to obesity prevention efforts, but as introducing new risks for children.

These messages thus represent important biopedagogies that require children and parents to negotiate risk and safety in play in the context of preventing obesity. Indeed, parents are instructed to free themselves of one fear (that is, the risks in outdoor play) while being vigilant of others (that is, decreased fresh air and sunlight, cyber-crime), a required negotiation in the name of obesity prevention. As Fullagar (2009) points out, 'leisure in this sense is inherently risky, which means pleasure and danger have to be constantly evaluated, taught and negotiated by adults who facilitate children's experiences' (p. 122).

Not surprisingly, the children in our study appeared to also negotiate between risk and safety in their discussions of play. Their discussions illustrate divergent perspectives that mirror the diverging discourses available to them regarding play, risk and safety. Marianne, a 10-year-old girl, reproduced the safety discourses around play when she talked about playing outside. For instance, she highlighted the importance of adult supervision of play:

Well, in our back alley, sometimes the kids playing are not supervised, and sometimes there are parents who come to ask us: 'have you seen my child, I don't see him anymore', so then it's like, 'you should supervise your child, it's dangerous!' ... At the park, well, I can't go alone ... I'm not allowed. And when we're in the alley, well, anything can happen, so my mom says she always has to be in the yard to supervise me. And when we are in the yard, she has to be somewhere close by where she can supervise us in the yard.

Lupton (1999) has suggested that risk can be viewed as a governmental strategy to manage populations and individuals. In this case, risk messages around play appear to mobilise a type of panoptic surveillance (Foucault 1977): Marianne not only reproduces the safe play discourse but individualises it in her judgement of her neighbours. By not abiding by these safety practices, Marianne's neighbours fail in their responsibility to manage their children's behaviour 'in the name of life and health' (Rabinow and Rose 2006: 197). Recalling Burrows (2009), we see that biopedagogies work not only at the level of the material body (that is, shaping physical bodies), but also work to produce and reproduce subjects (that is, families and children), as well as their practices and beliefs.

However, other children suggested that they enjoyed taking risks in their play and in this way they represented a resistance to safety prescriptions. For instance, Arman said he especially enjoyed doing acrobatics on the play module at school, although his teachers found it dangerous and did not permit it:

A: The teachers don't like it when your head is hanging down. They don't like it ... they find it dangerous.

I: And you?

A: It's cool. It's not dangerous, it's cool.

I: Why is it cool?

A: Because when you're hanging down you can make more figures than when you are upright ... I can hang upside down for hours and hours ... it's forbidden.

For Arman, who said that he had often done acrobatics and was very agile, being told that this kind of play was dangerous and forbidden was frustrating. However, although this restriction limited his ability to do acrobatics, he nonetheless engaged in these 'cool' and enjoyable acrobatics whenever he could, thus signalling a resistance to the adult discourses of risk around play.

Alain, a 9-year-old boy, similarly engaged in risks as part of his play. He said that learning to perform dangerous tricks on his bike was particularly exciting:

A: I like riding my bike ... So, you have the bike here and you have a bar that holds your seat [cross bar]. Well, I put my feet on that bar ... and then I stand up, except that I'm still holding the handle bars.

I: So you're standing on your bike?

A: Ya, because I'm going really fast, and I don't fall because I hold on pretty well. I'm also kind of used to it .... It took a long time before I knew how to do it. Before, I used to just put my feet on the bar, and I was afraid of standing up. Then I stood up a little. Then I got used to it, so I did the big standing figure.

I: Who taught you to do that?

A: No one, I learned it on my own.

I: Do other people find it dangerous?

A: Sometimes when I stand up, some people say, like my friends say, 'Stop, it's dangerous, you might fall and hurt yourself'. It's a little bit dangerous. The people who are just starting to bike ... they might fall easily. So, for them it's a bit dangerous.

While it often requires negotiation, resisting dominant discourses about risk in play, as in the case of Arman, and learning how to take risks, like Alain, may benefit children because it can inform the way in which children approach, judge and safely navigate future risks (Brussoni *et al.* 2012). Indeed, play advocates argue that removing risk from children's play leads to an underestimation of children's abilities, limiting the 'very experiences that help them to learn how to handle the challenges that life may throw at them' (Gill 2010: 1).

Discussion: shaping the actively playing child

Children in many industrialised societies are increasingly subjected to biopedagogies that have the potential to discipline and optimise their bodies and health (Harwood 2009). When play is taken up as a biopedagogical practice to promote physical activity, as in Canadian public health, certain representations of play (that is, being active and safe) tend to be promoted, while others (that is, being sedentary and risky) are obscured or marginalised. Indeed, the biopedagogical practices examined in this chapter appear to make particular subject positions available for children regarding play, physical activity and risk, which have the potential to marginalise some children's play experiences. For instance, naming children as 'active', 'sedentary', or as having 'basically done nothing all week' discursively constructs subject positions for children that encourage them (and their parents) to cultivate their bodies through exercise (Wright and Harwood 2009). These discourses appear to be reproduced, negotiated but also resisted by the children in our study: Arman, although uncertain of its exact meaning, repeats the 'truth' that one should play actively more, while Binati suggests that playing for exercise and to re-energise her body is a better form of play.

However, biopedagogical practices do not determine children's subjectivities. Inherent in these practices are also tensions that necessitate negotiation, and this was particularly evident in the multiple risk discourses around play that are in circulation in the public health texts. Such tensions make available multiple subject positions but this multiplicity also appears to open up a space for resistance (Alldred and Burman 2005). While Marianne reproduces the discourses of safety and surveillance regarding play, a form of resistance can be seen in Arman's refusal to abide by his teachers' safety prescriptions about his acrobatics.

Rail and Lafrance (2009) argue that biopedagogies are part of a 'neoliberal notion of individualism' that views individuals as 'capable of and responsible for changing their lifestyles through a variety of disciplinary techniques' (p. 76). The focus in public health on individual responsibility (for encouraging, role modelling and negotiating active play) appears to be important in the biopedagogical practices addressing children's play. Underlying the discourse on active play, children and families are urged to negotiate the risks of obesity and the risks of active play through the responsible management of leisure activities. Indeed, the way Marianne and Binati relate to exercise and safety in play characterises neoliberal self-governance (Rose 1999) in that their discussions also underscore a certain pleasure in demonstrating their responsible management of themselves.

What effects do these biopedagogies have on meanings of play? As we suggest at the outset of the chapter, focusing on active play as a biopedagogical practice for obesity prevention risks reshaping the meanings of play. Although public health organisations take a broad approach to increasing physical activity among children, by drawing on play as a means to do so reframes playing as an instrumental and productive activity. Given that children's subjectivities may be mediated by such public health discourses (that is, in campaigns, in schools), children may come to experience playing qualitatively differently than when there is no instrumental health purpose behind it. For example, Florence and Sebastien described 'sedentary' forms of play such as drawing, knitting, and reading as having important affective roles (for relaxing, calming, releasing the imagination). Yet in public health discourses, play that is not active, even if it is clearly affectively important for children, is neglected. We thus question whether playing, when it is promoted for physical activity and prescribed to be risk-free (but not overprotected), can still be characterised as possessing the qualities ('fun, freely chosen, personally directed, spontaneous') often considered fundamental to play.

As a governmental institution, public health wields a particularly strong normative and regulatory influence over the construction of health problems, over how the problem should be addressed, and over how the population is expected to relate to an issue (Bacchi 2009). Accordingly, biopedagogical practices act as authoritative and influential forms of governance which, through technologies of power and of the self, aim to regulate and discipline children's leisure activities (Wright and Harwood 2009).

We argue that by incorporating play within such public health obesity prevention strategies the meanings of play for children may be reshaped. We contend that the increasingly dominant active play discourse privileges particular forms of play while neglecting those that do not explicitly fit in the current mandates for physical health promotion. This, we argue, may have unintended consequences for children's wellbeing, particularly when the neglected forms of play are those that children highlight as important and might be as beneficial for their social and emotional wellbeing.

Acknowledgments

This study received financial support from a Canadian Institutes of Health Research (CIHR) graduate scholarship to SA, a CIHR new investigator award to KF and a Social Sciences and Humanities Research Council of Canada (SSHRC) grant (no. 410–2011–0860) to CF and KF. SA acknowledges Dörte Bemme for her generous analytical support.

Note

1   The "Physical Activity Report Cards for Children and Youth" are abbreviated to 'Report Card' in the remainder of this chapter.

References

Active Healthy Kids Canada (AHKC) (2010) *Healthy habits start earlier than you think*. AHKC: Report Card on physical activity for children and youth. Toronto.
AHKC (2011) *Today's after school special – inactivity. Canadian children missing the mark on physical activity in the after-school period*. Toronto, Canada: AHKC.
AHKC (2012) *Is Active Play Extinct? Report Card on Physical Activity for Children and Youth*. Toronto, Canada: AHKC.
AHKC (2013) About us: who we are. Available at http://www.activehealthykids.ca/AboutUs.aspx (accessed March 2013).
Alexander, S.A., Frohlich, K.L. and Fusco, C. (2014) 'Active play may be lots of fun … but it's certainly not frivolous': the emergence of active play as a health practice in Canadian public health. *Sociology of Health & Illness*. doi: 10.1111/1467-9566.12158.
Alldred, P. and Burman, E. (2005) Analysing children's accounts using discourse analysis. In Greene, S. and Hogan, D. (eds) *Researching Children's Experience*. London: Sage.
Arribas-Ayllon, M. and Walkerdine, V. (2008) Foucauldian discourse analysis. In Willig, C. and Stainton-Rogers, W. (eds) *The Sage Handbook of Qualitative Research in Psychology*. London: Sage.
Bacchi, C. (2009) *Analysing Policy: What's the Problem Represented to Be?*. Melbourne: Pearson Education.
Beausoleil, N. (2009) An impossible task? Preventing disordered eating in the context of the current obesity panic. In Wright, J. and Harwood, V. (eds) *Biopolitics and the Obesity Epidemic: Governing Bodies*. New York: Routledge.
Biddle, S.H., Gorely, T., Marshall, S.J., Murdey, I., *et al.* (2004) Physical activity and sedentary behaviours in youth: issues and controversies, *Journal of the Royal Society for the Promotion of Health*, 124, 1, 29–33.
Boufous, S., Finch, C. and Bauman, A. (2004) Parental safety concerns – a barrier to sport and physical activity in children?, *Australian and New Zealand Journal of Public Health*, 28, 5, 482–6.
Brussoni, M., Olsen, L.L., Pike, I. and Sleet, D.A. (2012) Risky play and children's safety: balancing priorities for optimal child development, *International Journal of Environmental Research and Public Health*, 9, 9, 3134–48.
Burrows, L. (2009) Pedagogizing families through obesity discourse. In Wright, J. and Harwood, V. (eds) *Biopolitics and the 'Obesity Epidemic': Governing Bodies*. New York: Routledge.
Canadian Society for Exercise Physiology (2011) *Canadian physical activity guidelines: for children 5–11 Years*. Ottawa: Canadian Society for Exercise Physiology.
Foucault, M. (1972) *The Archaeology of Knowledge*. London: Routledge.
Foucault, M. (1977) *Discipline and Punish: The Birth of the Prison*. New York: Random House.

Foucault, M. (1980) The politics of health in the eighteenth century. In Gordon, C. (ed) *Power/Knowledge: Selected Interviews and Other Writings*. New York: Pantheon, pp 1972–1977.

Foucault, M. (2008) *The Birth of Biopolitics: Lectures at the Collège de France 1978–1979* (G. Burchell, trans.). New York: Palgrave Macmillan.

Fullagar, S. (2009) Governing healthy family lifestyles through discourses of risk and responsibility. In Wright, J. and Harwood, V. (eds) *Biopolitics and the 'Obesity Epidemic': Governing Bodies*. New York: Routledge.

Gard, M. (2011) Truth, belief and the cultural politics of obesity scholarship and public health policy, *Critical Public Health*, 21, 1, 37–48.

Gard, M. and Wright, J. (2005) *The Obesity Epidemic: Science, Morality and Ideology*. New York: Routledge.

Gill, T. (2010) *Nothing Ventured: Balancing Risks and Benefits in the Outdoors*. London: English Outdoor Council.

Harwood, V. (2009) Theorizing biopedagogies. In Wright, J. and Harwood, V. (eds) *Biopolitics and the 'Obesity Epidemic': Governing Bodies*. New York: Routledge.

Canada, Health (2007) *Reaching for the Top: A Report by the Advisor on Healthy Children and Youth*. Ottawa: Health Canada.

Lupton, D. (1999) *Risk*. New York: Routledge.

McDermott, L. (2007) A governmental analysis of children 'at risk' in a world of physical inactivity and obesity epidemics, *Sociology of Sport Journal*, 24, 3, 302–24.

Markula, P. and Pringle, R. (2006) *Foucault, Sport and Exercise: Power, Knowledge and Transforming the Self*. New York: Routledge.

O'Brien, J. and Smith, J. (2002) Childhood transformed?, *Risk perceptions and the decline of free play, British Journal of Occupational Therapy*, 65, 3, 123–8.

O'Dea, J. (2005) Prevention of child obesity: 'first, do no harm', *Health Education Research*, 20, 2, 259–65.

ParticipACTION (2011a) ParticipACTION think again campaign. Available at http://www.youtube .com/watch?v=GM7HY2HqXEI&list=PLn9ck00ZhxkYVlk_itMNGnDdS5pqmcTOX&index=6 (accessed June 2012).

ParticipACTION (2011b) ParticipACTION toolkit: Think again. Available at http://www.participaction.com/resources-partners/toolkit/think-again/ (accessed June 2011).

ParticipACTION (2011c) Think your kids are active enough after school? THINK AGAIN. Available at http://www.participaction.com/pdf/par_schoolsout_englishforwebsite.pdf (accessed September 2011).

ParticipACTION (2012) Bring back play! Available at http://www.participaction.com/get-moving/bring -back-play-1/ (accessed July 2012).

ParticipACTION (2013a) A parent's guide to activity: tips on how to get your children to move more. Available at http://www.participaction.com/get-moving/tips/tips-for-parents/tips-for-parents-fun/ (accessed June 2012). No longer available online.

ParticipACTION (2013b) ParticipACTION: Active ways to play! Available at http://files.participaction. com/afterschool/afterschoolactivitytrackerengforwebsite.pdf (accessed June 2012).

Petersen, A. and Lupton, D. (1996) *The New Public Health: Health and Self in the Age of Risk*. London: Sage.

Public Health Agency of Canada (2008) *Healthy Settings for Young People in Canada*. Ottawa: Health Canada.

Public Health Agency of Canada (2012) The Government of Canada supports safe outdoor play spaces. Available at http://phac-aspc.gc.ca/media/nr-rp/2012/2012_0611f-eng.php (accessed September 2012).

Rabinow, P. and Rose, N. (2006) Biopower today, *BioSocieties*, 1, 195–217.

Rail, G. (2012) The birth of the obesity clinic: confessions of the flesh, biopedagogies and physical culture, *Sociology of Sport Journal*, 29, 2, 227–53.

Rail, G. and Lafrance, M. (2009) Confessions of the flesh and biopedagogies: discursive constructions of obesity on nip/tuck, *Medical Humanities*, 35, 2, 76–9.

Rail, G., Holmes, D. and Murray, S.J. (2010) The politics of evidence on 'domestic terrorists': obesity discourses and their effects, *Social Theory and Health*, 8, 3, 259–79.

Rich, E. (2011) 'I see her being obesed!': public pedagogy, reality media and the obesity crisis, *Health: An Interdisciplinary Journal for the Social Study of Health, Illness and Medicine*, 15, 1, 3–12.

Rose, N. (1999) *Governing the Soul: The Shaping of the Private Self*, 2nd edn. London: Free Association Books.

Shields, M. (2006) Overweight and obesity among children and youth, *Health Reports*, 17, 3, 27–42.

Tremblay, M.S., Kho, M.E., Tricco, A.C. and Duggan, M. (2010) Process description and evaluation of Canadian Physical Activity Guidelines development, *International Journal of Behavioral Nutrition and Physical Activity*, 7, 42, 1–16.

Veitch, J., Bagley, S., Ball, K. and Salmon, J. (2006) Where do children usually play?, *A qualitative study of parents' perceptions of influences on children's active free-play, Health and Place*, 12, 4, 383–93.

World Health Organisation (2010) *Population-based prevention strategies for childhood obesity: report of the WHO forum and technical meeting*. Geneva: WHO.

Wright, J. (2009) Biopower, biopedagogies and the obesity epidemic. In Wright, J. and Harwood, V. (eds) *Biopolitics and the 'Obesity Epidemic': Governing Bodies*. New York: Routledge.

Wright, J. and Harwood, V. (2009) *Biopolitics and the 'Obesity Epidemic': Governing Bodies*. New York: Routledge.

6

Parents' experiences of diagnostic processes of young children in Norwegian day-care institutions

Terese Wilhelmsen and Randi Dyblie Nilsen

Introduction

Today, close to 90 per cent of children aged 1–5 in Norway are enrolled in state-regulated day-care institutions[1] (Statistics Norway 2012). This coincides with the increasing role of health and educational systems, related to recent political emphasis on early intervention[2] in Norway (Arnesen 2012) and beyond (OECD 2006). Professionals[3] have been given greater responsibility than ever in monitoring and identifying behaviour that appears to be outside the norm and identifying 'the problem'. Parents participate in these diagnostic processes as laypersons. Parent–professional encounters are embedded in power relations, and critical research suggests that parents are often being silenced and subordinated in these processes (Hjörne and Säljö 2004, Hodge and Runswick-Cole 2008, Lundeby and Tøssebro 2008, Rogers 2011).

This chapter is based on a small study[4] that explored parental encounters with health and education professionals (Wilhelmsen 2012). Of particular interest to us were parents' experiences of taking part in diagnostic processes from the moment when initial concerns were raised about their children to the final diagnosis and selection of the means of intervention. Our analysis draws on in-depth interviews with parents of children (aged 4–8-years old) who were categorised as having 'special educational needs' while enrolled at regular early childhood education and care (ECEC) institutions or schools in Norway.

In the explorative analysis of the parents' accounts presented below we aim to illustrate decisive events during diagnostic processes in which particular children are constructed in a space of normality and deviance. We highlight parents' experiences by exploring the following question: how did parents participate in – and manoeuvre in response to – encounters with professionals during processes in which their children were constructed in a space of normality and deviance?

Our work is located in social studies of children and childhood or the sociology of childhood (here shortened to childhood studies). In so doing we are relying on an understanding of children and childhood as phenomena that are socially constructed in particular ways in diverse local and cultural contexts within generational relations (Alasuutari and Markström 2011, James and James 2004, Jenks 2004). In bringing parents' experiences to the fore, we hope to offer a nuanced understanding of childhood as a generational phenomenon (Alanen 2001, Mayall 2002). While not losing sight of parents as agents, we find it particularly important to account for the relations of power and control within which

Children, Health and Well-being: Policy Debates and Lived Experience, First Edition. Edited by Geraldine Brady, Pam Lowe and Sonja Olin Lauritzen. Chapters © 2015 The Authors. Book Compilation © 2015 Foundation for the Sociology of Health & Illness/Blackwell Publishing Ltd.

parent–professional encounters and constructions of children and childhood are embedded. In this study we built on the work of authors such as Foucault (1982, 1995) and his followers (for example, Bevir 1999a, 1999b, Coppock 2011, Jenks 2004) and on critical studies of disability and special and preschool education (for example, Arnesen 2012, Hjörne 2005, Ryan and Runswick-Cole 2008, Shakespeare 2000). We present the theoretical framework for this study first, followed by a description of the methodological approach. We will then present an analysis and discussion, closing with some final remarks.

Theoretical approach

A central achievement of childhood studies has been the groundbreaking promotion of research with child participants in such a way that children are valued as social beings in the present (Prout and James 1997). Expanding this effort, Mayall (2002: 21) states that the 'study of children's lives … is essentially the study of child–adult relations.' An emphasis both on conceptualising childhood as a generational phenomenon and on childhood as relational avoids conceptualising childhood as an isolated phenomenon (Alanen 2001, Mayall 2002, Qvortrup 2002). We agree with these efforts and we do not dispute the necessity of the inter-generational[5] aspect as such. Nevertheless, it might be fruitful to problematise the way that adults are usually simplified into one single generational category in a position of power (Qvortrup 2002). Based on our study with parents, we are differentiating between adults in different positions (see Alasuutari and Markström 2011). Focusing on parental experiences of encounters with child professionals provides an opening for deeper insights into adult intra-generational relations.

This study is grounded in a constructivist approach. As indicated above, we follow one of the basic tenets of childhood studies (Prout and James 1997) in viewing children as socially constructed (see Alasuutari and Markström 2011, Jenks 2004, Stainton Rogers and Stainton Rogers 1998). We conceive of 'the child as constituted socially, as a status of person which is comprised through a series of often heterogeneous images, representations, codes and constructs' (Jenks 2004: 77). Our study adds to research that sheds light on the manner in which diverse constructions of children and childhood have been (re)produced both historically and contemporarily (for example, Coppock 2011, Franck 2014, Hjörne and Säljö 2004, Nilsen 2012, Nind *et al.* 2011, Turmel 2008).

Power/knowledge
By interpreting children as discursively constructed, children have come to be understood contextually (Jenks 2004). The Foucauldian concept of discourse helps to account for complexities of power in adults' relations with children (Stainton Rogers and Stainton Rogers 1998):

> [T]he child, like other forms of beings within our culture, is presented through a variety of forms of discourse. These discourses are not necessarily competitive but neither is their complementarity inherent … the identity of children or of a particular child varies within the political contexts of those forms of discourse. Hence, the different kinds of 'knowledge' of mother, teacher, paediatrician, social worker, educational psychologist or juvenile magistrate, for example, do not live suspended in egalitarian harmony. (Jenks 2004: 78)

Foucault (1982, 1995) directs our attention to implicit forms of power and control, that are not necessarily experienced as controlling. Power is no property to be handed over or taken away. It is embedded in material and discursive practices (such as monitoring, testing and intervention measures). Language and knowledge are not neutral and the concept of discourse conceptualises power/knowledge relations. Discourses, such as medical, diagnostic or development discourses, offer particular kinds of perspectives, ethics, values, knowledge, explanations and truths (for example, Burman 2008a, 2008b, Jutel 2009, Ryan and Runswick-Cole 2008). These produce ways of understanding and defining children; consequently, these discourses also produce ways in which children are related to. Although it need not be the case, different discourses may challenge each other; and the ways in which children are constructed may be either in conflict or in agreement with one another.

Within each discourse certain kinds of perspectives, knowledge and truths are accepted, while others are excluded by being identified as invalid, false or unintelligent (Bevir 1999a). This also applies both to encounters between professionals and laypeople and to the ways in which particular children are constructed within intra-generational relations, for example, in diagnostic processes. Foucault (1982: 780) notes that we cannot disregard the fact that in society there is: "opposition to the power of men over women, of parents over children, of psychiatry over the mentally ill, of medicine over the population, of administration over the way people live". Although both laypeople and professionals may (re)produce the same discourses, the latter are given the authority to apply expert knowledge.

André Turmel (2008) investigated the history of how paediatrics and psychology started to compare and measure children, making statistics and charts and producing categories that came to be essential to professionals as well as to children, parents, institutions and policies. Deviation from 'the standardised child' is used to justify assessment; this leads to the legitimisation of early intervention and, consequently, to the construction of the child with 'special educational needs.' Scholars have provided a substantial critique of the discourse of child development and of age being a decisive benchmark for normal development (Burman 2008a, 2008b, Jenks 2004, Prout and James 1997).

Annemarie Jutel (2009) argued that diagnoses contribute to the maintenance of social order by differentiating deviance from normality. The norms and strategies in a diagnostic discourse help manage deviance by defining 'the problem' and separating 'true from false'. while also identifying treatment and providing an explanatory framework (Jutel 2009). A conclusive diagnosis also facilitates access to services and status.

Conceptualising agency

Research with parents (Rogers 2011, Singh 2004) indicates that parents are seldom passive receivers in parent–professional interaction; rather, they actively negotiate diagnostic issues in often shifting and flexible ways (Ryan and Runswick-Cole 2008). In discussing Foucault's writing on the issues of agents and power/knowledge, Mark Bevir argues that:

> Although agents necessarily exist within regimes of power/knowledge, these regimes do not determine the experiences they can have, the ways they can exercise their reason, the beliefs they can adopt, or the actions they can attempt to perform. Agents are creative beings; it is just that their creativity occurs in a given social context that influences it. (Bevir 1999b: 67)

We argue that, by viewing agents as social, contextualised and embedded in power relations, Bevir's conceptualisation is compatible with a relational view in childhood studies that departs from a contextualised social subject (Alanen 2001, Mayall 2002).

Although Foucault (1982, 1995) is mostly appreciated for his perspectives on power, he also emphasised that power is intrinsically related to resistance. Resistance presupposes power. In our study, some of the experiences the parents shared with us could be interpreted as acts of resistance. This point will be developed in the analysis that follows.

The methodological approach

This chapter is based on a study of parental experiences in parent–professional encounters with a particular emphasis on their experiences in relation to diagnostic processes in the context of an increased political emphasis on early intervention (Arnesen 2012). We learned about parents' initial concerns about their young children, assessment practices and identification of the problem, or the diagnostic label. Purposive sampling (Patton 2002) was used to recruit seven mothers for individual in-depth and semi-structured interviews (Kvale and Brinkmann 2009). The mothers chose to meet the interviewer in their own home. The fathers of the children participated in four of these interviews; the participation of fathers lasted either for the entire duration of the mother's interview or for part of it. Criteria for participation were (i) mothers with children who were, or had recently been, enrolled in day-care institutions, and (ii) a diagnostic process had started or was in process while the child was in day-care.

Norwegian legislation gives all children, independent of diagnosis or disability, the right to special educational assistance, provided that the child's special needs are recognised by health or educational professionals (Ministry of Education 2009). In this chapter, the use of the category children with special educational needs is understood as children who have been classified as such by professionals. We do not evaluate whether the needs do, in fact, exist. However, we acknowledge that special educational needs is a powerful category (Hjörne and Säljö 2004), the current importance of which is demonstrated in its widespread use in policy-making, administration and educational practice. The children in this study (4–8-year olds) were diagnosed with hearing or speech impairments, chronic illness, or behavioural disorders. Four of the children had been diagnosed with attention deficit hyperactivity disorder (ADHD) and two children were in the initial stages of a possible ADHD diagnosis. Although these cases provided rich data, it is not our task here to consider the large body of research concerning ADHD or the competing discussions and positions in this area of research (Timimi and Taylor 2004, Singh 2013).

The study was carried out in accordance with the ethical requirements of the Norwegian Ethical Board for Social Research. Informed consent was gained from the parents. They were informed about the possibility of opting out or refraining from answering questions at any time. The interviews were recorded and transcribed verbatim. Pseudonyms have been used to protect the anonymity of the participants and the third parties talked about.

During the interviews parents were encouraged to remember past experiences of the diagnostic process, to exemplify important events and to reflect on how they participated in this process. We recognise that the recollection and reconstruction of past experiences is complex (Riessman 2008). This chapter does not claim to describe 'what really happened' in the diagnostic processes, as knowledge produced in the course of research is constructed (Kvale and Brinkmann 2009, Søndergaard 2005, Stainton Rogers and Stainton Rogers 1998).

Analytical approach
For this chapter we carried out a thematic analysis (Patton 2002). Firstly, each author engaged in thorough readings and analytical reflections of the data; reflections and readings that were informed by the theoretical perspectives outlined above. From this initial

analysis, common themes and analytical questions were generated and subsequently refined as data were thoroughly discussed and related to theoretical perspectives, concepts and earlier research. Through this dialogical process of analysis (Nilsen 2005) we developed two closely related analytical threads in order to explore how parents participate in – and manoeuvre in – encounters with professionals during processes in which their children were constructed within a space of normality and deviance.

Parent–professional encounters are important events where children are spoken about and defined in particular ways (see Hjörne 2005, Hjörne and Säljö 2004). The first analytical thread addresses the finding that during such encounters and diagnostic processes, children become objectified subjects (see Foucault 1982). In other words, diverse constructions (or some may prefer 're-presentations') of particular children and related practices are brought to the fore. The parents recalled and shared these constructions and practices in the interview. In the analysis, we illustrate how parents encounter professional perspectives and constructions of their children, while also bringing their own lay understandings of their children to the fore.

The second analytical thread[6] addresses the question of how parents recall participating and manoeuvring in parent–professional encounters during diagnostic processes. In our analysis we illuminate the way that the parents described and reflected on manoeuvring between complying with and adapting to, and/or resisting the constructions and practices put forward by the professionals (as this was recalled and told in the interviews) while attending to issues of power and agency. Below we present and discuss the analysis in two sections, organised so as to follow the second analytical thread.

Adapting to children constructed as different

A key element of power embedded in early intervention policies is professionals' authority to identify and define a problem with a particular child (Shakespeare 2000). Initial concerns over a child's behaviour are key to the diagnostic process[7] (Franck 2014) and significant matters in parent–professional encounters (Hjörne 2005).

Adapting to initial concerns
In most of the situations described in the interviews, it was the staff at the day-care institutions who raised initial concerns of a child's potential differentness. In the interviews, parents recalled being offered a description of their child as different. An extract from the interview with Karen illustrates her response to this experience:

> We noticed that he [their son Aaron, 4-years old] was very active, so we thought, 'Okay, an active child.' But then we [the parents] started to get feedback from the day-care institution that he was interrupting others' play – well, it evolved into fighting, and he just went straight on and destroyed other children's play. … Then she [the preschool teacher] noticed, and we just like, yes, were told things that made us think, 'Wow, what is going on'?

Karen describes a conversation in which her (and her husband's) image of Aaron as a 'very active child' within a space of normality was challenged. Aaron's behaviour in peer relations had been pathologised and judged to be a problem (Franck and Nilsen 2015, Singh 2004).

Parents' responses to discussions about the observed differentness of their child vary a great deal (Ryan and Runswick-Cole 2008). However, discussions about a child's different-ness often impose expectations of parental adjustment to the information.

According to Karen, both she and her husband accepted the staff's description of their son. The other mothers in the study described similar responses of adaptation when con-fronted with initial constructions of their children as different and when accepting a pro-fessional's recommendations for further investigation. Nevertheless, as will be described further on, the parents differed as to whether they believed a diagnostic process was necessary.

The power of assessment devices and documented differentness

Monitoring children's development and conduct through assessment tools is essential within diagnostic processes. Parents' experiences of these tools can shed light on impor-tant moments in the diagnostic processes. During these critical points of parent–professional encounters, children are constructed through the continuous operation of power/knowledge relations between the two categories of adults. In what follows, we illustrate parental experi-ences with the evaluation tools.

The filling in of standardised assessment forms to evaluate and record the child's behaviour in the home setting is a form of parental contribution to the evaluation process. Sara recalled being asked to take part in this practice:

> We had to fill in different statements about Benjamin, sort of, and then they [the staff] filled out where on the chart he was, sort of. And we [the parents], we of course, saw that he was placed sort of a bit like … on his own. [With a small laugh].

The parents were presented with a diagram that portrayed Benjamin (aged 4 years at the time) as different. The chart placed him 'on his own,' indicating that he deviated from the normal standardised child. In their study of institutional procedures in diagnostic processes, Hjörne and Säljö (2004) suggest that using standardised assessment tools decontextualises children's behaviour; important environmental factors are not taken into consideration, and the problem is placed within the individual child (Franck 2013).

Sara recalled this visualisation of Benjamin's differentness as a decisive factor in their decision to continue with the evaluation process. She and her husband accepted the pro-fessionals' construction of their son. A diagram presented as visual evidence of a child's differentness compared with a normal child can be perceived as a strong argument in favour of the assessment (Turmel 2008).

Assessment tools can legitimise professionals' concerns about a particular child and pro-vide documentation that is usually presented to the child's parents in meetings such as parent conferences in ECEC (Alasuutari and Markström 2011). Benjamin's father highlighted his impression of the preschool teachers being well prepared for such a conference, and in dis-cussing the boy he emphasised 'that there were no speculations or qualified guessing, rather they brought with them certain forms – they had observed him professionally.'

Professionals' records of observations and standardised assessment forms are embedded in a powerful scientific discourse in which these artefacts, practices and results are regarded as producing objective knowledge on specific children (Turmel 2008). For Benjamin's father they provided trustworthy documentation and the 'truth' about Benjamin. This is made even more explicit in the interview with Ella. She described her meeting with the Child and Youth Psychiatric Service (BUP) and talked about testing as a reliable tool in evaluating her daugh-ter Anna:

Ella: [M]y brother got the diagnosis [ADHD] very quickly
Interviewer: Yes …
Ella: without a lot of testing and that kind of thing, and I don't want it to be like
                 that [with Anna]. I want to have her properly tested and that kind of thing,
                 you see. Because to start with medicines and all that, that … I couldn't bear it,
                 you see, if it doesn't work or if the diagnosis is wrong.

Even though Ella was convinced of the differentness of her daughter, she expressed her fear of an incorrect ADHD diagnosis and subsequent medicalisation, drawing on family history. Nevertheless, she acknowledged that proper testing was the best way of providing a valid result. Diagnostic processes operate in rigid systems grounded in a medical discourse of understanding children's special educational needs (Ryan and Runswick-Cole 2008). Within these systems, evaluation results serve as decisive indicators of perceived abnormalities in children, and results of standardised tools become forceful markers of truth. The cases of Benjamin's father and Anna's mother illustrate an agreement across professionals and laypersons within a medical discourse. Nonetheless, the normative truths constructed by assessment tools are questioned by some professionals (Franck 2013) and, as we will explore in the following section, by one mother in our study.

Parental critique and resistance

Although several forms of power are at play in parent–professional encounters, so too is agency. In this section, we consider parents' reflections on negotiations between themselves and professionals that impacted how they were able to manoeuvre as active agents in the diagnostic processes. Given our position that knowledge is socially constructed (Stainton Rogers and Stainton Rogers 1998), we explored whether parents reflected critically on the production of knowledge in these processes. Sara provided a critical parental voice, which we elaborate on below.

A critical voice
During the interview, Sara questioned an assessment form that she and her partner had been asked to fill out as part of the evaluation of their son. She started off by saying 'I think a lot of the questions were very, that is … a bit stupid, actually. But well, that's just me.' Later, she reflected on the demands placed on children by the assessment form:

Sara: When they are going to assess a 4 … 4-and-a-half – not even 5-year old, you
                 know – then it was [questions like]: 'Does he sit still at the dinner table?' Then
                 I think: Are there any 4-year olds who do that? Consequently, you think, like,
                 this is pointless – 'Does he understand that he might hurt someone?' Or, so –
Interviewer: Yes
Sara: To put it this way, in a way I felt that these were questions that actually were
                 about much older children. [Sara and interviewer laugh a bit, and soon after
                 she elaborates]. A lot of it I thought was redundant, as I didn't see the big
                 problem there and then. Wow – he's only 4-years old, you know, and then
                 they [the professionals] start to worry already!

This extract illuminates several important issues. Firstly, Sara seems critical about age being the determining factor for the construction of normality and deviance; something that is recurrent in standardised tools that are embedded in a development discourse (for example, Franck 2013). Secondly, Sara questions the normativity and context-dependence of expectations for a normal child at a specific age. This normativity is constructed in, and varies according to, certain contexts. Reflecting on the constructions of normality in criteria such as sitting still at the dinner table, Sara suggests the importance of contextualisation (Franck 2013, Hjörne 2005). Sara's critique of normative constructions appears to be indicative of her resistance to the basis on which her son was deemed to be deviant.

Generational relations – family history and experiences

Parents' responses to diagnostic processes are influenced by their emotions, family history and values (Bernheimer and Weisner 2007, Singh 2005). In the interviews parents used their family relations and generational history as a way to understand and compare their child's perceived differentness. Their own childhood conduct and experiences and that of their brothers, cousins and husbands were mentioned as possible explanations for the behaviour that had raised concern from professionals. Elin, for example, linked her daughter's possible diagnosis to her husband's dyslexia; Sara compared her son's high activity level and restlessness with her own childhood self and that of her side of the family. Ella recognised her daughter's behaviour because her brother had been diagnosed with ADHD. As such, by applying a relational, generational understanding (Mayall 2002) parents are actively using their lay knowledge and their own and family experiences to interpret their child's behaviour. This was illustrated in Sara's reflections on gender and her own childhood self:

> Well, I think more like – well boys are boys. I have been restless – a bit of a restless kid myself and I have nephews that were very active and full of life, you know. I recognised them in my children, in a way. And I am more like: 'Oh, this is okay!' ... But my husband was, he was [laughing] often – sort of felt that – but he is from the opposite side. They are sort of a very calm family and not – so there is a difference there.

While relating how her son Benjamin was constructed as deviating by day-care staff, Sara emphasised her own experiences and familial relations in order to reconstruct her child within a space of normality. Sara's statement also reflected her negotiations between contrasting family experiences. While she was drawing on family history – in which normality for children encompassed being restless, active and full of life – her husband had a contrasting family experience, which emphasised calmness. The father expressed a firm trust in professional knowledge, but Sara expressed her reluctance to start the diagnostic processes.

We should note that a family history with ADHD is, within a neurobiological framework, often connected to genetic inheritance (Barkley *et al.* 2002). Although this understanding is contested (Singh 2005, Timimi and Taylor 2004), neurobiological explanations are part of a powerful discourse that leaves little room for alternative understandings (Barkley *et al.* 2002). All parents who had children who were being assessed for ADHD were confronted with a medical discourse. Sara, for example, continued her reflections on family background by drawing on a medical understanding of heredity:

> And then I got to know that it is 80 per cent hereditary, ADHD; so then – no need to wonder where that came from! [Small laughter] Guilty! ... But we never talked about it, there is nobody in my family who has that diagnosis, in a way. Sort of, kids are kids, and – well we don't take it that seriously, so, more old school in that area.

Sara accepted the professional advice for further assessment. However, in the interview she also indicated that she was determined to understand her son within a space of normality. Thus, she constructed an alternative interpretation of her child's behaviour that was in line with her family history and experiences.

Hodge and Runswick-Cole (2008) argue that parents compromise their parental knowledge and view of their child in encounters with experts. While this is also reflected in our study, the complexity of diagnostic processes also initiates a variety of negotiations in the interplay between parents and professionals (Hjörne 2005), as well as between family members.

Parental resistance and agency
In the interview with Ella we learned how the lack of recognition of parental knowledge by day-care staff initiated parental agency. In the case of Ella this involved asking for a diagnostic process. In the following, we elaborate on this atypical case in our study, which provides valuable insights on how a mother manoeuvres persistently and with agency when conflicting child constructions are at play.

Ella and her husband had been working on getting their daughter Anna assessed for special educational needs in day-care since she was 3-years old. 'She started to throw toys and slam doors and – really – First I thought that yeah, yeah, that is the way it is, sort of. This is just a phase.' Ella's reference to her child's behaviour as 'just a phase' can be seen as within a developing-child discourse (Burman 2008a). Ella believed that Anna would mature and change. However, Anna's unwanted behaviour did not change and after consulting her parents (her brother had been diagnosed with ADHD), Ella decided to share her concerns with the day-care staff:

> And then we [the parents] asked the day-care institution what they thought of her. There, she was a normal child, like everyone else. 'She had maybe some problems sitting down quietly in circle time and things like that, but besides that, she is completely normal.' Then I thought, 'Yes, then it is probably just at home that she shouts and tries to bend the rules and does not want to listen.' Then we left and I didn't think that much about it anymore – not taking it any further. And we talked about it … at the parent conference, and then I asked them if they could observe, if they could take those tests, TRAS[8] and … I cannot remember the names now … But the different tests, so that they would test for things like that. So they were going to do that. And then they started to see a little bit, but it was still 'everybody was like that and.' So, yeah, yeah, all right. But I stuck to my beliefs, there is something that is not as it's supposed to be here. I do not feel … I see the difference when we are together with other children.

Ella continued communicating her concerns about Anna with the day-care staff, but according to her they viewed her daughter to be 'completely normal.' The parents felt that they were not believed.

Parents' struggles to be listened to are well known in the literature (Lundeby and Tøssebro 2008) and their knowledge is often overlooked (Ryan and Runswick-Cole 2008). Educational institutions often serve as gatekeepers and in order to get a child diagnosed, parents are dependent on professionals (Lundeby and Tøssebro 2008). Ella constructed her daughter as different, while being confronted with a non-complying response from day-care staff who continued to construct Anna as completely normal. We can trace the performance of agency in the recurrent initiatives by the mother, including getting her daughter observed and evaluated with the assessment tools that were available in the institution. Parents,' and often mothers' (Rogers 2011), experience of conflicting perspectives of a particular child's best interest is often recalled as being a demanding battle with professionals in the educational or health system (Hodge and Runswick-Cole 2008, Rogers 2011). In Ella's case, she decided to take the matter into her own hands, practicing agency by openly resisting the staff's judgement and advocating a diagnostic process by contacting BUP. Anna was 6-years old by the time professionals at BUP diagnosed her with ADHD.

It can be argued that mothers who push for their child to be diagnosed adhere to a medical discourse. However, as emphasised by Ryan and Runswick-Cole (2008), the mothers' choice of advocating a diagnosis may also be a result of their felt need to protect themselves from blame (Singh 2004) and the desire for more information about the child's behaviour, but it may also be a pragmatic political act aimed at barrier removal and to achieve increased impact in terms of help from the educational and health services. As noted above, labels serve as a recognition of the need for allocating resources to the matter (Jutel 2009).

Concluding remarks

In this analysis we explored how parents recalled their encounters with professionals during diagnostic processes in which their child was constructed within a space of normality and deviance. However, the children in question were constructed more towards deviance than normality. Grounded in a constructivist approach, our aim in promoting parents' voices was to illuminate the power/knowledge relations and agency in diagnostic processes. We applied Foucauldian conceptualisations of power to account for the complexities and nuances of childhood as a generational phenomenon and the constructions of particular children in adult intra-generational relations.

Discourses are tools by which we comprehend the social world, take action, construct ideas of children and childhood and create distinctions between normality and deviance. Parents are viewed as social and contextualised agents embedded in power relations. We explored various ways in which parents recall negotiating diagnostic processes, illuminating how they on the one hand adapted to powerful discourses, professional perspectives and practices, and how on the other hand they communicated their resistance.

Diagnostic processes are based on normative conceptualisations of children and childhood. As illustrated above, when professionals initiated concerns about a child, parents were confronted with an image of their child as different. Most of the parents adapted to these constructions and complied with further evaluations, although, with the exception of Ella, from the outset they had constructed their child as normal. In the interviews, parents said that, because they wanted to act in the best interest of their child, they trusted that the advice they received was concurrent with professional knowledge and practice. This implied that parents reconstructed their child as different, deviating from the norm as indicated by results from observation and assessment tools. However, Sara both adapted to professional constructions of her child as different as well as silently remaining determined to construct her child within a space of normality.

With respect to agency it is interesting to note that Ella was the only parent in our study who openly resisted professional judgements. This mother's actions resulted in an ADHD diagnosis that was of consequence to her daughter, the family, and the school. Even though we may think of Ella's initiatives as agency in the form of resistance, her reflections and actions are embedded in a diagnostic discourse reproducing power/knowledge relations in lay/professional encounters.

There is often a high threshold in challenging professionals' truths (Hodge and Runswick-Cole 2008). In our study, Sara, who compromised her parental knowledge, demonstrated this most clearly. She adapted to the professional knowledge embraced by her husband, even though her own family norms and experiences contradicted the kind of normality envisioned by the professionals. However, in the interviews Sara also questioned the normativity of the mapping tools. We might view her critical comments as silent resistance. Based on familial knowledge, Sara offered a substantial critique on issues that are taken for granted in scientific, medical, and child development discourses (Burman 2008a, Jutel 2009, Turmel 2008). By articulating her critical thoughts in the interview, this mother, from her lay position reflecting on her son's difference in relational terms, counteracted power/knowledge relations that constructed her son as deviant. Sara's experience and reflections indicate differences in values and constructions of children and normality across family generations. We might even be able to trace some modest historical changes in perceptions of normality. Conduct that parents experienced as normal in their own childhood might in contemporary society be subjected to categorisation and perceptions of deviance (Glogowska and Campbell 2004).

Burman (2008b: 224) asks, when professionals and parents conflict and construct particular children differently, '[w]ho can speak, from what points of view, with what authority and according to what criteria of expertise?'. When parent–professional encounters are about normality and deviance it is of utmost importance where particular children are placed in this space, as such placement has decisive consequences for the children and families in question as well as for professional practices in educational and health institutions (Hjörne 2005, Hjörne and Säljö 2004). Emphasis on early intervention establishes certain expectations of children's development features as well as parenting practices, making the family a site for surveillance by educational and health services (Rogers 2011). As pointed out above, normativity and what to expect of a child's conduct are dependent on context, and vary according to values and practices within families and educational institutions, cultures and history. Parent–professional encounters to identify and assess children for their possible special educational needs can be experienced as challenging for parents as well as for professionals. We argue that all parties can gain by listening to parents' voices, as it is necessary to take into account the fact that the home and the school are different contexts. Experts are in a powerful position, which needs to be reflected upon, and the same child might be constructed differently within and across these settings (Nind, *et al.* 2011). There is a need to recognise diversity in addition to take account of the familial knowledge base and parents' experiences.

Notes

1   We use the terms day-care and ECEC institutions interchangeably, as both translate as *barnehager* in Norwegian.
2   A discussion on intervention is beyond the scope of this chapter.
3   The term 'professional' refers here to a trained person with a specialised body of knowledge, such as a preschool teacher, a special educational needs teacher or a psychologist (Dale 1996).
4   The first author conducted this study (Wilhelmsen 2012) and carried out the interviews while employed as a research assistant for the research project, Children with (dis)abilities: practices and values in Norwegian day-care centres (see Franck 2013, 2014, Franck and Nilsen 2015) at the Norwegian Centre for Child Research, Norwegian University of Science and Technology. The project was directed by the second author and

funded by the Norwegian Research Council. We would like to express our sincere grati-
tude to the participants for sharing their stories. We would also like to thank the Norwegian Research Council for their funding and the helpful comments from the editors and
anonymous reviewers.

5   Alan Prout (2005) has discussed different generational approaches argued for in the sociology of childhood context and thus pointed out limitations of the strong argument
of focusing on inter-generational relationships on the basis of adult(hood)-child(hood)
binary differences. "Because of this it is difficult to see how intra-generational relationships can be properly acknowledged. Such intra-generational relations are themselves
very diverse, only very inadequately captured through the term peer [child] relations"
(Prout 2005:78). Within the sociology of childhood, analyses of intra-generational relations have elaborated on social and cultural practices among children. However, we focus
on adult intra-generational relations and practices in an effort to illuminate nuances
among adult groups. Discourses produced in adult intra-generational relations can as
such be thought of as a component of and interweaved in inter-generational practices
contributing to constructing children and childhood in diverse ways.

6   For the second analytical thread we have been inspired by other research in which young
children have been viewed as agents and their responses to institutional expectations with
strategies of both adaptation and resistance (Nilsen 2009). A study of day-care staff's
responses to regulation using a Foucauldian lens has also been helpful (Fenech and Sumison 2007).

7   In situations where teachers deem it necessary and have been given parental consent,
they will typically contact the Pedagogical and Psychological Service for guidance and
systematic assessment and identification of a problem or a diagnostic label.

8   TRAS is a commonly used age-dependent language development assessment tool in Norwegian ECEC, which also assesses children's social competence (Franck 2013).

References

Alanen, L. (2001) Explorations in generational analysis. In Alanen, L. and Mayall, B. (eds) *Conceptu-
alizing Child–Adult Relations*. Aldershott: RoutledgeFalmer.
Alasuutari, M. and Markström, A.M. (2011) The making of the ordinary child in preschool, *Scandinavian Journal of Educational Research*, 55, 5, 517–35.
Arnesen, A.L. (2012) Inkludering i det utdanningspolitiske barnehagelandskapet (Inclusion in
preschool educational policy). In Arnesen, A.L. (ed.) *Inkludering. Perspektiver i barnehagefaglige
praksiser (Inclusion: perspectives in preschool research and practice)*. Oslo: Universitetsforlaget.
Barkley, R.A., Cook, E.H., Diamond, A., *et al.* (2002) International consensus on ADHD, *Clinical
Child and Family Psychology Review*, 5, 2, 90–111.
Bernheimer, L.P. and Weisner, T.S. (2007) 'Let me just tell you what I do all day'. The family story at
the center of intervention research and practice, *Infants and Young Children*, 20, 3, 192–201.
Bevir, M. (1999a) Foucault, power and institutions, *Political Studies*, 47, 2, 345–59.
Bevir, M. (1999b) Foucault and critique. Deploying agency against autonomy, *Political Theory*, 27, 1,
65–84.
Burman, E. (2008a) *Deconstructing Developmental Psychology*, 2nd edn. London: Routledge.
Burman, E. (2008b) *Developments. Child, Image, Nation*. London: Routledge.
Coppock, V. (2011) Liberating the mind and governing the soul? Psychotherapeutic education, chil-
dren's rights and the disciplinary state, *Education Inquiry*, 2, 3, 385–99.
Dale, N. (1996) *Working with Families of Children with Special Educational Needs*. London: Routledge.

Fenech, M. and Sumison, J. (2007) Early childhood teachers and regulation: complicating power relations using a Foucauldian lens, *Contemporary Issues in Early Childhood*, 8, 2, 109–22.

Franck, K. (2013) Normality and deviance in Norwegian day-care institutions, *Childhoods Today*, 7, 1, 1–19.

Franck, K. (2014) Constructions of children in-between normality and deviance in Norwegian day-care centres. PhD thesis. Trondheim: Norwegian Centre for Child Research, Norwegian University of Science and Technology.

Franck, K. and Nilsen, R.D. (2015) The (in)competent child: Subject positions of deviance in Norwegian day-care centres, *Contemporary Issues of Early Childhood*, 16, 3.

Foucault, M. (1982) The subject and power, *Critical Inquiry*, 8, 4, 777–95.

Foucault, M. (1995) *Discipline and Punishment: The Birth of the Prison*. London: Vintage.

Glogowska, M. and Campbell, R. (2004) Parental views of surveillance for early speech and language difficulties, *Children & Society*, 18, 4, 266–77.

Hjörne, E. (2005) Negotiating the 'problem-child' in school: child identity, parenting and institutional agendas, *Qualitative Social Work*, 4, 4, 489–507.

Hjörne, E. and Säljö, R. (2004) 'There is something about Julia': symptoms, categories, and the process of invoking attention deficit hyperactivity disorder in Swedish school: a case study, *Journal of Language, Identity, and Education*, 3, 1, 1–24.

Hodge, N. and Runswick-Cole, K. (2008) Problematising parent–professional partnerships in education, *Disability & Society*, 23, 6, 637–47.

James, A. and James, A.L. (2004) *Constructing Childhood: Theory, Policy and Social Practice*. London: Palgrave.

Jenks, C. (2004) Constructing childhood sociologically. In Kehily, M.J. (ed) *An Introduction to Childhood Studies*. London: Open University Press.

Jutel, A. (2009) Sociology of diagnosis: a preliminary review, *Sociology of Health & Illness*, 31, 2, 278–99.

Kvale, S. and Brinkmann, S. (2009) *InterViews: Learning the Craft of Qualitative Research Interviewing*. Thousand Oaks: Sage.

Lundeby, H. and Tøssebro, J. (2008) Exploring experience of 'not being listened to' from the perspectives of parents with disabled children, *Scandinavian Journal of Disability Research*, 10, 4, 258–74.

Mayall, B. (2002) *Towards a Sociology for Childhood, Thinking from Children's Lives*. Buckingham: Open University Press.

Ministry of Education (2009) *St. meld. nr. 41, 2008–2009, Kvalitet i Barnehagen (Quality at day-care centres)*. Oslo: Ministry of Education (White Paper).

Nilsen, R.D. (2005) Searching for analytical concepts in the research process, Learning from children, *International Journal of Social Research Methodology*, 8, 22, 117–35.

Nilsen, R.D. (2009) Barndomssosiologiens kritikk av sosialiseringsbegrepet og en alternativ forståelse. (Sociology of childhood's critique of the socialisation concept and an alternative understanding), In Markström, A.M., Simonsson, M., Söderlind, I. and Änggård, E. (eds) *Barn, barndom och föreldraskap. (Children, childhood and parenting)*. Stockholm: Carlssons Bokförlag.

Nilsen, R.D. (2012): Flexible spaces – flexible subjects in 'nature.' Transcending the 'fenced' childhood in day-care centres? In Kjørholt, A.T. and Qvortrup, J. (eds) *The Modern Child and the Flexible Labour Market: Early Education and Care*. Basingstoke: Palgrave Macmillan.

Nind, M., Flewitt, R. and Payler, J. (2011) Social constructions of young children in 'special', 'inclusive' and home environments, *Children & Society*, 25, 5, 359–70.

OECD (2006) *Starting Strong II: Early Childhood Education and Care*. Paris: OECD.

Patton, M.Q. (2002) *Qualitative Research and Evaluation Methods*, 3rd edn. Thousand Oaks: Sage.

Prout, A. (2005) *The future of childhood*. Abingdon: RoutledgeFalmer.

Prout, A. and James, A. (1997) A new paradigm for the sociology of childhood? Provenance, promise and problems. In James, A. and Prout, A. (eds) *Constructing and Reconstructing Childhood*: Contemporary Issues in the Sociological Study of Childhood, 2nd edn. London: Falmer Press.

Qvortrup, J. (2002) Sociology of childhood: conceptual liberation of children. In Mouritsen, F. and Qvortrup, J. (eds) *Childhood and Children's Culture*. Odense: University Press of Southern Denmark.

Riessman, C.K. (2008) *Narrative Methods for the Human Sciences*. Thousand Oaks: Sage.

Rogers, C. (2011) Mothering and intellectual disability: partnership or rhetoric?, *British Journal of Education*, 32, 4, 563–81.

Ryan, S. and Runswick-Cole, K. (2008) Repositioning mothers: mothers, disabled children and disability studies, *Disability & Society*, 23, 3, 199–210.

Shakespeare, T. (2000) *Help*. Birmingham: Venture.

Singh, I. (2004) Doing their jobs: mothering with ritalin in a culture of mother-blame, *Social Science & Medicine*, 59, 6, 1193–205.

Singh, I. (2005) Will the 'real boy' please behave: dosing dilemmas for parents of boys with ADHD, *American Journal of Bioethics*, 5, 3, 34–47.

Singh, I. (2013) Brain talk: power and negotiation in children's discourse about self, brain and behaviour, *Sociology of Health & Illness*, 35, 6, 813–27.

Stainton Rogers, R. and Stainton Rogers, W. (1998) Word children. In Lesnik-Oberstein, K. (ed.) *Children in Culture. Approaches to Childhood*. Basingstoke: Macmillan.

Statistics Norway (2012) Kindergardens, 2012, final figures. Available at https://www.ssb.no/en/barnehager (accessed July 2013).

Søndergaard, D.M. (2005) At forske i komplekse tilblivelser. Kulturanalytiske, narrative og poststruktural-istiske tilgange til empirisk forskning (Research in complex becomings. Cultural analytical, narrative and post-structuralistic approach to empirical research). In Jensen, T.B. and Christensen, G. (eds) *Psykologiske og pædagogiske metoder (Psychological and pedagogical research methods)*. Roskilde: Roskilde Universitetsforlag.

Timimi, S. and Taylor, E. (2004) ADHD is best understood as a cultural construct, *British Journal of Psychiatry*, 184, 8–9.

Turmel, A. (2008) *A Historical Sociology of Childhood: Developmental Thinking, Categorization and Graphic Visualization*. Cambridge: Cambridge University Press.

Wilhelmsen, T. (2012) Parent-practitioner collaboration in Norwegian day-care institutions. Unpublished MPhil thesis Trondheim: Norwegian Centre for Child Research, Norwegian University of Science and Technology.

7

The meaning of a label for teenagers negotiating identity: experiences with autism spectrum disorder

Lise Mogensen and Jan Mason

Introduction

In the past two decades autism has increasingly been defined as a social problem. During this time a growing number of children and young people have been diagnosed with one of a range of autism spectrum disorders (ASD) (Matson and Kozlowski 2011). This increase has been attributed (in part) to the widening of the diagnostic criteria for ASD (Gernsbacher *et al.* 2005, Matson and Kozlowski 2011). The labelling of children with autism[1] is, however, a complex decision with many implications (Hodge 2005, Nadesan 2005). On one hand, the policy decision to diagnose or label children has significant advantages for children and their families in terms of delivery of services (Ho 2004, Nadesan 2005). In particular, a diagnosis is used to determine the nature and quantity of services provided to children in education systems. Children without a diagnosis, who behave in a manner perceived as different from the norm, may be interpreted and responded to as lazy or lacking interest in educational activities, based on assumptions that children generally learn and develop in the same way (Ho 2004). The early detection of significant impairments can be a prompt for the development, by teachers, support staff and parents, of focused educational plans and of specialised help to assist students achieve academically (Ho 2004, Nadesan 2005).

On the other hand, potential disadvantages for children are inherent in the assumptions and stereotypes associated with labelling them as autistic, and with the medical processes which accompany such a diagnosis (Hodge 2005, Nadesan 2005). Firstly, the pathologising of difference that a diagnosis brings may result in a sameness of treatment for children with this diagnosis, despite their individual strengths, achievements and interests (Ho 2004). In this process the diagnostic label may become 'more significant than the nature of the child' (Hodge 2005: 2), as in situations where children become objectified because they are associated with, or even named as, the diagnosis (for example, 'the autistic boy in year seven'). Secondly, the asymmetrical relations embedded in the medical, diagnostic process can position the child as passive or inferior and as having needs that are abnormal (Ho 2004). These notions are informed by Goffman's (1963) theory of social stigma by which particular labels have the power to spoil the identity of the individual.

The implications of the diagnostic process and the labelling that accompanies it have received little attention in the literature in terms of what it means in the lives and experiences of the children and young people who receive a diagnosis of autism. An extensive literature review, conducted by the first author (and researcher) (Mogensen 2011), highlighted

Children, Health and Well-being: Policy Debates and Lived Experience, First Edition. Edited by Geraldine Brady, Pam Lowe and Sonja Olin Lauritzen. Chapters © 2015 The Authors. Book Compilation © 2015 Foundation for the Sociology of Health & Illness/Blackwell Publishing Ltd.

the fact that research about autism has primarily been based on what is commonly referred to as the medical model. In this model the researcher adopts an expert role, which has been critiqued for treating the child as an object, in contrast to that of a subject whose views are included in the data (Prout 2002). It has also been critiqued for emphasising deficiencies in those diagnosed and thereby ignoring their qualities as persons. Alternative constructions of both the child and disability have been promoted in the literature in recent decades (for example, Connors and Stalker 2007, Davis *et al.* 2003).

The literature shows that connecting the principles of childhood sociology and disability studies in research can significantly contribute to understanding the lives of disabled children and young people from their own experiences (for example, Connors and Stalker 2007, Davis 2006). Epistemologically, sociology of childhood theory was considered relevant to this research because it recognises children 'as active in the construction … of their own social lives, in the lives of those around them and of the societies in which they live' (Prout and James 1990: 8). Acknowledging children as social actors who are able to contribute knowledge about issues that are important in their lives, such as having a diagnosis, emphasises the importance of taking their view seriously and placing them centrally in research.

Using a critical disability studies perspective was important for this study because of the way the social model of disability (Oliver 1990) differentiates disability from impairment. It enables us to understand the disabling effects of structural, social and attitudinal barriers on disabled people's lives as separate from individual experiences of physical, cognitive or sensory impairments (Morris 2001, Oliver 1996). Difference and identity are two contested concepts in critical disability studies theory (for example Oliver 1996, Shakespeare 1996) that resonate strongly with findings in this research. Identity as a concept has different meanings in different contexts (Shakespeare 1996) but in terms of disability, Oliver (1996) argues that disabled people are those who can be identified as such (by the presence of an impairment or externally imposed restrictions) or those who actively identify as such. Currently, these concepts have received limited attention in research with children and young people diagnosed with autism.

One aim of this research was to learn about the lives of a small group of young people diagnosed with autism, from their own experiences. Another aim was to use methods to facilitate their direct participation in the study. In this chapter we present findings about individual experiences of having a diagnosis of autism as shared by five young people in this research. These findings contribute to our understanding of the significance that receiving a diagnosis of autism had for these young people's active construction of identities, and the meanings they attributed to the diagnosis.

Methodology and methods

The theories informing the research reported here, contributed to a particular use of phenomenology and ethnography for developing an inclusive, collaborative, participatory approach with the participants. Phenomenology was relevant to this research, as it involves setting aside personal beliefs and, in Crotty's (1998) terms, enables the 'privileging of personal experiences' of the young participants and thereby widening the sociological knowledge about their individual lives and experiences. The use of ethnography provided flexibility in allowing the researcher to observe and interact with the children in social settings and enabled them to actively contribute to the direction of the research process (Christensen and Prout 2002, Davis 1998). For example, in this research the young people were consulted prior to commencing (and during) data collection on their preferences for methods of communicating with the researcher. A flexible use of methods allowed the researcher to individualise and change communication strategies according to each participant's preferences and abilities.

The five young people who contributed to the findings presented here were aged between 13 and 19 years of age (teenage), diagnosed with different forms of autism. These participants were recruited through the website of Autism Spectrum Australia and the organisation's school newsletters. Institutional ethical approval was obtained for this project and consent was treated as an ongoing process throughout the research. All names used in this chapter are pseudonyms.

The methods used in this research were flexible and were allowed to change. The researcher offered the participants a range of communication options (including face-to-face interviews, drawings, photos, communication cards and e-mails) for sharing their views in ways suited to them individually. The face-to-face interview was the most common choice by participants initially, but after the first two visits two individuals changed to e-mail due to their time constraints. Communication strategies were also flexible, depending on individual style and requirements. For example, people diagnosed with autism sometimes have difficulty in responding to the open-ended questions typically associated with qualitative interviews (Beresford *et al*. 2004). Therefore, the researcher took direction from the way in which the individual participants communicated with her during interactions with them (on average in three sessions per participant) and some open-ended questions were broken down into a more structured format.

Thematic analysis was carried out across the data collected from the participants (transcripts, e-mails and photos on a communication board). An interpretative framework (Richards 2005) was used to explore how themes related to the broad research question topics and the theoretical underpinning of the project. Firstly, the researcher identified initial strong or recurring topics. These initial topics were listed, and possible connections were made with theoretical concepts relating to childhood sociology and disability studies. Thereafter, links between individual topics were explored to develop the themes. This process was iterative and identified common and divergent perspectives within and across data inputs, which formed the basis for the construction of new understandings about the lives of young people diagnosed with autism.

As part of the collaborative approach, and to strengthen research rigour and the trustworthiness of the analysis, the young people were encouraged to provide feedback on summaries of the findings as well as on the research process. Two participants provided feedback on the research process and four participants commented on their own contributions. Feedback from the young people showed that three of them felt empowered by being able to contribute their own views, while for two participants being able to direct and decide on research methods was more significant.

In the following sections of this chapter we present findings from the views and experiences shared by five research participants. In the final section of the chapter we discuss the significance of these findings.

Findings

The findings presented here illustrate the meanings the diagnosis of autism had for the way the young people negotiated identity. The accounts show a variety of experiences and views about learning of and being labelled with autism, in terms of the young people's struggles with personal identity, their social relations and the ways in which they negotiated impairment.

Meanings of the diagnosis of autism at the level of individual personal identity

The meanings that a diagnosis of autism had for the young people at a personal level, presented here, are indicative of the diversity and complexity of experiences of having a diagnosis. While individual participants variously described the diagnosis as being oppressive, positive or even liberating, for several individuals it also facilitated their having some control in their lives.

Diagnosis as oppressive

Kim (age 18) described her experience of being diagnosed as oppressive. With help from her mother, she explained that she had not wanted anything to do with the diagnosis, because it meant 'difficulties' and 'made everything so much harder'. The diagnosis had confronted her with issues of her difference from others, of which she had not previously been aware:

Mother: Kim has in the past said that up until she was 8 … she didn't think she was different at all. She just lived in her own little world and was quite happy doing what she was doing. But then as soon as the intense intervention sort of stuff happened, evolving around ASD specifically, all of a sudden there was a label and that is when you started hating …
Kim: Yeah, the label and what came with it …
Mother: The fact that there was so much focus put on her all of a sudden … And she was … yeah would that be right?
Kim: Yeah …
Researcher: Were you told of it [autism] then (when she was 8)?
Kim: I was probably told but I just didn't understand what it meant until like the end of last year.

Kim explained that what came with the label, was intense, early intervention directed by a health professional. She experienced this 'sudden focus' on her as an effort to change her and frame her identity, in ways that, at that time, she did not understand. The mainly negative feelings Kim associated with the diagnosis of autism meant she had to struggle with a personal sense of identity of being different. Interactions with others and, in particular, with health practitioners confronted her with ways in which she was different and outside the norm:

Researcher: Did you feel different?
Kim: Yeah …
Researcher: From other people?
Kim: I felt it … but like I didn't notice it until that – just special things – at intervention and places. … And then I felt different and it was … like an outsider sort of … I don't know why, I couldn't fit in. I couldn't fit in … I couldn't talk … I got lost.

Diagnosis as liberating

In contrast to Kim, Ian (age 18) and Anna (age 16) experienced the diagnostic process as liberating – as a means of situating themselves in relation to normative experience. Their experiences of receiving a diagnosis were connected with their understandings of identity, in terms of the ways in which the diagnosis enabled them to integrate knowledge about their condition in their lives. Ian explained how he used the diagnosis of Asperger's syndrome, when given 2 years before the research interviews, as part of a reflexive process to understand his self within his biography:

> Um I started to look at my life completely differently. ... Well, I noticed that um ... but I never really looked at it ... but all throughout my life ... I was sort of ... I was always a bit weird, and I noticed I had little habits and things ... and this thing that I eventually was diagnosed with ... that condition ... looking back on my life and thinking yeah I saw a lot of it there, where previously I just thought it was normal.

The knowledge inherent in the diagnosis enabled Ian to gain insights into the 'habits and things' which characterised how he lived his life and to confront the ways that he felt his life differed from normative life experiences:

Researcher: Right. So once you were diagnosed, you saw things that were different?
Ian: Um, yeah ... I had symptoms back then which I didn't know I had ... so little habitual things and little patterns and things.

For Ian, being able to apply the diagnostic label to himself enabled him to reframe his problems and incorporate them into an acceptable sense of self, legitimising his experiences of difference, while still recognising the negative connotations commonly associated with the label:

> [W]hen she ... like she [his specialist] diagnosed me with Asperger's and stuff and just ... it just put everything into perspective for me because ... um ... a lot of people think 'Oh, it's a label' and all of a sudden it has to be some sort of prejudice – but I think that is sort of like a secure sort of thing for me. And just finding out that problems that I was dealing with were real problems and that they actually had names and labels and that they have diagnosis and treatments for that sort of thing. And that was a really secure thing for me. I wanted to be labelled because I suddenly knew what I could do and I knew there was a way I could cope with that problem once it had been identified. It was like a diagnosis in a way, saying that 'Oh, for this certain thing like you use this certain method and it works well'.

Diagnosis as facilitating control

For Anna the liberation gained from a diagnosis was that it provided her with a sense of gaining control in her life. It gave her a reason for feeling different from others and she was resentful that the diagnosis had been withheld from her until recently (3 months before the research interviews). She was beginning to recognise that the knowledge provided by the diagnosis could have helped her in earlier attempts to develop a frame for making sense of her experiences:

Anna: I had just been through months of problems and questioning why ... [things were happening] she (her mother) had known long enough ...

Researcher: So you feel that it would have been helpful to know about … ?
Anna: Yeah …
Researcher: Do you think things would have changed much for you if you had known earlier?
Anna: Yeah … it would have … if I'd known before.

There was a sense that Anna had been struggling for control over things happening to her in terms of what Huws and Jones (2008) have described as the 'absent presence' of autism. Anna's experience resonates with the argument made by some autistic self-advocates that it is important for diagnosed individuals to be informed that they have a diagnosis of autism as soon as possible. While most will already know, or feel, that they are different from others, 'they will suffer deeply from not knowing why' (Princes-Hughes 2004, cited in Davidson and Henderson 2010: 174).

For Ian, actively exploring and using knowledge of the diagnosis also helped him to gain some control in his life:

> It was really helpful because I suddenly understood myself a bit more. Because I read these books about heaps of people who had Asperger's in their lives or that – and I found out that there were certain similarities that all Asperger's people had with each other.

Seeing a common identity with others with whom he shared characteristics, contributed for Ian, to his positive experiences of who he was, in a similar way to that described by other people diagnosed with Asperger's syndrome who choose the label for themselves and emphasise the way they differ from social norms (for example Brownlow and O'Dell 2006, Davidson and Henderson 2010).

Autism as positive identity

For Lucas (age 16), autism and 'being different' were positive and fundamental parts of his self-concept. In contrast to Anna, autism was something he had 'always' known about, and the diagnosis had formed a significant part of his childhood. This knowledge meant that Lucas did not have the same struggle to understand his experiences of difference. Lucas framed his identity in relation to the diagnosis of autism and with a distinct sense of pride in being exactly as he was, including where he saw himself as different from the norm, as illustrated in the extract below from an e-mail response to a question of whether there was ever a time when he wished away autism from his life:

> Never, I believe that it was pure chance and genetics that I am this way, and it gives my class group a more serious look on things, my friends notice two sides to me, the more proactive and punctual Lucas, and the mysterious out- of-school Lucas, I say mysterious, as [a] few people think I work for ASIO [Australian Security Intelligence Organisation]. This may be because I have an interest in the subject of Intelligence and that I can say things and know a lot about security subjects, and the fact that I disappear when I'm not on school grounds. This two sided me is a trait of Autism, and I feel my peers admire me because of it. … when I'm in a relaxed environment the real me comes out, and I think they are taken by that, also general comments like 'my gosh Lucas, you are soo mysterious'.

Lucas's account shows how he asserted his identity within his own interpretations of the diagnosis. He actively structured his identity around difference and through his objects of interest, choosing to focus on aspects that contributed specific qualities to his personality such as being punctual, knowledgeable and mysterious.

These findings clearly show that the personal meanings and experiences young people attribute to a diagnosis of autism are complex and multifaceted according to the context in which the diagnosis is given and how young people understand it in relation to their personal biography. One young person, Dylan (aged 13) said the diagnosis of autism was unimportant to his personal identity.

Dylan, who had had the diagnosis explained to him by his sister when he was 9, asserted that it was not significant for him, answering an emphatic 'No,' in response to the researcher's question: 'Do you think it [autism] makes you different from your friends in any way?' However, he indicated that others, adults in particular, saw him as different. He interpreted this difference positively in terms of the allowances that were sometimes made for him, explaining: 'I know that if I wasn't autistic my Mum wouldn't let me get away with much stuff' and 'I think I get a bit of easier work' at school. So although Dylan indicated that the diagnosis was not significant for his self-identity, he recognised that it had a meaning and a function – in perhaps reducing some of the typical school expectations and the way others saw him.

Meanings of diagnosis for identity at the socio-relational or public level

The dilemma of disclosure and social identity: stereotypes and negative attitudes
The participants suggested that too much focus was placed on the negative connotations attached to the diagnosis in society. They felt that public attitudes generally showed a lack of understanding about autism, typically constructing the differences in terms of deficiencies. These negatives were aspects of the diagnosis that the participants resisted as part of their identity. For example, Lucas criticised the 'stereotype of an autistic or borderline autistic, and of Aspergers, as people who are anti-social, can't handle relationships (sexual and otherwise) and know a lot about trains'. He spoke of the need for what he referred to as 'a more in-depth awareness' of 'the nature of autism,' explaining:

> [T]here is no definite diagnosis for any case of borderline autism, autism, Asperger's, ADD/ADHD ... we are all different.

Kim suggested that the broader society needs to recognise that 'we are not stupid ... we can think for ourselves.'

This awareness of stereotypes and attitudes towards the diagnosis of autism meant that some of the young people were reluctant to disclose their diagnosis to others. Anna and Kim both struggled with the fear that disclosing the diagnosis would for them result in being treated as different:

Researcher: Do your friends know [about your diagnosis]?
Anna: Nooo I don't tell them.
Researcher: Do you think it would make life easier for you if they knew ... sometimes?
Anna: Yeah.
Researcher: But at the same time you don't really want them to.
Anna: No.
Researcher: Why don't you want them to know?
Anna: I just want them to think about me the way they think about me now.

Researcher: Do you think they would think about you differently if they knew?
Anna: Yeah.

When Kim was asked whether any of her friends knew about the diagnosis, she responded:

> I didn't want to tell them at first because I wanted them to have their own opinion before they find out something that could … you know, let them treat me differently … I didn't want to be perceived as different.

Kim and her mother described how Kim had become proficient at executing social strategies, described in previous research as 'masquerading' (Carrington and Graham 2001), allowing her to adapt to various social contexts and being perceived as normal. When asked to elaborate, Kim asked her mother to describe the way she worked at conveying a picture of her self to fit normative expectations:

Mother: I describe. OK. Kim has told me that because she spent so much time observing what she calls NT[2] behaviour and working out how people tick that she's worked out that there is certain characteristics of people. Like she has studied it so much that she can pick how … what someone is like … the way they behave sort of describes to her what they're like as a person. And then she is able to sort of put on like a mask, she puts on a mask that allows her to fit with that person's character so she can relate to them … or at least fit … is that right?
Kim: Yes.
Mother: Without feeling um …
Kim: Uncomfortable … Yep.
Mother: Uncomfortable … So she is quite often in character when she is talking to people, depending on who they are.

In contrast to the two young women, Lucas was more relaxed about his peers knowing about his condition. He was comfortable with his diagnosis and the idea of being different in ways that worked for him socially:

> [I]t doesn't bother me at all, my friends have some idea about me being unusual, but I'm not sure that they know a complete diagnosis, and I don't think it really matters.

The findings presented in this section clearly indicate that social experiences were significant for the way the participants understood themselves and related to the diagnosis. Feelings of being different could be detrimental to their sense of self when connected with lack of social competence. They seemed uncomfortable with the connotations of incompetence and negative stereotypes associated with autism that seem to persist in society, while still acknowledging certain personal limitations as part of the condition.

Meaning of the diagnosis in terms of negotiating impairments

Impairment and losing control
The young people did not talk about the social effects of autism as impairments but referred to their specific difficulties, or personal faults, flaws or limitations. Anna and Ian both gave

examples of how they experienced the effects of impairments in their engagements with friends, as having difficulties with understanding certain social interactions. Ian explained:

> I've got some of my faults ... I guess um the friendship thing – it has always been a big sort of problem for me ... I go too far in some jokes, sort of thing. Sort of – I don't understand that there's a certain boundary that you don't cross when you're speaking to people. ... And I can do that unintentionally, just not even knowing I'm doing it.

Ian and Anna also both talked about impairment in terms of losing control of the self. Inappropriate anger was a significant issue which they related to their diagnosis:

Ian: I really lose it ... or something, so I can get angry quite a bit ... um ... just snapping at people over nothing.

Anna: The fact about ... it's not normal ... I get angry at Mum, and when she asks a question I sometimes yell the answer at her ... I don't know but it just comes out ... I can't control it.

It was at the social relational level that the meanings of their diagnoses in terms of impairment, as defined by medical practitioners, impacted on and required active negotiations from the young people, as they lived their lives in various social contexts.

Context, especially school, was significant for the young people's individual experiences of living with difference and of lacking control. Kim described a sense of losing control of her feelings, as related to her diagnosed impairments, after having changed schools. Kim experienced the effects of the new environment and the demands that followed, as losing control in ways that meant she had to make a decision to confront her differences:

Kim: I went to boarding school then that's when we had to sort of open up and discover about it because of problems being with the stress issues and stuff like that ... I can be quite unfocused. And that was hard to begin with cause [sic] I didn't really want to. But then sort of had to. I had to make that decision.

Mother: The environment at boarding school was such that it was such a high level of stress all the time. Kim started saying things like 'I feel like I'm becoming autistic again' or 'I feel like I'm not controlling it anymore'. 'It throws me ... I used to be able to control it, now I can't'.

Even though Kim had identified the boarding school environment as being stressful, she internalised her difficulties and attributed her lack of control to her diagnosis using the term, 'becoming autistic again'. Kim explained that while she tried 'not to use Autism as an excuse', she sometimes felt that the diagnosis was necessary in validating experienced difficulties and to obtain support from teachers in order to achieve, according to normative expectations in the school context.

Ian recognised how leaving the school environment was liberating in terms of enabling him to experience broader social relations, as talked about in the extract below in terms of his experiences at church and in his newfound employment:

> I don't really think I am all that different after all, as I have recently found a nice group of people at church who will accept me for who I am. Not to say I don't have to try my best anymore, but rather, I can be allowed to contribute to other people just like I have always wished I could. Other than the example of church, there have been some other

areas within my new life that have revealed to me that I am probably just as normal as the next teenager. One more of these areas can be found in the form of my current employment – it is here that, once again, people enjoy my company and make me feel very valued. I have begun to think that my life has been very limited at school and I just haven't been able to experience many friendships beyond my peers.

Ian's new experiences outside of school not only enabled him to feel useful and valued, they had the effect of 'normalising' him as a person.

In another context, Kim had found health professional–client relations disempowering in terms of the professional's attitude and control over prescribed interventions. She considered how the professional's condescending attitude toward her emphasised her inferior status:

Kim: I found it very patronising with all these cards and things.
Mother: So it became more of an issue of feeling like an idiot rather than … 'cause that is what she said. She used to hate – you know – those PECS cards and Boardmaker – she just hated it!
Researcher: OK, so what do you think would have been helpful for you?
Kim: I don't know. I really – I just didn't like the patronising manner. I still cannot stand being spoken down to …
Mother: … and once you said to me, that it was like they tried to get you to work on areas that weren't relevant … but it would have been helpful if they had helped in other areas.
Kim: Yeah.

It was clear that Kim's experiences of early intervention had been significant in shaping the way she related to her diagnosis. Kim's inferior, 'idiot' status was reinforced for her when she experienced interactions as defining her needs and interventions, in ways that lacked meaning for her and took away her control.

Impairment and taking control

To several participants the notion of losing control of self implied a lack of competence. Some of them described how they used strategies in negotiating social relations to exert control over their impairments in different contexts. In addition to masking her differences, Kim's efforts to become 'normal' involved gaining control in social situations by working hard to 'fix what was wrong' with her, in order to overcome her differences. Lucas also explained how, over time, he had consciously worked to acquire certain skills to overcome perceived social limitations:

[Y]ou know how people with autism generally have really bad social skills … I've tried to teach myself good social skills … Over 12 years I have taught myself through trial-and-error, thinking and learning from people to gain social skills.

Lucas described how his preferred mode of social interaction, communicating online, enabled him to have a sense of control and security because he could stay in his comfort zone. Ian and Kim both explained that maintaining control in their everyday lives required ongoing planning and effort, learning skills that would conceal or diminish differences:

Ian: It takes a lot of time and effort and just um, just thinking ahead before you do something to keep everything … to actually keep things under control …

Kim: Years ahead. Yeah plan every single day ... everything would go like ... not con-
         sciously, but pretty much the next hour, to the next, to the next. I will just do a plan
         to the week, to the month to the year.

The findings presented here relate to struggles for control associated with having a diagnosis
of autism. For the young people these experiences were additional to everyday struggles for
control typical of the socially structured period of teenagehood, in the school and sometimes
the family. The young people experienced a regular undermining of their social competence
as persons, on the basis of their age, in ways described in findings from research with children
and young people more generally, where they tell us the importance of day-to-day control in
their lives (for example Mayall 2002).

Discussion

Children diagnosed with autism are typically portrayed as being significantly different from
other young people and generalisations are made about their lives. These generalisations tend
to define the experiences of children diagnosed with autism as either positive or negative.
However, the participatory research reported here indicates that when we hear from young
people directly, we learn that there is more complexity and heterogeneity in the ways in which
they engaged in making sense of their diagnoses than is evident in the literature. While the
diagnosis was associated with negative experiences – of being stigmatised and treated differently from non-diagnosed young people, it was for some young people associated with
positive experiences in terms of better understanding oneself. It legitimated difference and
empowered them to negotiate living lives of difference. In the discussion we focus on the
significance, for the young people, of a diagnosis of autism for personal identity, for social
relational processes and for facilitating control in their own lives.

Significance of diagnosis for personal identity
In relation to self-identity, the findings highlight the significance of the labelling process for
young people who at times struggled to understand who they were, in terms of Giddens'
(1991: 53) description of 'the self as reflexively understood by the person in terms of her or
his biography'. In the case of Kim the diagnosis was experienced as negative and restrictive
in her interactions with health professionals and in discovering limitations she did not know
she had before she was labelled with autism. However, for some other young people the diagnosis provided a sense of liberation and understanding of self. For Ian, seeing a common
identity with others with whom he shared characteristics contributed to positive experiences
of who he was. For Lucas, the uniqueness of the characteristics he attributed to autism was
significant to the way he constructed his identity in positive terms. The accounts of Ian and
Lucas reflect reports in the literature of people diagnosed with Asperger's syndrome who
choose to identify with the label and emphasise the way they differ from social norms (for
example Brownlow and O'Dell 2006, Davidson and Henderson 2010). Dylan's discussion of
his experiences contrast with those reported by Kim, Ian and Lucas, in indicating that for
some young people diagnosed with autism, the experiences associated with the label may not
have significant implications for the way they construct their identity.
   The diversity of experiences of these young people contrasts with the typically homoge-
neous portrayals of children in more traditional research about autism. These findings also
support the comment by Tom Shakespeare (1996) in a discussion on 'disability identity'. He
refers to the fact that 'identity is a complex field' (p. 94) and that, while numerous disciplines

use the word 'variously and in different contexts' (p. 94), the metaphor 'provided by the concept of identity as narrative which focuses on the stories we tell about ourselves and our lives' (p. 99) has value for understanding key approaches to disability identity.

Significance of diagnosis for social relations
It was in their interactions with others, that participants' experiences reflected the complexity of having a potentially stigmatising label. While the participants were generally accepting of their own differences from others, some of the young people resisted autism as a social or public identity. They experienced relationship issues attributable to the broader cultural representations of autism and to persistent disabling attitudes in society, similar to those described more broadly by writers in disability studies (Shakespeare 1996, Thomas 1999). Goffman (1963) has referred to experiences of stigma as highlighting 'undesired differentness' from 'the normals' (p. 44) – an attribute of relationships that is 'deeply discrediting' (p. 3). Recent research more specifically on autism, (for example Davidson and Henderson 2010) highlights problems with disclosing the diagnosis at the public or socio-relational level, even when people may consider their diagnosis helpful at the personal level. For young people, issues of disclosure may become particularly significant in attempts to fit in with peers (Humphrey and Lewis 2008). The act of trying to pass as normal is not an uncommon theme in the disability literature. The perceived stigma associated with a diagnosis leads some people to go to great lengths to deliberately mask or conceal their differences (for example Goode 2007, Thomas 1999), and their experiences illustrate complex interrelations between the direct effects of impairment and the effects of disablism (Thomas). Thomas (1999) has suggested that while such strategies might provide an immediate sense of control, long term, the fear of being discovered may have negative psycho-emotional effects. This issue was highlighted by Kim who actively used masquerading in an effort to pass as normal and to hide the feelings of inferiority that she attributed to autism.

Some of the findings presented here contribute a unique insight into how some children might experience being diagnosed with autism and early intervention practices. While the impacts of health professionals' attitudes on children's experiences are rarely discussed in the literature about autism, it was clear that Kim attributed her negative feelings toward the diagnosis to her early experiences of intervention and the responses she received from health professionals. Kim's experiences highlight the significant implications of a diagnosis for sense of self-worth, in a context where the medical meaning of a diagnosis is that of being deficient and is experienced as oppressive. Shakespeare (1996) proposes that such internalised oppression occurs because people are 'socialised into thinking of disability in a medical model way' (p. 104).

Significance of a diagnosis for facilitating control
The findings indicate that a major factor in determining whether the diagnosis was experienced as an advantage or a disadvantage was the extent to which it facilitated agency and control for the young people. Where individuals experienced their diagnosis as helping them understand themselves and gaining control in their lives, they considered the label an advantage. Where the young people associated autism with a lack of control, or when it impacted negatively on their identity and social relations, the label was experienced as a disadvantage. The importance of children and young people having agency and control in their own lives is acknowledged in research and policy which, in line with the UN Convention, argues for greater participation for children in decision-making about their own lives (United Nations 1989). In the research reported here, in the context of having a diagnosis of autism, control, or the lack of it, appears crucial in the young people's negotiations of their development of

identity and in their everyday social relations. These findings contribute important knowledge about the experience of autism to the dialogue in the literature on the advantages and disadvantages of this diagnosis (Hodge 2005, Nadesan 2005).

Conclusion

The young peoples' experiences of being diagnosed with autism inform us of the way in which these diagnoses can impact on children and young people so labelled. These findings illustrate that knowledge from those who live with the diagnosis can add to and also challenge dominant understandings about young people with a diagnosis of autism. In particular, it adds knowledge in highlighting the significance of structural factors embedded in social policies and the practices associated with them. Acknowledging the significance of structural factors contributes challenges to the policies and practices that continue to marginalise young people with impairments, when diagnosis is interpreted as defining difference from a norm. This point is emphasised by young people's descriptions of how, in disabling environments, the diagnosis of autism itself became a context for experiences of difference.

The findings support McDonald's (2008) suggestion that social policy developed for and about children has a significant role in creating and promoting identities of those who are its object. In illustrating the extent to which the framing of autism is associated with the ordering of social relations and normative expectations for those with autism, the findings point to the importance of promoting policies and practices which not only minimise the stigmatisation and marginalisation of those with a diagnosis of autism but also provide the spaces for children and young people to experience a sense of control in their own lives.

Acknowledgements

We wish to thank the young people and their families who contributed their time, experiences and knowledge to this project. We greatly value the contributions made by Annie McCluskey as the second supervisor on this research project.

Notes

1   For brevity we use the term autism in the remainder of this chapter. The term ASD is often used in policy documents but inconsistently in the literature. At the time of the research ASD encompassed a broader range of diagnoses including that of Asperger's syndrome, which has been eliminated in the recently (2013) published DSM-5.
2   NT, neuro-typical: a description people diagnosed with autism use about non-diagnosed people in autism advocacy forums.

References

Beresford, B., Tozer, R., Rabiee, P. and Sloper, P. (2004) Developing an approach to involving children with autistic spectrum disorders in a social care project, *British Journal of Learning Disabilities*, 32, 4, 180–5.
Brownlow, C. and O'Dell, L. (2006) Constructing an autistic identity: AS voices online, *Mental Retardation*, 44, 5, 315–21.

Carrington, S. and Graham, L. (2001) Perceptions of school by two teenage boys with Asperger syndrome and their mothers: a qualitative study, *Autism*, 5, 1, 37–48.

Christensen, P. and Prout, A. (2002) Working with ethical symmetry in social research with children, *Childhood*, 9, 4, 477–97.

Connors, C. and Stalker, K. (2007) Children's experiences of disability: pointers to a social model of childhood disability, *Disability & Society*, 22, 1, 19–33.

Crotty, M. (1998) *The Foundation of Social Research: Meaning and Perspective in the Research Process*. Sydney: Allen & Unwin.

Davidson, J. and Henderson, V. (2010) 'Coming out' on the spectrum: autism, identity and disclosure, *Social & Cultural Geography*, 11, 2, 155–70.

Davis, J. (1998) Understanding the meanings of children: a reflexive process, *Children & Society*, 12, 5, 325–35.

Davis, J. (2006) Disability, childhood studies and the construction of medical discourses: questioning attention deficit hyperactivity disorder: a theoretical perspective. In Lloyd, G., Stead, J. and Cohen, D. (eds) *Critical New Perspectives on ADHD*. New York: Routledge.

Davis, J., Watson, N., Corker, M. and Shakespeare, T. (2003) Reconstructing disability, childhood and social policy in the UK. In Hallett, C. and Prout, A. (eds) *Hearing the Voices of Children: Social Policy for a New Century*. London: RoutledgeFalmer.

Gernsbacher, M., Dawson, M. and Hill Goldsmith, H. (2005) Three reasons not to believe in an autism epidemic, *Current Directions in Psychological Science*, 14, 2, 55–8.

Giddens, A. (1991) *Modernity and Self-identity*. Cambridge: Polity.

Goffman, E. (1963) *Stigma: Notes on the Management of Spoiled Identity*. Englewood, Cliffs: Prentice-Hall.

Goode, J. (2007) Managing disability: early experiences of university students with disabilities, *Disability & Society*, 22, 1, 35–48.

Ho, A. (2004) To be labelled, or not to be labelled: that is the question, *British Journal of Learning, Disabilities*, 32, 1, 86–92.

Hodge, N. (2005) Reflections on diagnosing autism spectrum disorders, *Disability & Society*, 20, 3, 345–9.

Humphrey, N. and Lewis, S. (2008) 'Make me normal': the views and experiences of pupils on the autistic spectrum in mainstream secondary schools, *Autism*, 12, 1, 23–46.

Huws, J.C. and Jones, R.S.P. (2008) Diagnosis, disclosure, and having autism: an interpretative phenomenological analysis of the perceptions of young people with autism, *Journal of Intellectual & Developmental Disability*, 33, 2, 99–107.

McDonald, C. (2008) The importance of identity in policy: the case for and of children, *Children & Society*, 23, 4, 241–51.

Matson, J.L. and Kozlowski, A.M. (2011) The increasing prevalence of autism spectrum disorders, *Research in Autism Spectrum Disorders*, 5, 1, 418–25.

Mayall, B. (2002) *Towards a Sociology for Childhood: Thinking from Children's Lives*. Buckingham: Open University Press.

Mogensen, L. (2011) 'I want to be me': learning from teenagers diagnosed with autism using collaborative, participatory research. PhD thesis. Social Justice and Social Change Research Centre, School of Social Sciences, Sydney: University of Western Sydney.

Morris, J. (2001) Impairment and disability: constructing an ethics of care that promotes human rights, *Hypatia*, 16, 4, 1–16.

Nadesan, M. (2005) *Constructing Autism: Unraveling the 'Truth' and Understanding the Social*. London: Routledge.

Oliver, M. (1990) *The Politics of Disablement*. Basingstoke: Macmillan.

Oliver, M. (1996) Defining impairment and disability: issues at stake. In Barnes, C. and Mercer, G. (eds) *Disability: Exploring the Divide*. Leeds: Disability Press.

Prout, A. (2002) Researching children as social actors: an introduction to the Children 5–16 programme, *Children & Society*, 16, 1, 67–76.

Prout, A. and James, A. (1990) A new paradigm for the sociology of childhood? Provenance, promise and problems. In James, A. and Prout, A. (eds) *Constructing and Reconstructing Childhood: Contemporary Issues in the Sociological Study of Childhood*. London: Falmer Press.

Richards, L. (2005) *Handling Qualitative Data: A Practical Guide*. London: Sage.

Shakespeare, T. (1996) Disability, identity and difference. In Barnes, C. and Mercer, G. (eds) *Disability: Exploring the Divide*. Leeds: Disability Press.

Thomas, C. (1999) *Female Forms: Experiencing and Understanding Disability*. Buckingham: Open University Press.

United Nations (1989) Convention on the rights of the child. Available at http://www.ohchr.org/en/professionalinterest/pages/crc.aspx (accessed 14 November 2014).

8

What am I 'living' with? Growing up with HIV in Uganda and Zimbabwe

Sarah Bernays, Janet Seeley, Tim Rhodes and Zivai Mupambireyi

Introduction

Enormous progress has been made in the efficacy of treating children born with HIV. Perina-tally infected children can now lead long, productive lives, providing that they have contin-uous access to anti-retroviral treatment (ART) (Busza *et al.* 2013, Heymann *et al.* 2008). In high-income settings the almost complete success in reducing mother-to-child transmis-sion means that paediatric HIV has now become an adolescent epidemic, with those already infected surviving into adulthood (UNAIDS 2012). Yet we know surprisingly little about what it is like to grow up with HIV and ART, especially in sub-Saharan Africa where almost all (91%) of the estimated 3.4 million HIV-positive children live (World Health Organization 2013). Despite the impressive clinical progress in improving survival rates and life expectancy, children's lives continue to be characterised by substantial biomedical and social uncertain-ties (Domek 2006). In our chapter we draw on the accounts of perinatally infected chil-dren aged 11–13 years old, living in Uganda and Zimbabwe, as well as those of their car-ers and healthcare workers. We examine the children's experiences of living with HIV on ART, where HIV is relatively common and yet these experiences are also silenced, as well as surrounded by uncertainty. We aim to describe how children articulate 'living with' and 'growing up' with HIV and how this is shaped through their relationships with the adults around them.

Background

The potentially transformative effects of ART on HIV have been well documented (Camp-bell *et al.* 2011, Castro and Farmer 2005). In both high-income and low-income settings there have been radical changes in the illness narratives of people living with HIV, characterised by narratives of disruption and shattered lives in the time before ART, to narratives of readjust-ment and restoration post-ART (Davies 1997, Robins 2005). ART is popularly represented globally by a collective narrative of enabling a return to normal life by having turned HIV into a manageable chronic illness (Russell and Seeley 2010, Wouters 2012).

Yet studies also contest the linearity of the post-ART experience, noting that clinical recovery can lead to a mixed array of emotions and social outcomes (Seeley and Russell

Children, Health and Well-being: Policy Debates and Lived Experience, First Edition. Edited by Geraldine Brady, Pam Lowe and Sonja Olin Lauritzen. Chapters © 2015 The Authors. Book Compilation © 2015 Foundation for the Sociology of Health & Illness/Blackwell Publishing Ltd.

2010), as has been shown with other illnesses (Shapiro *et al.* 1997). The rhetoric surrounding the global scale-up of ART has been very promising; however this conceals the significant variation in the lived experiences of treatment and its social effects, including between individuals, across settings, and over the course of the illness trajectory (Goudge *et al.* 2009, Seeley and Russell 2010, Wekesa and Coast 2013). Importantly, the relationship between treatment uptake and the decline in the stigma of HIV is not universal (Abrahams and Jewkes 2012, Bernays *et al.* 2010, Maughan-Brown 2010). The need or desire to maintain a pragmatic silence in relation to HIV continues to persist in many settings and this not only threatens the capacity to engage with ART (Bond 2010), but suggests that the process of normalising HIV through ART is socially complex, slow and uneven (Bernays *et al.* 2010, Gilbert and Walker 2009).

Understanding children's HIV treatment experiences

Two core overlapping concepts that have been influential in understanding individuals' responses to chronic illness, including HIV, are biographical reinforcement, characterised by an individual born with a chronic condition facing life disrupted by 'socially-set standards and cultural prescriptions of normality' (Williams, 2000: 50) and transition, characterised by an active adaptation towards incorporating illness and its treatment into daily life and identity (Russell and Seeley 2010). Children born with HIV, who have started ART at an early age, have no experience of life pre-HIV to use as a reference point or embodied knowledge of normalcy without illness. Rather, these children's remembered normative experiences are more likely to revolve around the illness experience and the taking of HIV treatment. Their experience of biographical reinforcement may be most particularly felt through changing life circumstances brought about, for example, through the death of a parent and having to negotiate new care, home and school environments (Daniel *et al.* 2007). Children's experience of growing up with HIV and ART may, to some extent, be articulated as a form of social rebirth (Seeley and Russell 2010), in keeping with a narrative of transition, for ART may afford novel social opportunities associated with good health and positive interaction with peers. Yet despite ART, children's social lives may be hindered by the irreversible visual markers of HIV, such as scars resulting from skin disease or stunted growth, leaving them noticeably smaller than their peers.

Despite the vast numbers of children infected and affected by HIV in sub-Saharan Africa, documenting the effect of the HIV epidemic on children has been neglected (Skovdal *et al.* 2013). Firstly, there has been a tendency for studies to focus on the experience of children and young people in high-income and low-prevalence settings (Mellins and Malee 2013). While the findings from research in industrialised settings may have some relevance for children living in sub-Saharan Africa, such as the role of silence in managing perinatal HIV (Fielden *et al.* 2011), the vast clinical, social, material and epidemiological variations between (as well as within) these contexts are likely to shape HIV experiences differently. Secondly, there has been a methodological and ethical preference for research to focus on the adults in children's lives as proxy representations of their experiences. The primary exception to this is the research that has been done with young carers, where the agentic capacity of children has been more readily recognised (Andersen 2012, Evans and Becker 2009, Skovdal *et al.* 2009). This research blind spot in part reflects the history of the availability of global paediatric HIV treatment and the relative novelty of this surviving cohort, as well as the highly sensitive and relational nature of paediatric HIV as an illness, but it also demonstrates a generalised regional and disciplinary trend in which researchers have been slow to embrace the role of children in research.

Researching children's narratives of HIV experience

The once hegemonic conceptualisation of children as passive, developing and 'unfinished' persons is a relatively outdated idea in the sociological literature (Prout and James 1990). However, its effect on research design in studies with children has been far-reaching, with researchers tending to position children as objects of research rather than participants in the process (Kirk 2007). Theorists increasingly cast children as competent contributors to social life; a social competence achieved through living in the world (Prout 2000). But empirical studies show that this is bounded by specific contexts, the various structural and relational features shaping their lives and their biological vulnerabilities as well as the extent of their experience (Berman 2000, Hutchby and Moran-Ellis 1998).

Given this relational complexity, we explore children's lived experience of growing up with HIV through the narratives that they and the adults around them tell about their lives and the role of HIV within them. Cognisant of the debate around the privileging of narrative methods in illness contexts (Thomas 2013), we do not consider these narratives to be transparent, hyper-authentic representations of experience. Rather, analysing these narratives becomes an opportunity to illuminate how experience is represented through a process in which power is contested and negotiated (Mazanderani *et al.* 2013). Our consideration of narratives involves examining the broader context in which stories are told, attentive to the socially constructed and performative nature of how illness experience is represented in interview accounts. This is revealing about wider social and economic conditions, as well as more localised processes, values and norms that frame which narratives come to dominate and shape the accepted representations of illness experience (Mishler 2005). Furthermore, narratives can be a means to understand the evolution of an illness and the fluid evaluation of an individual's past and future in light of changing circumstances (Ochs and Capps 1996).

The consideration of these concerns has important theoretical implications for how we recognise and understand narrative resistance and subsequently the evolution of illness narratives. Children's narratives may be subsumed or shaped by those of adults (Bluebond-Langner 1978), who themselves are informed by and interpret the language and narratives about HIV that circulate within their broader community. But whether alternative accounts are recognised as resistant narratives may rely on the capacity to be heard, which relies in part on their access to language in order to hold a recognised perspective, as well as the willingness of the audience to listen (Pols 2005). This feeds into our understanding of the evolution of narratives as illnesses and societies change and the pace at which these revised versions are accepted as being legitimate, making it increasingly difficult to separate out the individual from the collective experience, as neither exist in a vacuum but are inextricably connected.

Given the link between collective and individual experience and power, our purpose is to consider how the narratives of children, which may be significantly shaped by the stories available to them, and their experience of growing up with HIV affect their capacity to represent alternative experiences. Specifically, we examine how perceptions of children's well-being, health and illness engage with and manage the dialectic of hope and uncertainty inherent in paediatric HIV at this point in the epidemic.

Methods

Study design

We draw on findings from a prospective, qualitative study (2011–2013) conducted with children aged 11–13 years old perinatally infected with HIV across three sites in Uganda and one in Zimbabwe. We conducted 104 baseline in-depth interviews and then followed up 60 of these children for 16 months through two further in-depth interviews (15 per site) and in the Zimbabwe site 12 out of 15 of these children also kept an audio diary. Twenty of the children from the baseline sample participated in three focus groups (FGDs) in Uganda and Zimbabwe at the end of the data collection period.

Our approach is influenced by the theoretical framework of bounded agency, which focuses on the influence of structure, while allowing space for individual agency, in constructing an individual's experience (Evans and Becker 2007). Specifically, our study includes separate interviews with 40 adult carers (10 per site) and 20 healthcare workers in the clinic (5 per site) because we are interested in the relational influences in children's lives that contribute to framing and shaping their experiences. This inclusion gives a fuller picture of the children's experiences by recognising how children's personhood and agency are shaped by intergenerational relationships (Evans and Becker 2009).

All the children were participating in the Anti-Retroviral Research for Watoto clinical trial (ARROW), from 2007 to 2012. It was conducted with 1200 children aged 6 months to 14 years. Participants began HIV treatment at enrolment and the trial assessed two different management strategies for giving first line anti-HIV drugs (ARROW Trial team *et al.* 2013). While the trial interventions were not a focus of the qualitative study's investigation the trial acted as a recruitment pool for the qualitative study sample. We focused on children aged 11–13 years both because they have been especially neglected in research and to explore the interim period post-disclosure, which in both Uganda and Zimbabwe is encouraged from the age of 8, and prior to them becoming a focus for HIV prevention and sexual health initiatives.

Sampling

Of the 104 children involved at baseline there were 58 girls and all participants were distributed across the age-range. To be included they had to have been aware of their HIV diagnosis for at least 6 months. The baseline sample from each site represented a significant proportion of those eligible for inclusion. We then followed a reduced sample of 15 from each site for two further interviews ($n = 60$). We adopted a theoretical sampling strategy informed by the findings of the baseline, having identified orphanhood status and knowledge of perinatal transmission as important characteristics shaping their experiences. In the follow-up sample there were 25 boys and 35 girls, reflecting the trial sample among this age group. They were evenly spread across the age range, with 19 participants aged 11, 21 aged 12 and 20 aged 13 years. Of this sample of 60 children, 22 were double orphans, 32 had lost either their father or their mother and only six had both parents alive. Fifteen of the children in the sample did not know about perinatal transmission. The 20 healthcare workers who were invited to participate were selected because they all had high levels of contact with the children in the clinics. They included doctors, nurses, counsellors and pharmacists. Of the 40 carers who were interviewed, 23 were parents of the children, 15 were other biological relatives and two were non-biologically related carers. Seventeen of these carers were themselves HIV-positive, with five others reporting that they were HIV negative and the status of the remaining 18 was unknown.

Data collection and analysis

Most of the interviews took place in private rooms at the clinics and involved just the participant and the local interviewer. The interviews were semi-structured, shaped by the relevant topic guide, and were tailored to the individual. Being encouraged to talk about HIV and asked for their opinion by an adult were relatively novel experiences for most of the children. However, our task-based approach alongside the repeat interview design, in which children met with the same interviewer each time, enabled rapport to develop and children reported growing in confidence to talk as the study progressed.

Ethical approval was provided by all the appropriate committees in Uganda and Zimbabwe, as well as the London School of Hygiene and Tropical Medicine. All data were collected with the participants' written informed consent. For the children's interviews this involved the informed consent of their carer (parent or guardian) and the assent of the child. Interviews lasted between 30–120 minutes and were primarily participant-led. Participants received a transport refund and refreshments for each interview, and those participating in the FGD also received a t-shirt. All interviews and FGD were tape recorded and conducted in the language of the participant's choice (Luganda, Shona or English). Data were transcribed verbatim, translated for equivalent meaning and checked by the interviewer. We approached translation as both a technical and discursive process and discussions were held within the team during both the initial translation process and through the analysis to ensure that the complexity of concepts was conveyed.

Data collection and analysis were conducted iteratively, informing each subsequent phase of data collection. We used a combined thematic and narrative analytical approach. Initially, we compiled case summaries, amalgamating interview and field-note data for each participant. Carer interview data were included in the summaries for the related child, with particular attention being paid, through the drafting of extensive analytical memos, to relationship dynamics and points of congruence and diversion between the adults and children's accounts.

We managed the thematic coding of the full dataset into primary and detailed subthemes using NVivo 8. Our narrative approach involved paying attention to whether particular stories were repeated across the interview transcripts. We considered whether there was a narrative similarity across the accounts, in terms of there being common ideas and patterns in how, for example, the children described their experiences and whether this differed from those of the adults. This enabled us to identify both the personal narratives, which were the stories that participants gave to describe their own experiences, and the broader, cultural narratives about HIV, which they were responding to in their accounts to contextualise their own experiences and structure how they made sense of HIV in their everyday lives. Through this approach we identified a dominant narrative about children growing up with HIV that appeared to encapsulate the current common representation of the illness experience, and an alternative narrative, in which children themselves engaged with and contested this dominant narrative. All names used are fictitious.

Findings

Constructing HIV through a language of sickness

We found that children's experience of HIV is largely constructed in relation to a language of sickness. Although all the children involved in the study were themselves on ART and most were relatively healthy, almost without exception they associated HIV with illness and weakness. The children described people living with HIV as being visibly ill and depicting them as 'thin and small', sometimes physically short, with 'scars and wounds all over their bodies', as someone who 'doesn't want to eat' and has 'thinning hair'. It was only with prompting that they mentioned people on HIV treatment. The children's accounts were littered with horror stories about the physical appearance of other people living with HIV, 'even your hair becomes brownish and it drops out when you comb it like a cancer patient' (FGD). This was not just a question of being identified as HIV positive through signs of poor health but also a consequence of ideas about HIV positivity that ignored the relatively stable health that someone on ART might enjoy.

Let me be normal

Despite this characterisation many children did not consider themselves to be sick, describing themselves instead as being strong and appearing healthy. This created a tension. Given the dominant imaging of people living with HIV, they struggled to recognise themselves within this picture of 'sickness', as Anita (aged 12) describes: 'Ha! I wasn't worried about an illness that maybe I have HIV ... I wasn't worried and I never counted myself among those that have it!'

However, in spite of the disassociation children made between their own state of health and those of other 'sick' people living with HIV, many carers continued to emphasise their child's vulnerability and propensity to sickness. Many children were singled out by their carers as being weaker than the other children in the household because they 'are sick' and required 'special care'. Job's grandmother, for example, insists that he carries a smaller amount of water than other children because of the fear that 'his body may weaken a bit'.

However, Job (13 years old) does not consider himself weaker than the others and asks to be allowed to do the same as the other children, saying: 'I think I am fine'. The challenges that Job has in resisting the restrictive parameters his grandmother imposes, regardless of his opinion, is indicative of the struggle that children encounter in trying to shape and define their own experience of living with HIV. So, while at an individual level the children, like Job, might perceive themselves to be 'healthy', in this social context at the level of the household and broader community they are defined through an association with sickness that inextricably accompanies their HIV status.

All the children, in describing the impact of HIV on their own appearance, emphasised that a valuable effect of ART lay in its capacity to render HIV virtually invisible, whereas prior to ART it had been obvious on their bodies and many children had been teased and ostracised as a result. The children invested heavily in concealing and disguising their HIV status in order to be indistinguishable from their peers and considered normal. The value of ART was in the opportunity that it gave to maintain this impression of normalcy, rather than in enabling someone to become healthy. This appearance of normalcy was precarious and constantly vulnerable to disruption, not only by the telltale physical indicators of previous illnesses but the activities accompanying continuous adherence to treatment, such as having to leave school every day at a certain time to take their pills and the special treatment they received from adults. If the children could successfully negotiate these risks and continue to maintain an appearance of normalcy some sense of well-being was achieved. However, this was firmly located in a denial of illness rather than an attainment of health.

Boundaries of HIV talk

Despite the difference in priorities noted between some adults and children, there was a general consensus that children's HIV should be managed in relative silence. Once the diagnosis had been disclosed, HIV was rarely talked about in the household and the children were discouraged from discussing it with anyone else. We identified two exceptions to this pattern of silence: medicalised talk and past illness stories.

Medicalised talk

Post-disclosure, even outside the clinic, HIV was communicated almost exclusively through discussions about the symptoms of illness and HIV medicines, such as adherence reminders about treatment and clinic appointments. Mary (12 years old) describes how her aunt consistently reminded her of the precariousness of her health: 'If you do not take drugs you fall sick and die'. There was little to no discussion of the ways in which HIV influenced and shaped their social lives and the role that HIV may play in the future. For example, although many children had been disclosed to by their primary carer, the experience of Samuella (11 years old), who said that she had 'not spoken about it with Daddy since then', was very common. On the rare occasion when the children did break the silence to initiate discussion about HIV, for example to ask how long they had to take drugs or their futures, often their questions went unanswered or were dismissed as being unnecessary and the children were discouraged from 'thinking too much'. Charity (13 years old) would take herself away from everyone when she thought about HIV and explained that 'each time I recover from having deep thoughts I pretend to have forgotten about it and I will join others and laugh with them'. Martha (12 years old) used to ask many questions about HIV, such as 'Why am I like this? Why am I HIV positive?' She, like many other children, was strongly discouraged from voicing her questions and anxieties about growing up with HIV. Martha's cousin explained how 'no one brings up such conversations' and surmises that 'she now doesn't think a lot about it because no one tells her such things any more'.

Past illness stories
We identified one other exceptional circumstance in which HIV was talked about. This was the selective rehearsal of past illness narratives in which children and their carers recounted the child's particular illness story prior to treatment initiation. Charity (13 years old), in common with many of the children, describes her past illness in vivid, embodied terms:

> When we went [to hospital] for the second time I could not breathe properly and I told my mother that I was failing to breathe … She called the nurses and I was put on oxygen. Then I started to breathe well. So each time I think of it I will say 'I could have been dead by now and there would be no one by the name Charity'.

Whether experiences were reported or remembered, they formed a pivotal feature of the children's memory of the past and were central in defining their present experiences.

The narrative pattern in both children and carers' accounts follows a dominant structure in which talk about their experience of living with HIV is divided into 'then' (ill, weak, hospitalised, small) and 'now' (on ART, stronger, healthier, *looking* normal). Isaiah's aunt recalls his situation prior to starting ART and how he reflects on the difference between then and now:

> The thing was, he was continuously sick, in bed and there was a time he was unconscious and they told people he had passed away. In fact, when you ask Isaiah, he still remembers that incident and at times he tells me that, 'Mum, one time my granny told people I was dead because she thought I was about to die but can you imagine that I am alive!' If you asked him about that time he can tell it to you because by the time I picked him from that place his brain was working fine and he could understand what was going on.

It is striking that these stories can be told in some detail by the children and the carers even though they generally occurred at least 3 years beforehand, prior to starting in the ARROW trial. However, when asked how they were disclosed to, which is likely to have been more recently, the children commonly say that they cannot remember. This suggests that these illness stories are more likely to have been retold and reinforced in their memory.

Silencing talk of non-adherence and the future
In considering why the retelling of illness stories, between the carer and the child, is legitimate and encouraged it becomes clear that they are used to motivate continued adherence.
The threat that 'you'll be sick again, like you were before' is used to scare the children into
maintaining adherence.

There were many reasons why maintaining adherence was challenging, including managing the side effects, which were exacerbated by household food insecurity; protecting against
disclosure by being identified as taking treatment; feeling tired or overwhelmed by the relent-
less, daily doses; or forgetting. Children expressed their frustration at the lack of sympathy
that they received when struggling to take treatment every day and how they felt that adults
commonly dismissed the broader psycho-social reasons that underpinned instances of non-
adherence. As Jacob (11 years old) says: 'When they hear they call you stupid and think that
you are lying to them ... because for them they don't take it'.

Children described times when they had felt like not taking treatment any more or stop-
ping; although they said that they rarely acted on it. When asked why or how they had managed to resist these inclinations they responded by using their illness stories to illustrate how
bad it had been when they had not taken their drugs. As Charity (13 years old) explains, 'I
take my pills every day and I don't skip them because when I was sick each time I think of
it I feel like crying'. The sense of fear surrounding the ongoing risk and the imperative of
avoiding the past is also voiced by some of the healthcare workers when counselling a child
once an adherence problem is identified:

> You try to remind them [the child] how they were when they came to ARROW. Then
> they will say 'I was not going to school', 'I was not able to do this and that' and you will
> ask them if they want to go back to the same situation.

These forms of HIV talk may inadvertently dismiss or fail to engage with the social challenges children face in sustaining their adherence. Furthermore, the children reported that if
they did miss treatment they were unlikely to tell anyone about it because, 'I'll be scolded or
beaten'. They had learnt to edit out the features of their experience that are not well-received
and do not fit within the dominant representation of their experience. In turn, the silence that
exists around non-adherence further feeds and shapes the dominant script around growing
up with HIV on ART.

Although these narratives appear to play a valuable role in making sense of the past and
present, the future is rarely mentioned. Children are told 'not to think about it'. When the
future is discussed, though, it is in uncertain, anxious terms. While carers hoped that their
children would grow up to lead 'normal lives', a number of them expressed concern about
the exceptional 'burden' that these children carry in growing up with HIV in relation to risk
and limited opportunity, especially about their future sexual and reproductive lives. Jovia's
brother compares his life, growing up HIV negative, and his sister's:

> I started enjoying myself a long time ago and if they discovered HIV now and I start
> drugs, at least I will have moved and have done what I have done. But the child will never
> enjoy herself ... So you will find that all her life that she will be in danger; you have
> removed that [free sexual] act from her and even if she becomes an adult, she will go for
> it fearfully ... She has not any hope.

These rare spaces for selective discussion about HIV, medicalised talk, illness narratives and
the interviews themselves, all converge to form a script around the experience of perinatal

HIV, which emphasises that their current position is threatened by an absence of resilient health. The relevance of these memories as a way of 'knowing' about HIV may be particularly important when their knowledge of HIV and the management of HIV in other forms are limited.

Children's protest talk: 'but I am not sick'
While the children's interpretation of their illness experiences does appear to be heavily influenced by the talk both around and readily available to them, there are instances in which they contest this characterisation of their health. Crucially, both the medicalised talk and past illness stories described above are led by adults and are legitimised as acceptable forms of discussion about the child's HIV. However there is one additional, but rare, form of talk adopted by the children alone, which we characterise as protest talk.

Although the language used by the children appears to percolate into how children articulate their conditions, in describing themselves as sick, there are times when children are quick to follow this statement by emphasising, 'but I feel fine'; 'but I am strong'. These limited, but common, expressions allude to the complexity of their lived experience in being at once described as sick but *feeling* well. For example, having spoken about the visible indicators of illness displayed by people living with HIV, Rose (13 years old) describes her own appearance quite differently: 'I'm well, nice looking and beautiful. I have no scars, I'm not sick'. Unlike the more negative tone of the carers, when discussing her future aspirations, she explains how she thinks about the future: 'I told myself, on the earth there is no one who will never die, even that one who is not sick dies, and yet you who have HIV you remain alive'. Similarly, Grace (13 years old) asserts her sense of health, explaining that she does not perceive that HIV limits her opportunities or capacity: 'I am just a happy person because there is nothing that I cannot do; I can do all the chores. I can do everything … I am healthy and look strong'.

Rudo (12 years old) encourages other HIV-positive children to avoid being presumed to be sick by trying to participate in everything:

> It's better for people to be taken by surprise to say 'Ah, this child may be thin and we were thinking that she is sick but she is very hardworking'. But on your own you will know that you are on pills and the pills are making you strong and have the energy.

While such positive talk, which protested against the normative characterisation of their experience, was present in children's accounts it was in subtle forms and only occasionally articulated. Most commonly it was silenced within everyday talk. For example, Job (13 years old) had not told his grandmother that he felt able to carry the same amount water as the other children his age. Where it is articulated, though, this may indicate the embryonic forming of resistance narratives, in that they contest the normative characterisation. This narrative does not deny the challenges inherent in living with HIV but instead aims to prioritise the opportunities for health and well-being brought by living well on ART.

Discussion

We have noted that the lived experiences of children have been constructed through the symbiotic relationships between children, their carers and healthcare workers and the broader discourses through which these individuals are influenced. This relational complexity shapes how children consider and articulate what it is like to grow up with HIV. However, the capacity these three groups have to shape their accounts is not equal but, rather, filtered through a prism that reflects the distribution and negotiation of power between the parties involved (Mazanderani, Locock, and Powell 2013). This can be seen by how talk outside the medical frame is inadvertently shut down, with children discouraged from talking or even thinking about HIV in their everyday lives. This serves to frame the experience of HIV as singularly biomedically felt and embodied, often ignoring the social effects (Waitzkin 1991). Such edited talk, with silence indicative of disquiet about the social implications, suggests that 'living with' and 'growing up with' HIV continues to be imbued with social uncertainty.

This limits children's autonomy to articulate their experience along alternative lines as their sense-making is narrowed by the narrative grids available to them to frame their experiences (Wilkinson 1988). However, this is contested to some degree through the presence of protest talk as well as silences, but recognising its subtle manifestations depends on our capacity to notice such talk (Hendry and Watson 2001). Notably, this emerging alternative narrative appears to have little influence on how adults recount children's experiences. Instead the adults' emphasis on these children's ongoing vulnerability to sickness reinforces their biographical status as different from other children. This illustrates the inherent challenges that children face in achieving a sense of normalcy when growing up with HIV, despite the apparent invisibility of HIV when it is successfully controlled by treatment; and is indicative of the limited nature of their transition from illness to health. Our analysis illuminates the effect of bounded agency on children's articulation and experience of living with HIV, as it is through the exploration of this relational complexity that we can observe the influences which shape their narratives.

Silence and illness stories as disciplinary

The HIV experience script that is created does not just reflect how adults may narrow the articulations of children directly, but illustrates how children also engage with and interpret the narrative frameworks that define what constitutes acceptable talk. Children learn to edit adherence slippages and problems out of their reported treatment experience. Taking a Foucauldian perspective, this form of silencing not only highlights the importance of examining how power is operationalised through who is, and who is not, allowed to speak, but also in considering which subjects are silenced. Children may see that silence on the subject of non-adherence is a tool for their social and cultural survival (Fielden *et al.* 2011). This silence, if ignored or not heard, appears to strategically accommodate and reproduce the dominant narrative, which neglects the prominence that social concerns may play in conditioning the experience of growing up with HIV. This, in turn, limits the opportunities that there may be to diverge from the accepted script and articulate alternative narratives.

The illness narratives told by carers and children form a central organising thread in the representations of the children's experience. The accepted structure of this narrative, told through multiple discourses, pivots around HIV pre-ART and the rejuvenating effects of the successful initiation of treatment. The hopes generated by ART are illustrated and consolidated by the telling of these past illness stories. This may also function, in part, as a moralising discourse to engender ongoing discipline and commitment to adherence, as well as, by extension, to become a stratagem of blame for non-adherence. Furthermore, in discrediting talk of non-adherence, this dominant narrative may also serve to resist the unwelcome and disquieting narrative that articulates how, despite the opportunities brought about by ART availability, its long-term efficacy may be disrupted by the social challenges that accompany long-term adherence to ART. Together, these patterns of talk act in the service of a medicalised HIV identity, which silences alternatives and, in ignoring these social challenges, neglects these children's desires to focus on appearing normal as a means to achieving a sense of well-being.

Challenges to realising normalcy
We have shown how illness narratives and medicalised talk firmly assert the language of sickness within the characterisation of these children's experiences. This undermines a quest for ordinariness (Kralik 2002), in which the opportunity to diminish the centrality of their HIV diagnosis in their lives is made more difficult by the prominence given to illness events in shaping their present narratives. Although ART renders the illness virtually invisible, talk around treatment appears to reinforce the presence rather than alleviation of this 'sickness' (Hunleth 2013, Williams 2000) and, as such, who/what risk becoming fixed as commensurable and inextricable (Ezekiel *et al.* 2009). Ironically, perpetuating HIV's association with the discrediting attributes of sickness exacerbates the social challenges people encounter in maintaining exemplary long-term adherence and benefitting from the clinical opportunities afforded by ART.

The focus on the certainty of the past and the absence of a script to articulate the everyday realities of long-term HIV treatment in the present may indicate the doubt that circulates about the future for these children as they grow up with HIV. Therefore, the linguistic tension in their protest talk and the challenges that children encounter in articulating the relative buoyancy of their health may be indicative of the broader struggle to negotiate what the present and future looks like and means for individuals growing up with HIV, their households and the healthcare sector in these contexts. Settings which are characterised by burgeoning but precarious access to ART, high levels of orphaning and stretched resources that are available to meet the potentially complex needs of these children.

However, that there is protest talk at all suggests the presence of some embryonic resistance to this dominant narrative, which attempts to contest the equivalence attributed to being HIV positive on ART and being considered 'sick'. Through this, some children describe how living with HIV under these conditions involves living in a liminal state in which apparent binaries, such as health and sickness, strength and weakness and invisibility and spoilt identity, exist in an everyday tension. The presence of protest talk and the opportunities afforded by ART, if access is secure and households are given adequate adherence support, suggests that children would benefit from a shift in focus towards looking at how to foster and maintain resilience (Kia-Keating *et al.* 2011, Luthar *et al.* 2006). Emphasising the possibilities that are available to those growing up with HIV on ART, rather than the more singular focus on them as 'at risk' to themselves and others (Busza *et al.* 2013, Mellins and Malee, 2013), may alter the current vocabulary used to describe this population and contribute to accelerating the development of alternative narratives that reflect children's experiences of growing up with HIV.

Acknowledgements

The authors wish to thank all the children and carers who participated in the ARROW social science sub-study for the time and information they shared with us. We are grateful to Hellen Nakyambadde, Olive Kabajaasi and Rachel Kawuma for data collection and their contributions to analysis. We thank the ARROW Trial team led by Prof Di Gibb for their support and the Department for International Development of the UK Government through the Medical Research Council (G0300400) for funding this study.

References

Abrahams, N. and Jewkes, R. (2012) Managing and resisting stigma: a qualitative study among people living with HIV in South Africa, *Journal of the International AIDS Society*, 15, 17330. doi.org/10.7448/IAS.15.2.17330.

Andersen, L.B. (2012) Children's caregiving of HIV-infected parents accessing treatment in Western Kenya: Challenges and coping strategies, *African Journal of AIDS Research*, 11, 3, 203–13.

ARROW trial team, Kekitiinwa, A., Cook, A. and Nathoo, K. *et al.* (2013) Routine versus clinically driven laboratory monitoring and first-line antiretroviral therapy strategies in African children with HIV (ARROW): a 5-year open-label randomised factorial trial, *Lancet*, 381, 9875, 1391–403.

Berman, L. (2000) Surviving on the streets of Java: homeless children's narratives of violence, *Discourse Society*, 11, 2, 149–74.

Bernays, S., Rhodes, T. and Jankovic Terzic, K. (2010) You should be grateful to have medicines: continued dependence, altering stigma and the HIV treatment experience in Serbia, *AIDS Care*, 22, S1, 14–20.

Bluebond-Langner, M. (1978) *The Private Worlds of Dying Children*. Princeton: Princeton University Press.

Bond, V. (2010) It is not an easy decision on HIV, especially in Zambia: opting for silence, limited disclosure and implicit understanding to retain a wider identity, *AIDS Care*, 22, S1, 6–13.

Busza, J., Besana, G.V., Mapunda, P. and Oliveras, E. (2013) I have grown up controlling myself a lot. Fear and misconceptions about sex among adolescents vertically-infected with HIV in Tanzania, *Reproductive Health Matters*, 21, 41, 87–96.

Campbell, C., Skovdal, M., Madanhire, C., Mugurungi, O. *et al.* (2011) We, the AIDS people: how anti-retroviral therapy enables Zimbabweans living with HIV/AIDS to cope with stigma, *American Journal of Public Health*, 101, 6, 1004–10.

Castro, A. and Farmer, P. (2005) Understanding and addressing AIDS-related stigma: from anthropological theory to clinical practice in Haiti, *American Journal of Public Health*, 95, 1, 53–59.

Daniel, M., Apila, H.M., Bjørgo, R. and Lie, G.T. (2007) Breaching cultural silence: enhancing resilience among Ugandan orphans, *African Journal of AIDS Research*, 6, 2, 109–20.

Davies, M. (1997) Shattered assumptions: time and the experience of long-term HIV positivity, *Social Science & Medicine*, 44, 5, 561–71.

Domek, G. (2006) Social consequences of antiretroviral therapy: preparing for the unexpected futures of HIV-positive children, *The Lancet*, 367, 9519, 1367–1369.

Evans, R. and Becker, S. (2007) *Hidden young carers: the experiences, needs and resilience of children caring for parents and relatives with HIV/AIDS in Tanzania and the UK: stakeholder report.* Nottingham: School of Sociology and Social Policy, University of Nottingham.

Evans, R. and Becker, S. (2009) *Children Caring for Parents with HIV and AIDS: Global Issues and Policy Responses.* Bristol: Policy Press.

Ezekiel, M.J., Talle, A., Juma, J.M. and Klepp, K. (2009) When in the body, it makes you look fat and HIV negative: the constitution of antiretroviral therapy in local discourse among youth in Kahe, *Social Science & Medicine*, 68, 5, 957–64.

Fielden, S., Chapman, G. and Cadell, S. (2011) Managing stigma in adolescent HIV: silence, secrets and sanctioned spaces, *Culture, Health and Sexuality*, 13, 3, 267–81.

Gilbert, L. and Walker, L. (2009) They (ARVs) are my life, without them I'm nothing – experiences of patients attending a HIV/AIDS clinic in Johannesburg, *South Africa, Health and Place*, 15, 4, 1123–9.

Goudge, J., Ngoma, B., Manderson, L. and Schneider, H. (2009) Stigma, identity and resistance among people living with HIV in South Africa, *SAHARA*, 6, 3, 94–104.

Hendry, J. and Watson, C. (2001) *An Anthropology of Indirect Communication*. London: Routledge.

Heymann, S., Clark, S. and Brewer, T. (2008) Moving from preventing HIV/AIDS in its infancy to preventing family illness and death (PFID), *International Journal of Infectious Diseases*, 12, 2, 117–19.

Hunleth, J. (2013) ARVs as sickness and medicine: examining children's knowledge and experience in the HIV era in urban Zambia, *AIDS Care*, 25, 6, 763–6.

Hutchby, I. and Moran-Ellis, J. (1998) *Children and Social Competence*. London: Falmer.

Kia-Keating, M., Dowdy, E., Morgan, M.L. and Noam, G.G. (2011) Protecting and promoting: an integrative conceptual model for healthy development of adolescents, *Journal of Adolescent Health*, 48, 3, 220–8.

Kirk, S. (2007) Methodological and ethical issues in conducting qualitative research with children and young people: a literature review, *International Journal of Nursing Studies*, 44, 7, 1250–60.

Kralik, D. (2002) The quest for ordinariness: transition experienced by midlife women living with chronic illness, *Journal of Advanced Nursing*, 39, 2, 391–400.

Luthar, S.S., Sawyer, J.A. and Brown, P.J. (2006) Conceptual issues in studies of resilience: past, present and future research, *Annals of the New York Academy of Sciences*, 1094, 105–15.

Maughan-Brown, B. (2010) Stigma rises despite antiretroviral roll-out: a longitudinal analysis in South Africa, *Social Science & Medicine*, 70, 3, 368–74.

Mazanderani, F., Locock, L. and Powell, J. (2013) Biographical value: towards a conceptualisation of the commodification of illness narratives in contemporary healthcare, *Sociology of Health & Illness*, 35, 6, 891–905.

Mellins, C. and Malee, K. (2013) Understanding the mental health of youth living with perinatal HIV infection: lessons learned and current challenges, *Journal of International AIDS Society*, 16, 1, 18593. doi.org/10.7448/IAS.16.1.18593.

Mishler, E.G. (2005) Patient stories, narratives of resistance and the ethics of human care: a la recherche du temps perdu, *Health*, 9, 4, 431–51.

Ochs, E. and Capps, L. (1996) Narrating the self, *Annual Review of Anthropology*, 25, 19–43.

Pols, J. (2005) Enacting appreciations: beyond the patient's perspective, *Health Care Analysis*, 13, 3, 203–21.

Prout, A. (2000) Children's participation: control and self-realisation in British late modernity, *Children and Society*, 14, 4, 304–15.

Prout, A. and James, A. (1990) *Constructing and Reconstructing Childhood: Contemporary Issues in the Sociological Studies of Childhood*. London: Falmer Press.

Robins, S. (2005) Rights passages from 'near death' to 'new life': AIDS activism and treatment testimonies in South Africa. IDS Working Paper 251. Brighton: Institute of Development Studies.

Russell, S. and Seeley, J. (2010) The transition to living with HIV as a chronic condition: working to create order and control on anti-retroviral therapy, *Social Science & Medicine*, 70, 3, 375–82.

Seeley, J. and Russell, S. (2010) Social rebirth and social transformation? Rebuilding social lives after ART in rural Uganda, *AIDS Care*, 22, S1, 44–50.

Shapiro, S., Angus, L. and Davis, C. (1997) Identity and meaning in the experience of cancer: three narrative themes, *Journal of Health Psychology*, 2, 4, 539–54.

Skovdal, M., Magutshwa-Zitha, S., Campbell, C. and Nyamukapa, C. *et al.* (2013) Children's role in the community response to HIV in Zimbabwe, *Journal of the International AIDS Society*, 16, 18468. doi.org/10.7448/IAS.16.1.18468.

Skovdal, M., Ogutu, V., Aoro, C. and Campbell, C. (2009) Young carers as social actors: coping strategies of children caring for ailing or ageing guardians in Western Kenya, *Social Science & Medicine*, 69, 4, 587–95.

Thomas, C. (2013) Negotiating the contested terrain of narrative methods in illness contexts, *Sociology of Health & Illness*, 32, 4, 647–60.

UNAIDS (2012) *UNAIDS Report on the Global Aids Epidemic 2012*. Available at http://www.unaids.org/en/resources/publications/2012/name,76121,en.asp (accessed 16 July 2014).

Waitzkin, H. (1991) *The Politics of Medical Encounters: How Patients and Doctors Deal with Social Problems*. New Haven: Yale University Press.

Wekesa, E. and Coast, E. (2013) Living with HIV post diagnosis: a qualitative study of the experiences of Nairobi slum residents, *BMJ Open*, 3, 3, 5. e002399.

World Health Organization (2013) *Global update on HIV treatment 2013: results, impact and opportunities*. Geneva: WHO/UNAIDS.

Wilkinson, S.R. (1988) *The Child's World of Illness: the Development of Health and Illness Behaviour.* Cambridge: Cambridge University Press.

Williams, S.J. (2000) Chronic illness as biographical disruption or biographical disruption as chronic illness? Reflections on a core concept, *Sociology of Health & Illness*, 22, 1, 40–67.

Wouters, E. (2012) Life with HIV as a chronic illness: a theoretical and methodological framework for antiretroviral treatment studies in resource-limited settings, *Social Theory & Health*, 10, 368–91. doi:10.1057/sth.2012.12.

9

Food, risk and place: agency and negotiations of young people with food allergy
Marie-Louise Stjerna

Introduction

Against the background of a heightened risk awareness in children and their wellbeing in contemporary society (Lee *et al.* 2010), the case of child food allergies is of particular interest. The prevalence of food allergies is increasing; in the Western world up to 12% of children, depending on the definition, are affected (Burks *et al.* 2012). The most common food allergies among children are to milk, egg and nuts (Arias *et al.* 2009). Allergic reactions to food occur shortly after exposure, with symptoms varying from mild oral itching to the life-threatening reaction, anaphylaxis. As the avoidance of certain foods and the management of symptoms is the only treatment, food allergy requires constant risk management. Children with food allergy face the risk of encountering allergens, the dangerous food, in a variety of situations in everyday life and are therefore children at risk. Constant vigilance by the parents and the child is necessary, but there also needs to be communicated with others to ensure different social arenas are safe for the child. The meaning of this constant vigilance is still not fully understood and the purpose of this chapter is to explore children's management of risk in their everyday lives.

Previous research on food allergies has demonstrated that children as young as 7-years old are aware of the risks involved in a serious allergic reaction (Klinnert and Robinson 2008). Further, the experience of anaphylaxis can lead to increased concern about their allergies and parents' protective practices (Herbert and Dahlqvist 2008). Severe allergic reactions also increase when children reach adolescence (Bock *et al.* 2001), which may be due to teenagers' willingness to take risks, as well as their faulty perceptions of risks (Klinnert and Robinson 2008). In addition to the health risk of an allergic reaction, young people can face a social risk in how others perceive them (DunnGalvin *et al.* 2009) and may take risks to fit in with their peers (Sampson *et al.* 2006).

Earlier research on children's experiences of risk in and outside their home has found that children's risky landscapes differ from their parents, and are more experiential and oriented to the here and now (Kelley *et al.* 1997, Murray 2009, Valentine 1997). Studies have also demonstrated how young people's lived experiences of places affect their risk perceptions (see, for example, Mitchell *et al.* 2001). Children and young people may also experience their allergies or other health issues differently, depending on the place and social context. For example, children with asthma may experience certain places as dangerous, or 'dirty'

Children, Health and Well-being: Policy Debates and Lived Experience, First Edition. Edited by Geraldine Brady, Pam Lowe and Sonja Olin Lauritzen. Chapters © 2015 The Authors. Book Compilation © 2015 Foundation for the Sociology of Health & Illness/Blackwell Publishing Ltd.

(Rudestam *et al*. 2004). Similarly, DunnGalvin *et al*. (2009) have demonstrated that children with food allergies begin to experience places as safe or unsafe when they reach school age.

Sociocultural theories of risk (Tulloch and Lupton 2003) highlight the importance of contextualising risk in everyday experiences of different social contexts and places (Henwood *et al*. 2008, Holloway and Valentine 2000). Risk is not seen as something given but as a dynamic phenomenon, which individuals interpret by developing strategies to manage risk in the local contexts where they spend time. When they interact with each other and the physical environment, they also interpret and (re)construct risk – they are doing risk.

In the research tradition of childhood studies, children and young people are seen as active social agents who are not only shaped by the processes, milieus and social relations around them, but also shape them. Indeed, the health and wellbeing of young people is both subject to adult control and also influenced by their own choices (Christensen and James 2008, Mayall 2002). However, children's agency is not unconstrained, but inflected with power. In contrast to liberal models, the point of departure in this chapter is a social model of agency that recognises the social embeddedness of agency and children's differences (Valentine 2011). Power and agency have also been important themes in research on children and food. Power may be negotiated in eating practices and there is 'the tension between controlling children on the one hand, whilst acknowledging their growing autonomy on the other' (Punch *et al*. 2011a: 2). Drawing on the term foodscape to describe places where children encounter food and eating during the day, Brembeck (2009: 141) shows that some of these local contexts offer children a 'free zone for experimentation', away from adults' direct supervision. Power and children's agency is of particular interest in relation to allergies, since an allergy entails additional restrictions for children. Yet, like other health research, allergy research has mainly focused on adult rather than child informants (James *et al*. 2011) and there is a dearth of studies exploring young people's perspectives of the challenges they face when eating in a variety of social contexts.

Young people's lived experiences of food allergies are shaped within wider discourses around childhood, such as childhood vulnerability, age and responsibility (James and James 2012) and societal consumption and eating ideals. Consumption choices such as food and smoking have been shown to be important as identity markers, expressing either similarity or difference from others (see for example, Denscombe 2001, Wills *et al*. 2009). Restricted food options may therefore have consequences for the young person's understanding of the self. Of importance are also local negotiations and agreements about how to manage food allergy risk in different social arenas (Rous and Hunt 2004). These norms may be reflected in institutional arrangements and cultural practices of adults and children. Young people with food allergies are therefore both positioned by others and position others within interaction processes in different contexts and peer groups where the tensions between conformity and individuality have to be managed (Valentine 2000).

The aim of this chapter is to explore young people's management of food allergy risks in relation to food, eating and place. Specifically, it focuses on young people's accounts of agency and negotiations in the avoidance of health risk as well as social risk: how they avoid risky food, cope with allergic reactions and manage social risk related to interaction with others, together with their expectations of the future.

Method

The findings presented in this chapter are derived from individual interviews with 10 young people with food allergies, six girls and four boys aged 11–17 years. These interviews were part

Table 1   *Interview participants' details and allergies*

Participants (pseudonyms) and age (years)	Allergies
Adrian (13)	Nuts, peanut, almonds
Alva (15)	Milk protein, peas
Clara (13)	Peanuts
David (14)	Milk protein, eggs
Isabella (11)	Milk protein
Joel (14)	Nuts, peanuts, apple and pear peel
Joanna (16)	Milk protein, egg, nuts, fruit, vegetables
Molly (15)	Nuts, peanuts, sesame seed
Sophia (15)	Nuts, peanuts, legumes, stone fruits, seeds
Vincent (17)	Nuts, peanuts, fish, eggs

of a larger multi-methodological study in 2012 and 2013 of young people's own experiences of food allergies, which also included focus groups and visual research methods. Six participants were recruited from a patients' organisation for people with asthma and allergies and four from a children's hospital. The participants were informed about the study by the staff and the researcher then contacted those who had expressed an interest in participating. All the participants had been prescribed an adrenaline auto-injector to be administered immediately in case of a severe allergic reaction (Simons 2010). They had various food allergies and were either allergic to a single food or to various foods (see Table 1).

The study was approved by the Ethics Committee at Karolinska Institute and informed consent was obtained from the participants and their parents.

The interviewees' accounts are constructed from their conversations with a researcher (Kvale and Brinkmann 2009) and in the present study the researcher told the participants that little is known about how young people themselves view life with a food allergy. She emphasised that the information about their experiences would be very valuable and encouraged them to speak about things they considered important. To elicit their own reflections, the participants were first asked about what came to mind upon hearing the term food allergy. A topic guide was used which included open-ended questions about how their allergy was discovered and subsequent events, the everyday management of their allergy at home, school and other places, others' attitudes to their allergy and how they perceived their future life. The participants were interviewed at home or at a summer camp for children with allergies and asthma; the interviews lasted between 25 minutes and an hour and were digitally recorded and transcribed. Their accounts differed in terms of detail, but all interviewees were willing to share their experiences and some of them took the opportunity to express issues they considered important.

Data were analysed thematically (Braun and Clarke 2006), focusing on the young people's perspective on the meanings of food allergy risks. Two major themes were identified: the management of, on the one hand, the health risk and on the other hand, the social risk across different settings. The analysis focused on how these themes were linked to each other, as well as their implications for the young people's agency.

Management of health risks

Health risks and shared responsibility in different places
The management of health risks in different social contexts and places involves dependence on others. Despite constant vigilance, the participants described the impossible task that total risk avoidance presents, as the measures that others take to ensure that food is safe

never appear fully trustworthy. Public places appear particularly precarious, while the home is depicted as a safe zone where family members adjust to the young person's needs. Parents ensure that the young person with an allergy can eat the same food as the rest of the family. The home is often free from the foods they are allergic to, as Adrian says:

> At Mum's we never ever have anything with nuts in it, well traces of nuts can, my little brother can have sweets sometimes, but never anything with nuts in it. At Dad's it's probably a bit more, well, with nuts, we have biscuits with nougat in and that but I'd rather they weren't there when I'm at home, but I feel, when Mum and Dad cook I feel almost completely safe. There are few things … well, especially with mum, I knew she'd never like risk anything. (Adrian)

In the above account Adrian indicates that, even if the home is regarded as a safe zone one has to be alert there too; a challenge that increases in public places. Here, Alva describes the experience of the constant threat of an allergic reaction:

Alva: Imagine if I eat something, just imagine, it could happen at any time, it's really frightening.
M-LS: So that's what you think.
Alva: If those who prepare food in different places don't know what they're doing, then it's really risky and I wonder whether I should eat that sandwich or not. Have they used the right sort of butter? If not, I'll be really, really ill.

Like Alva, others also mention that the health risk is severe or life-threatening, hence consuming certain foods involves great risk. As Alva's account illustrates, food allergy risk management involves issues of trust or mistrust of the vigilance and understanding of others — family, friends and a wider circle of actors, such as school staff, restaurant chefs, food and airline companies. Even though not all the participants in this study who are allergic to peanuts know if they react to airborne allergens, knowing that it is possible to have an allergic reaction just from breathing in small particles of peanuts influences their experiences of the risk involved. Several of them mention that they are worried when they travel by aeroplane. Other public places, such as buses or institutions like school, may also be regarded as unsafe. For example, Sophia says that she thinks it is 'a bit scary' when people around her consume sweets with nuts. Like several of the other participants she feels comfortable asking her friends to be careful when she is around, but in other situations, the participants say they may just leave the place.

Ultimately, the participants say they feel responsible for making their own assessment of different places and the safety of the food served. For example, Molly explains that she always carefully examines the school lunch: 'You have to be really careful to check, just to be sure, even though you know the school isn't allowed to serve nuts'. The level of responsibility one is able to assume varies with age, according to some participants' accounts. Molly says that when she was younger and allergic to egg she was served lasagne at school. Luckily, the teachers discovered the mistake before she had consumed too much, as Molly says:

> They really panicked and started phoning mum every 20 minutes to tell her what had happened and also, like, say if I was starting to react, but I hadn't had very much so nothing happened but all the same they were still, like, they handled it very well. (Molly)

This dialogue between Molly's teachers and her mother about the incident at school illustrates that the management of food allergy risk is 'shared, spread over more than one body/self' (Tulloch and Lupton 2003: 20). Accordingly, food allergy management emerges as a 'social project' involving several actors: the child and others. This also means that the 'risk management is carried out *through* social interaction' (Stjerna *et al.* 2014: 138) and the relationship between risk and trust are in different ways intertwined in the young people's stories. For example, Joanna stresses that she 'is fed up' with people confusing her potentially life-threatening milk protein allergy with lactose intolerance and she usually avoids eating out. Here, Joanna talks about her summer holiday and how her mum is involved in buying a pizza for her:

> We usually do it this way that I don't go with mum when she's going to order. Mum and my little sister go together while I stay in the caravan because, well, if I come with them I can become really unsure, it's better if I just say to mum that I trust you, I trust you to sort this out together with the kitchen staff.(Joanna)

The shared aspect of managing a food allergy risk emerges as an issue of who can be trusted and which places can be regarded as safe and unsafe. Being able to judge this and to control the dangers by, for example, extra vigilance during the school lunch and leaving an unsafe place is part of young people's allergy management and competence. Risks are not always easy to assess, however.

Trying to control the uncontrollable
As we have seen, allergy management has to be carried out in different social contexts and it impacts on young people's everyday life and how they anticipate their future. Reflecting on her future life with allergy, Isabella says she can never be totally safe, but only increasingly better at managing her allergy:

Isabella: When I was little it was mum and dad who knew everything, without them I was helpless, but now I feel that I can look after myself, I know that I can't eat certain things and I know what I can and cannot eat, so I hope, yes, I think it will be fairly easy, I mean when I move into a home of my own, I'll have everything milk free in any case and that feels really good.
M-LS: Mm.
Isabella: But of course it will affect my life, I'll never really be able to go to real parties, like I'll never be able to drink alcohol or, well, do a lot of things, because then you can lose control and eat whatever and become really ill, not know what you're doing, that'll never happen in my life, because I can't, it mustn't happen and it makes me think, how will it be if I want to go partying with my friends?

While allergy management at home may become easier, managing Isabella's allergy in some social contexts and situations may become more problematic. She must never lose control, because then her life may be endangered, illustrating the powerful restrictions to her life her allergy dictate and the responsibility she needs to assume. She repeats several times that she 'has to be very mature for her age' or else 'it will not work'. Similarly, Joel explains that he has to remember to inform 'new people' about his allergy and to always bring his adrenaline injectors, which he keeps in his school bag:

> You see, we have those lockers [in school]. Imagine if I'm lying like unconscious and they have to take the key out of my pocket and open the locker and everything, that like takes time, maybe they don't know how. But I don't think it'll be like that, it's just that it can happen. (Joel)

Joel's account illustrates that the feeling of loss of control, being very vulnerable and relying on others to know what to do is particularly pertinent if there is an allergic reaction. At the same time he also gives examples of how he tries to regain control and, like some of the other participants in this study, he has instructed his friends what to do if he has an allergic reaction. Some of the participants have had severe reactions and describes it as a frightening experience:

> People have to help me and like phone somebody or stick the syringe into my leg, but I don't understand what's happened until afterwards, while it's going on it's just a matter of surviving or something, of breathing. (Alva)

Here, the loss of control, the dependence on others and the experience that one's life is threatened emerge as aspects of the experience of a severe allergic reaction. This is also in line with previous research, which demonstrates that fear of death is 'particularly associated with not being able to breathe' (DunnGalvin *et al.* 2009: 562). Even if they have never experienced a severe reaction, the knowledge that it might happen seems to permeate the lives of the participants in this study. This agrees with the studies by DunnGalvin *et al.* (2009) and Fenton *et al.* (2011), in which the life or death aspect is a central theme. Here, Joanna talks about her fear of having a severe reaction:

> I'm like terrified because it's bound to happen sometime. I don't think I can live my life without ever getting a allergic reaction, because I'm bound to get one, that's what I believe. Like, I'm almost certain that I will and it feels like every day could be that day in some way. (Joanna)

The management of risk associated with food allergy is presented as trying to control the uncontrollable and the existential aspects of allergy management comes to the fore. Allergy risk emerges as being highly unpredictable, as a risk that may occur at any time. At the same time young people take measures to control the risk, such as informing their friends what to do in case of an allergic reaction. To these young people a severe reaction also means an experience that temporarily results in loss of control: this is part of their life and it is essential to trust others to deal with such situations. Thus, the threat of a severe reaction seems to have an impact on the young peoples' agency and influence over their own lives, demonstrating a tension between own sense of responsibility and their dependence on others: which is the shared aspect of allergy management.

Management of social risks in different places

At school
In institutions such as schools the needs of the allergic individual must be balanced with the needs of the many (see for example, Punch *et al.* 2011b). The child's allergy must be managed, while at the same time all children should be treated as equally as possible. Usually, others understand and respect the allergy of participants in this study, although some may forget (both adults and peers) and may have to be reminded. But the young people also provide examples of when people ignore their allergy or even question if they 'really are allergic'. Alva, who has a contact allergy to milk protein and 'may develop eczema and turn red and spotty' if someone touches her with milk on their hands, describes an incident at school: 'then there was a time when I was like in fifth grade there was someone who tried to pour milk over me because they didn't believe me'. Previous research has shown that teenagers with a food allergy experienced 'a lack of understanding of the seriousness of food allergy

among classmates' (Monks *et al.* 2010: 1539). This same study revealed that the young people also had friends whom they had informed about their allergy and who supported them (see also Fenton *et al.* 2011), which is in line with the results of this study. The present study also demonstrates that, even though there are examples of occasions when those who are nut allergic are forgotten in school, there seems to be a general awareness of the allergy:

> Because they [teachers] know that there are pupils who have nut allergy, so they always remind us if we are going on an excursion or the like and at the beginning it is always like: 'Right, who's allergic?' So in the end everyone finds out that you are allergic and it's actually quite nice that everybody knows about it, it's not even as if I'm the only one with nut allergy in my class, there are two more. (Molly)

However, awareness does not rule out all uncertainty:

> When we were going to have a sleepover [as part of a class excursion] I thought quite a lot about it, what if someone forgot or didn't remember. (Joel)

During the school day children's lives are highly regulated, both temporally and spatially. However, the lunch time period is less structured and may give room for children to display more agency, where children organise themselves while eating and relaxing and form peer groups during lunch breaks (Valentine 2000). Research has shown that, from the perspective of children, it is the social rather than nutritional aspects that are their priority with regard to school meals. Daniel and Gustafsson (2010) found that what children disliked most were things that they perceived as an intrusion on their interactions with friends, such as seating arrangements. In the present study, the participants provided accounts of situations when they felt 'odd' or were unable to fully participate in the same way as their peers. David[1] has to follow a certain lunch-time routine every day at school, which affects his access to social life at school:

> I have to go straight to the kitchen and get my food. My friends they don't have to eat the school lunch if they don't like what's on the menu, but I have to go there because they have fixed it just for me, so for this reason sometimes I have to sit by myself. (David)

Alva cannot have her lunch at a special table for those who are allergic to food, since others may 'spill stuff or take the wrong spoon', and thus she must fetch her food from the school kitchen, which makes her feel 'odd'. Earlier, she had to sit at a special table reserved for her, but now she chooses seats more freely; someone just has to 'wipe the table' before she sits down. She says that she is 'lucky to have friends who sit with her at lunch time'. They understand her allergy and 'choose to drink water for her sake'.

How the home economics classes are organised also influences the school day for those pupils who are allergic. For example, Joanna says that sometimes they bake in class and it works fine because they only use 'her' butter and flour. To be treated fairly and equally is important. Isabella says she thinks it is unfair that during outdoor days the other pupils are served 'tasty pasties with minced meat and an ice cream in a cone' and she is served an ice lolly:

> So if I think it's wrong, they say: 'Yes, but you were offered an ice cream as well, weren't you?' but I reply that 'Just because, yes but if we, well what if I put it like this: if somebody's in a wheelchair and everybody's sitting round a lovely table, is it right that the one in the wheelchair should have to sit at another table because the wheelchair won't fit under that table? That isn't really right either, it's the same thing'. (Isabella)

Isabella explains that she has learned to 'make a stand' and that she knows 'her rights'. So the social consequences of safety arrangements have an influence on the young people's well-being at school.

Public places
Public places pose a number of particular challenges. During breaks at school the pupils may have access to places that are less supervised by adults:

> My school is very close to a food store so we are allowed to go shopping there during long breaks, sometimes I do and I go with my friends and they buy these pastries, sugar buns from the bread counter, things like donuts and Danish pastries and I can't: it feels like a limitation. (David)

Brembeck (2009) argues that in smooth foodscapes such as the nearby shop and playground, it is the 'relative invisibility of the childish foodscape to authorities, such as teachers and health experts that becomes an important factor supporting children's agency' (p. 141). As evident in the above example, however, an allergy to certain foods may prevent participation in the more hedonistic and pleasurable aspects of food and eating that peers engage in. Brembeck *et al.* (2013) found, in a study where children were encouraged to explore their foodscapes, that sugary and fatty tastes made them 'exhilarated and happy', at the same time as they were well aware of the dominant discourses of healthy and unhealthy eating. Rather than the issue of healthy versus unhealthy eating, the risk of an allergic reaction is the stronger theme in the present study. In the above account, it is not the health risk of mistakenly eating something the young person is allergic to that is in focus, but not having the opportunity to share the same experience as many of your peers – also evident in the following excerpt:

> Then my friends eat chocolate sometimes and they say they think it's really tasty, but of course I don't know, it's frustrating not to know what it tastes like. (Alva)

In line with Alva's reasoning, some of the participants say that they do not like it when others focus on the things that they as individuals with a food allergy cannot do: 'So you can't eat sweets and you can't eat those things and they just become like really annoying: "Oh you poor thing!"' (Adrian). Similarly, Joanna says she wishes she could think of something to say just to silence people when they focus on the things she cannot eat. It appears that when others draw attention to their limited consumption opportunities this just makes the situation harder to bear and even positions them as different. An unplanned visit to a friend's house might mean that the food allergic individual is not able to participate in the family dinner. Therefore, Alva always brings noodles in her bag. This way, she and her friend can eat the same food 'because I don't like eating different food, I want to eat the same as the others'. Evidently, food and eating are fundamentally about togetherness and connecting to people (see for example, Caplan 1997).

The participants' fairly limited possibilities for being able to eat food served in public places is perceived as 'restricting and boring'. For example, they always eat the same safe products or go to the same restaurants, such as McDonald's. While teenagers are generally thought to prefer fast food, Wills *et al.* (2009) found that a central aspect of middle-class teenagers' identity-forming work was to avoid fast food. In this study, McDonald's, which has an allergy policy, becomes a symbol of not being able to choose to eat what and where you want:

> It kind of works with the apple pie and the cinnamon bun at McDonald's but like how much fun is that all the time? (Joanna)

Concern is also expressed about how others will have to adjust to participants' restricted consumption opportunities. For example, Adrian says that in the future, when he is older and going to have lunch, it might not 'sound so fun' to go to McDonald's. Similarly, Joanna says:

> Just think if someone doesn't want to be with me because I can't like go for a latte or whatever it might be, you know, things like that, just simple things, that are simply part of life for many people but can never be that for me. (Jonnna)

When the content of a product that has previously been regarded as safe changes, the options are further reduced for the individual who has a food allergy:

> So then I think like, 'Hey why don't we go for an ice cream?', but no, that's not an option because the only one I can eat now is an ice lolly. They have stopped making all the others. Before I used to be able to eat nearly half of the ice creams, but now they just keep disappearing and then you are not free, you are trapped in a little box. (Isabella)

The strength of the metaphor —'to be trapped in a box' — illustrates the challenge experienced by participants in not participating in some of the normal, everyday things in life, like enjoying an ice-cream, having lunch or a coffee. Young people with food allergies have to manage their limited consumption opportunities, as well as their peers' responses to their restricted food options.

Discussion

This chapter contributes to the emerging body of work exploring young people and food by illustrating the complexities of risk management in this early phase of life when the individual is faced with, an external and (often) invisible threat, which has to be managed on a daily basis within different social contexts, as well as in relation to the eating ideals of today. How they perceive food allergy risks *and* their lived experience of different social contexts and places influences their understanding of self as young people with food allergy and as food consumers.

Age, accountability and everyday risk management

The awareness that an allergic reaction may be severe or life-threatening together with the difficulty of total risk avoidance, creates uncertainty and is an everyday threat to these young people. The analysis demonstrates the high risk-awareness of participants in this study: there are accounts of responsibility and maturity and a lack of accounts of risk-taking practices. This may be an effect of the methodology of the individual interviews and participants not wanting to tell an adult interviewer about such behaviour,[2] but the results of this study support the analysis of Gallagher *et al.* (2012) which found that anaphylaxis in adolescents was not necessarily seen as the result of 'irresponsible' teenage practices, such as alcohol use. They found that the 'stereotypes of teenagers as reckless appear inaccurate and over-generalised' (p. 396) and that it is, rather, the task of avoiding food allergy risk that appears as challenging.

How the participants in this study construct themselves as young people with a food allergy is related to how they understand age. Looking back, they regard themselves as having become more able to manage their food allergy with age. But there is also the idea that to manage their condition they have to be 'very mature'. As in their transition to adult life, they have to take more responsibility for themselves in some respects than would have been expected *for their age*. Importantly, this quest for responsibility is in contrast to the idea of teenagers as being willing to take risks and transgress boundaries and may reflect the fact that life with a food allergy at a young age involves the experience of differentness with regards to expectations of a normal teenage life, because they are forced to manage the health risks related to their condition.

As we have seen, managing a food allergy means, to some extent, trying to control the uncontrollable. A reaction can occur at any time and to experience a severe reaction entails temporary loss of control and feelings of vulnerability, placing limits on agency. At the same time, the strategies the young people develop to avoid an allergic reaction can be understood as responses to this uncertainty as well as as manifestations of their agency.

The relational aspects of agency

A strong theme in this study is the dependence of these young people on others to manage their allergy risk. In the risk literature, an individualistic risk perspective which conceptualises the human actor as rational and atomised is generally accepted, yet like Tulloch and Lupton (2003) who found that several of the adult interviewees put forward the notion of risk as being something that is shared, managing a food allergy risk emerges in the present study as a shared process: the participants describe having to learn how to manage their food allergy risk and take personal responsibility, while they are also dependent on others' understanding and vigilance to manage the risks.

Further, in addition to managing the allergy risk itself, young people with food allergies have to manage social risk and, in line with the findings of DunnGalvin et al. (2009), the participants' risk experiences vary between different social contexts and places. The analysis reveals that the participants are positioned differently in different places. Drawing on a social model of disability, as described by Pitchforth et al. (2011) the disability emerges in the encounter with the outer world, in social, cultural or physical barriers (Oliver and Barnes 2010). For example, the school's responses to the participants' allergy affect their access to social life and participation in school life. From their perspective, some practices at school seem to be more inclusive than others, such as when everybody uses 'their products' in home economic classes, or more excluding, such as when safety arrangements at times prohibit them from eating lunch with their friends. In this process, however, young people are not just docile bodies but also actively challenge norms around eating practices and, for example, question the equivalence of their food to non-allergic pupils' food.

Our way of eating implies a meaning-making process which involves a classification of an 'us' (who eat in the same way) and 'others' (who eat differently than us) (Fischler 1988). Not being singled out as other seems to be an important part of the young people's understanding of themselves as food consumers in this study. At the same time, they are happy when others understand their allergies, suggesting their self-understanding is also about being respected as being different, as well as being included in different social contexts and places that involve eating. Indeed, this study shows how the teenagers ally themselves with friends who understand their allergy and are willing to adjust to their needs.

The importance of place and young people's agency managing food allergy risk

Places that are relatively free from adult supervision, where children without allergies have the opportunity to experiment with their agency in relation to food (Brembeck 2009), may be regarded as unsafe for those with a food allergy. Consequently, public places and a range of commercial establishments such as restaurants, local food shops and cafeterias are not as accessible to young people with a food allergy as to others. In particular, they are not able to choose what and where they would like to eat. Young people's limited ability to engage in food consumption can be seen as an example of the 'commodification of childhood and youth' (Valentine 2000: 258). Valentine argues that young people are confronted with the same media and economic actors and are expected to make the same consumption choices as adults. More generally, young people are therefore at risk of making the wrong consumption or identity choices compared to their peers. Brembeck *et al.* (2013) also found that children's foodscapes were highly commercialised and that brands and commercial messages were part of their worlds. These children were well aware that food stores used strategies to make people buy more food, but they also imagined people enjoying themselves in activities in consumer landscapes, such as shopping in food stores. This chapter demonstrates that the pressure that might be entailed from our consumer society – that we should all strive to make the right food choices, but also happily engage in consumption – might be increased if one is restricted by a food allergy.

The young people's accounts show that different food allergies in themselves seem to provide different conditions in communication and negotiations with others. If the allergy and its consequences are well-known it may be easier to gain an understanding from others, compared to if the allergy is less known. As Rous and Hunt (2004) state, today peanuts have become 'emblematic of the wider issue of allergies' (2004: 825). In this study, it is clear that a nut allergy is rather expected and normalised at school. However, a milk protein allergy seems to raise more questions among others, according to the participants. While school is supposed to be a nut-free zone, milk is served at lunch time. The participants in this study, a heterogeneous group, therefore face different challenges in their allergy management. Yet the analysis shows a consistent and complex pattern of adjustment regarding the young people's allergy management in their everyday life.

Parents provide a safe home environment for the child. This is not to say that the child is passive, but that others to a great extent adjust to the young person's needs at home. At school young people's adjustment patterns are more complex. The young person has to deal with health risks as well as social risks and may experience exclusion in some situations. At the same time, the participants give examples of how others adjust to their needs and how they themselves try to exert an influence on their situation. According to these young people, the food offered at public places is mostly not adjusted to their needs. Moreover, even if they inform others about their allergy it is difficult to know whether they can rely on having food served that actually is safe for them, constraining their agency in public places. Social risks are rather prominent, given that the young people with a food allergy, for example, cannot experiment with food to the same extent as their peers or freely choose what and where they would like to eat. Altogether, their possibilities of exerting agency in different places and situations has implications for their social identity.

To conclude, this chapter demonstrates the social embeddedness of agency: how young people's management of health risks associated with a food allergy takes place in social interaction with others and how different social contexts and places pose particular challenges. What we see is not agency as a voluntary or authentic choice, but rather, that young people with a food allergy are managing a complicated balancing act between their own competence to manage different types of risks and their dependence on other's understanding and competence. This suggests that young people's agency is indeed of a relational character and is distributed between themselves and the social networks and institutions of which they are a part.

Acknowledgements

I want to thank the young people who participated in this study. I also want to thank Inga-Lill Bjöörn at the Swedish Asthma and Allergy Association and Mirja Vetander, Gunnar Lilja, Caroline Nilsson, Magnus Wickman and Eva Östblom at the Sachs' Children and Youth Hospital who helped me to get in contact with young people with a food allergy. The research was funded by a postdoctoral grant from the Anna Ahlströms and Ellen Terserus foundation at Stockholm University. I am grateful to Neneh Rowa-Dewar and Liz Adams Lyngbäck for their insightful comments on an earlier version of this chapter and the constructive advice provided by the two anonymous reviewers.

Notes

1 This example comes from a focus group interview in which David took part.
2 To reach out to more risk-prone individuals a different recruitment strategy might have been necessary.

References

Arias, K., Waserman, S. and Jordana, M. (2009) Management of food-induced anaphylaxis: unsolved challenges, *Current Clinical Pharmacology*, 4, 2, 113–25.
Bock, S.A., Munoz-Furlong, A. and Sampson, H.A. (2001) Fatalities due to anaphylactic reactions to foods, *Journal of Allergy and Clinical Immunology*, 107, 1, 191–3.
Braun, V. and Clarke, V. (2006) Using thematic analysis in psychology, *Qualitative Research in Psychology*, 3, 2, 77–101.
Brembeck, H. (2009) Children's 'becoming' in frontiering foodscapes. In James, A., Kjorholt, A.T. and Tingstad, V. (eds) *Children, Food and Identity in Everyday Life*. Basingstoke: Palgrave Macmillan.
Brembeck, H., Johansson, B., Bergström, K., Engelbrektsson, P., *et al.* (2013) Exploring children's foodscapes, *Children's Geographies*, 11, 1, 74–88.
Burks, A.W., Tang, M., Sicherer, S., Muraro, A., *et al.* (2012) ICON: food allergy, *Journal of Allergy and Clinical Immunology*, 129, 4, 906–20.
Caplan, P. (ed) (1997) *Food, Health and Identity*. London: Routledge.
Christensen, P. and James, A. (2008) *Research with Children. Perspectives and Practices*, 2nd edn. Abingdon: Routledge.
Daniel, P. and Gustafsson, U. (2010) School lunches: children's services or children's spaces?, *Children's Geographies*, 8, 3, 265–74.
Denscombe, M. (2001) Uncertain identities and health-risking behaviour: the chase of young people and smoking in late modernity, *British Journal of Sociology*, 52, 1, 157–77.

DunnGalvin, A., Gaffney, A. and Hourihane, J.O. (2009) Developmental pathways in food allergy: a new theoretical framework, *Allergy*, 64, 4, 560–8.

Fenton, N.E., Elliot, S.J., Cicutto, L., Clarke, A.E., *et al.* (2011) Illustrating risk: anaphylaxis through the eyes of the food-allergic child, *Risk Analysis*, 31, 1, 171–83.

Fischler, C. (1988) Food, self and identity, *Social Science Information*, 27, 2, 275–92.

Gallagher, M., Worth, A., Cunningham-Burley, S. and Sheikh, A. (2012) Strategies for living with the risk of anaphylaxis in adolescence: qualitative study of young people and their parents, *Primary Care Respiratory Journal*, 21, 4, 392–97.

Henwood, K., Pidgeon, N., Sarre, S., Simmons, P., *et al.* (2008) Risk, framing and everyday life: epistemological and methodological reflections from three socio-cultural projects, *Health, Risk & Society*, 10, 5, 421–38.

Herbert, L.J. and Dahlqvist, L.M. (2008) Perceived history of anaphylaxis and parental overprotection, autonomy, anxiety, and depression in food allergic young adults, *Journal of Clinical Psychology in Medical Settings*, 15, 4, 261–9.

Holloway, S.L. and Valentine, G. (2000) Spatiality and new social studies of childhood, *Sociology*, 34, 4, 763–83.

James, A. and James, A. (2012) *Key Concepts in Childhood Studies*, 2nd edn. London: Sage.

James, A., Kjorholt, A.T. and Tingstad, V. (2011) *Children, food and identity in everday life*. Basingstoke: Palgrave Macmillan.

Kelley, P., Mayall, B. and Hood, S. (1997) Children's accounts of risk, *Childhood*, 4, 3, 305–24.

Klinnert, M.D. and Robinson, J.L. (2008) Addressing the psychological needs of families of food-allergic children, *Current Allergy and Asthma Reports*, 8, 3, 195–200.

Kvale, S. and Brinkmann, S. (2009) *InterViews. Learning the Craft of Qualitative Research Interviewing*, 2nd edn. Los Angeles: Sage.

Lee, E., Macvarish, J. and Bristow, J. (2010) Risk, health and parenting culture, *Health, Risk & Society*, 12, 4, 293–300.

Mayall, B. (2002) *Towards a Sociology of Childhood. Thinking from Children's Lives*. Maidenhead: Open University Press.

Mitchell, W.A., Crawshaw, P., Bunton, R. and Green, E.E. (2001) Situating young people's experiences of risk and identity, *Health, Risk & Society*, 3, 2, 217–33.

Monks, H., Gowland, M.H., MacKenzie, H., Erlewyn-Lajeunesse, M., *et al.* (2010) How do teenagers manage their food allergies?, *Clinical & Experimental Allergy*, 40, 10, 1533–40.

Murray, L. (2009) Making the journey to school: the gendered and and generational aspects of risk in constructing everyday mobility, *Health, Risk & Society*, 11, 5, 471–86.

Oliver, M. and Barnes, C. (2010) Disability studies: disabled people and the struggle for inclusion, *British Journal of Sociology of Education*, 31, 5, 547–60.

Pitchforth, E., Weaver, S., Willards, J., Wawrzkowicz, E., *et al.* (2011) A qualitative study of families of a child with a nut allergy, *Chronic Illness*, 7, 4, 255–66.

Punch, S., McIntosch, I. and Emond, R. (2011a) Introduction. In Punch, S., McIntosch, I. and Emond, R. *Children's Food. Practices in Families and Institutions*. New York: Routledge.

Punch, S., McIntosch, I. and Emond, R. (2011b) *Children's Food. Practices in Families and Institutions*. New York: Routledge.

Rous, T. and Hunt, A. (2004) Governing peanuts: the regulation of the social bodies of children and the risks of food allergies, *Social Science & Medicine*, 58, 4, 825–36.

Rudestam, K., Brown, P., Zarcadoolas, C. and Mansell, C. (2004) Children's asthma experience and importance of place, *Health*, 8, 4, 423–44.

Sampson, M.A., Munoz-Furlong, A. and Sicherer, S.H. (2006) Risk-taking and coping strategies of adolescents and young adults with food allergy, *Journal of Allergy and Clinical Immunology*, 117, 6, 1440–45.

Simons, F.E. (2010) Anaphylaxis, *Journal of Allergy and Clinical Immunology*, 125, 2, S161–81.

Stjerna, M.-L., Vetander, M., Wickman, M. and Olin Lauritzen, S. (2014) The management of situated risk: a parental perspective on child food allergy, *Health*, 18, 2, 130–45.

Tulloch, J. and Lupton, D. (2003) *Risk and Everyday Life*. London: Sage.

Valentine, G. (1997) 'Oh yes I can'. 'Oh no you can't': Children and parents' understandings of kids' competence to negotiate public space safely, *Antipode*, 29, 1, 65–89.

Valentine, G. (2000) Exploring children and young people's narratives of identity, *Geoforum*, 31, 2, 257–67.

Valentine, K. (2011) Accounting for agency, *Children & Society*, 25, 5, 347–58.

Wills, W., Backett-Milburn, K., Lawton, J. and Roberts, M.-L. (2009) Consuming fast food: the perceptions and practices of middle-class young teenagers. In James, A., Kjorholt, A.T. and Tingstad, V. (eds) *Children, Food and Identity in Everday Life*. Basingstoke: Palgrave Macmillan.

10

Negotiating pain: the joint construction of a child's bodily sensation
Laura Jenkins

Introduction

As assumptions about the nature of childhood have developed, the view that the child is merely subject to social forces is increasingly being rejected in favour of a new sociology of childhood that frames the child as a social actor (Moran-Ellis 2010). This emergent paradigm, which stands in contrast to a traditional framework that positioned children as passive victims of external influences (Alanen 1988), instead understands childhood as a social construction; a negotiated set of social relationships in the early years of human life (Prout and James 1997). Alongside this, the concept of intergenerational relations has been highlighted as being useful in understanding children's experiences of childhood, particularly the ways in which children's lives are structured through their relationships with adults (Mayall 2001a).

Parallel developments are evident in the way listening to children's voices is increasingly promoted in both policy (Department of Health 1989, Lansdown 2001, UN 1989) and social science method (Prout and James 1997), with a move towards research that explores children's experiences in their own terms (Prout 2002). Constructing children as agents in their own lives is operationalised in terms of granting them the status of participants and constructors, specifically in social science research (Prout and James 1997). Utilising participatory methods has been advocated as a means by which to address the inherent power relations involved in the research process (Moran-Ellis 2010, Prout 2002), in addition to interactionist analysis that subjects aspects of everyday life to detailed and critical reflection (Prout and James 1997).

Interactionist methodologies address concerns about how children interact with each other and with adults, and how they shape as well as are shaped by the various locales of their lives (Prout 2002). Conversation analysis (CA), in particular, has proven to be a useful way of examining how talk is used to manage social relationships and construct identities (Drew 2005), seeking to describe in extensive detail the structures and patterns that enable us to understand how speakers do what they do and understand what others do (Schegloff 2005).

CA has been applied to talk about pain, but in institutional settings. This has proven to be a valuable means by which to describe how the revelation of pain emerges in the sequential progression of certain medical actions and activities (Heath 1989) and to highlight children's agency in terms of how children are able to solicit parental assistance in ways that underline

Children, Health and Well-being: Policy Debates and Lived Experience, First Edition. Edited by Geraldine Brady, Pam Lowe and Sonja Olin Lauritzen. Chapters © 2015 The Authors. Book Compilation © 2015 Foundation for the Sociology of Health & Illness/Blackwell Publishing Ltd.

the role of the child as the primary informant (Clemente 2009). CA's systematic approach to examining the fine detail of interaction represents a unique tool for exploring the emerging sociology of childhood's focus on children's agency and social relationships (Prout and James 1997).

In contrast to interactionist methodologies that seek to explore intergenerational relations by asking children to describe their experiences of childhood (for example, Mayall 2001b), the current study used CA to analyse video-recordings of talk between children and their parents. It investigates the negotiation of the status of symptoms of illness and pain as expressed by children to their parents in everyday settings. It considers children's agency in their health in terms of how the nature, severity and authenticity of their sensations (including pain) are socially constructed and managed on a turn-by-turn basis, shaped by contributions from both children and parents. It investigates how children's rights to report on their own experience are produced, accepted or resisted by children and parents, evidencing the social construction of childhood and children's agency in the micro-detail of concrete instances of naturally occurring talk. These findings are discussed in terms of their implications for how authority and rights to access an experience or knowledge about illness are constructed in the claims embedded in talk.

Aims

The objectives of this study are to present a systematic and detailed examination of video-recorded episodes in which children express bodily sensations, including pain, in everyday family life, and to reveal the way in which the characterisation of the bodily sensations are shaped by contributions from both children and parents. The analysis investigates intergenerational relations by specifically seeking to (i) examine how children exert agency and how the nature of their sensation is formulated in their expressions of bodily experience; (ii) reflect on how a parent's response reworks the nature of the child's experience; and (iii) describe how a child's right to report on their own sensation is negotiated in the subsequent interaction.

Method

The analysis in this chapter is based on a corpus of video-recordings of family mealtimes. Full ethical clearance was granted by Loughborough University's ethical committee. The participants were recruited via voluntary support groups for families with children with chronic health concerns, on the basis that talk about a child's health and their body may be more prevalent in such families. Organisations that focused on diabetes, heart conditions and allergy distributed information about the project to approximately 600 potentially eligible families in the UK. The adults and children of three families responded and signed consent forms. They were given a video camera and asked to film between 10 and 15 meals. When to film was at the participants' discretion (with the exception of mealtimes in which guests attended who had not given informed consent to be recorded), and even after having filmed a meal they were able to delete any recordings they did not wish to submit to the study. The participants were told that they had the right to withdraw their data at any time, including after the point at which they had returned the camera and all the recordings they had made.

Table 1   *Participants' details*

Family	Number of meals filmed	Age of children	Recruitment Source	Health conditions
Edwards	14	Lanie (4 y) Finley (15 m)	Support group	Lanie has a congenital heart condition
Hawkins	14	Jack (9 y) Charlie (5 y)	Support group	Jack has type I diabetes
Jephcott	17	Haydn (6 y) Isabelle (4 y)	Support group	Haydn and Isabelle have food allergy and intolerance issues
Amberton	13	Emily (7 y) Jessica (4 y)	DARG Archives	None recorded
Crouch	13	Katherine (5 y) Anna (3 y)	DARG Archives	None recorded

m, month; y, year

Recordings from a further two families were accessed through an archive of recordings kept by the Discourse and Rhetoric Group at Loughborough University.[1] These families were recruited on the basis that they ate their meals together, and in this study these particular families provide a broader data set and offered a potential comparison with the families in which particular health issues were of concern. In total, the five families recorded 71 mealtimes, totalling 32 hours of data. This represented an amount of data that was both manageable, in terms of being systematically searched, and sufficient, in terms of yielding the collection of interactional phenomena forming the focus of this study. The participants were all white and of middle socioeconomic status. Each family included a heterosexual married couple and two children under 10 years old (see Table 1 for more details). All names have been changed.

Like Clemente's (2009) study and other CA work in medical sociology (for example, Parry 2004, Pilnick and Zayts 2012), this chapter provides a data-driven analysis of talk-in-interaction. CA sets out to understand the elementary properties of social action (Schegloff 1992), in order to understand how talk is used to manage social relationships and construct, establish, reproduce and negotiate identities (Drew 2005) (For a more in-depth description of CA's analytic assumptions and method see Drew 2005, Heritage 1984, Schegloff 2007). The selected extracts were transcribed using the conventions developed by Gail Jefferson and supplemented by Hepburn in relation to distress and upset (Hepburn 2004, Jefferson 2004) (Table 2).The analysis in this chapter focuses on a collection of sequences in which children initiate an expression of bodily sensation, including pain. It describes the components of children's expressions, the character of the parents' responses and the nature of the subsequent conversation, revealing the way in which children exert agency and participate in talk about their bodies.

Findings

The corpus of mealtimes contained various talk relating to health, pain and the body, such as discussions about a friend being treated in the burns unit, talk about a child's medication, parents' reports of pain or parents initiating enquiries into a child's wellbeing. This study focused specifically on sequences in which children initiated expressions of bodily sensation, on the basis that they were more prevalent in the data and represented a distinct set of phenomena for elucidating commonalities in how they were formulated and delivered. In total,

Table 2   *Transcription conventions*

[ ]	Square brackets mark the start and end of overlapping speech.
↑	Vertical arrows precede marked pitch movement.
Underli<u>ni</u>ng	Indicates emphasis.
CAPITALS	Mark speech that is hearably louder than surrounding speech. This is beyond the increase in volume that comes as a by product of emphasis.
°I don't know°	'Degree' signs enclose hearably quieter speech.
#My tummy hurts.#	Hash signs denote creaky delivery
(0.4)	Numbers in round brackets measure pauses in seconds (in this case, 4 tenths of a second).
(.)	A micropause, hearable but too short to measure.
((grabs head))	Additional comments from the transcriber, e.g. about embodied actions.
my tu:mmy h:ur:ts	Colons show degrees of elongation of the prior sound.
.hhh	Inspiration (in-breaths).
Yeh,	'Continuation' marker, weak rising intonation.
what sorry?	Question marks signal stronger, 'questioning' intonation, irrespective of grammar.
Right.	Full stops mark falling, stopping intonation ('final contour'), irrespective of grammar.
I'm probably s-	hyphens mark a cut-off of the preceding sound.
>I know<	'greater than' and 'lesser than' signs enclose speeded-up talk.
solid.= =We had	'Equals' signs mark the immediate 'latching' of successive talk.

For more detail see Jefferson (2004) and Hepburn (2004).

33 expressions of bodily sensation which initiated new sequences were produced by children. These were found in 20 mealtimes across all five families. A careful descriptive account of these pain expressions is provided elsewhere (Jenkins 2013).

In this corpus episodes containing expressions of physical experience rarely contain what is described in CA as an adjacency pair. This is a simple unit of talk containing a turn from one speaker, followed by a second turn (a response) from another speaker (Schegloff 2007). Instead, they often involve extended sequences in larger stretches of talk during which the nature of the sensation is negotiated. Sequence organisation is an orderly turn-by-turn process that provides slots where adults or children can resist or accept the diagnostic work of the other speaker, display understanding, repair their own or another speaker's talk of the previous turn and negotiate the nature of the bodily sensation and the response. Extensive stretches of talk can be built as a way of dealing with difficulties in the talk, such as negotiating the nature of the child's experience (Schegloff 2007).

In this analysis I show how the character of the sensation is initially formulated within the child's report and embodied in these reports are claims of unmediated access to their experience, and the right to report on these sensations. In their responses parents also make claims about the nature of the child's experience, its severity and its authenticity, and potential remedies. The analysis that follows describes the strategies by which children can accept or resist the claims embedded in these responses.

Example 1: Child accepts adult's non-serious interpretation
In this first example, Lanie's report that her tummy hurts is responded to by Dad, who claims that he doesn't think it hurts and suggests an alternative, non-serious interpretation of the sensation:

Extract 1: Edwards 5: 16.58–17.04 You're quite full

```
67 Lan:    Oh my tu:mmy h:ur:ts.
68 Dad:    I ↑ dont think it hurts Lanie. Its probly just
69         cause you're quite full.
70         (0.5)
71 Lan:    Yeah.
```

In line 67 Lanie reports that her tummy hurts, producing a lexical formulation that identifies the location ('tummy') and the nature of the sensation as hurting. As with many of the lexical formulations in this collection, this formulation is characteristic of an announcement; an assertion relating to a current, speaker-specific event (Schegloff 1995). Connected with this it contains an indication that the reported condition is current such that the recipient would not be aware of it (Maynard 1997, Schegloff 1995). The turn is prefaced with an 'oh,' which signals a change of state, displaying the newness of this feeling (Heritage 1984). By announcing the condition as news, and claiming ownership of the sensation, the child treats the adult as unknowing, that is, as not having access to the child's experience.

Dad produces a second pair part with no delay, asserting that he doesn't think her tummy hurts, and provides the explanation 'It's probly just cause you're quite full' (line 68). Dad resists Lanie's characterisation of the sensation as 'hurting,' and formulates an alternative explanation which minimises the seriousness of the experience, invoking the notion that it is normal and ordinary; fullness rather than pain. It also does so with an orientation to the potentially disaligning nature of the explanation, employing the terms 'think' and 'probly', which soften the strength with which Dad asserts this knowledge. In this way the epistemic claim (that is, the extent to which Dad asserts rights to knowledge about the diagnostic explanation underpinning Lanie's experience) is weakened.

After a short delay Lanie responds in third position on line 71 with a receipt that aligns with Dad's explanation. This token 'Yeah' provides an acceptance of the less serious interpretation, making no issue with Dad's epistemic claims to access her experience, but which nonetheless positions Lanie as able to confirm or refute the assessment. It is a minimal post-expansion, designed to close the sequence (Schegloff 2007).

This extract demonstrates the way in which the nature of the sensation, produced initially by the child, is reworked by the response, and the alternative formulation is accepted by the child in third position. The child demonstrates rights to report on their bodily sensations, and to accept or deny reworked interpretations of the sensation. An explicit acceptance of the parent's interpretation of their sensation is rare in this data corpus. Elsewhere, the sequential space following an adult's response is used by the child to resist an adult's formulation of the nature of the experience, as the next example shows:

Example 2: Child resists adult's formulation that the expression is exaggerated
In the next extract, Dad has offered Jack second helpings of dinner. As we join the talk, Dad is scraping the spoon in the saucepan, causing a high-pitched sound.[2] As Jack is accepting the offer he puts his hands on his ears and before completing his turn produces a cry of pain:

Extract 2: Hawkins 11:10.05–12.29 Bit over the top

```
130 Jack:      Okay[    I'll have some        ]
131                [((Jack puts hands on ears))]
132 Dad:       chicken.=
133 Jack:      =AH: .hh A:H:
134            (1.5)
135 Mum:       He doesnt li:ke that sound. ↑ You
136            do'are a bit over the top [(    )]
137 Jack:                          [But it ] Doe:s
138            give me like that.
139 Mum:       >I know< but it's a bit th:eatrical isn't
140            it.
```

In line 133 'AH: .hh A:H:' provide no detail as to the nature of the pain, although the embodied actions in response to scraping sounds from spooning food from the saucepan provide sources by which the other participants can infer the source. After a 1.5 second gap, Mum asserts 'He doesn't li:ke that sound.' which, according to the person reference seems to address Dad regarding Jack. She formulates Jack's experience in terms of a preference rather than sensations or unpleasant feelings. She then changes to the first person, addressing Jack in the next unit of talk, known in CA as a turn construction unit or TCU (Sacks *et al.* 1974) saying '↑You do'are a bit over the top.' The expression of pain is packaged as disproportionate to the level of pain actually experienced, undermining the legitimacy of his expression. The present-tense formulation offers the description as an instance of a more generalised pattern, and in this way produces 'being over the top' as a dispositional character of the speaker (Edwards 1995).

The end of Mum's turn on line 135–136 is inaudible, and Jack, in third position, produces a turn in overlap that seems defensive, either of his experience or his actions, with the contrastive term 'But' which is produced in turn-initial (at the start of the turn) and places an emphasis on 'does' when he says 'it Doe:s give me like that.' Mum goes on to assert '>I know< but it's a bit th:eatrical isn't it'. The tag question 'isn't it' produces the assertion as if Jack should be in agreement. In this way Mum orients to the notion that other speakers have privileged access to their own experiences, with specific rights to narrate them (Sacks 1984) and invites Jack to agree.

In Extract 2 it is possible to see how claims to knowledge about Jack's experience are negotiated. Participants in interaction have been shown to display sensitivity to what they have rights to know, how they know it, and whether they have rights to say it, and they constantly manage their and others' rights to describe or evaluate states of affairs (for a more detailed discussion of epistemics see Heritage 2012; Raymond and Heritage 2006). Mum's initial response displayed an understanding of Jack's report, reworking the expression in terms of its authenticity. As in example one, Jack uses the third position to assert his rights to confirm or deny Mum's claims, in this case resisting the embodied assumptions about both the nature of this expression, and Jack's 'theatrical' disposition more generally.

Example 3: Child resists parent's serious diagnostic explanation
Whereas Extract 2 provides an example of the child resisting a response which undermines the legitimacy of the bodily sensation, in Extract 3 the child resists a diagnostic explanation

that pathologises the reported sensation. This mealtime is breakfast and the extract begins 15 minutes into the meal, following a lapse in talk, when Lanie asserts that her tummy hurts, a sensation that Mum proposes will be alleviated by drinking water as the pain is probably caused by constipation:

Extract 3: Edwards 5:15.50–16.50 Probably a bit constipated

```
05        (10.7)
06 Lan:   [     #My tu:mmy        ] [ hur:ts:.# ]
07        [((Lanie leans heads))] [((Lanie puts hand on tummy))]
08        [      (1.9)            ]
09        [((Lanie puts hand in lap))]
10 Mum:   Mm thi:nk (1.6) need to have full day:, of
11        getting you drinking cause I think you're probly
12        a bit (1.2) co:nstipay::ted,
13        (0.9)
14 Lan:   I ar:m't,
15 Mum:   Mm:, either that or you've got a tummy bug.
16        (2.5)
17 Lan:   U:h
18        (1.0)
19 Lan:   I've got no:thing you two,
```

On line 6 Lanie produces an assertion that her tummy hurts, claiming unmediated access to this sensation, conveying information related to the nature of the pain and her experience of upset without marking her epistemic rights to remark on the matter (Heritage and Raymond 2005). Lanie's formulation is followed by a gap of 1.9 seconds. While Mum (or Dad) may be chewing at this point, they both display the ability to talk through a mouthful elsewhere, and this gap signals some sort of delay, indicating a dispreferred response (Pomerantz 1984).

Mum's turn beginning in line 10 is formulated as an assertion that proposes a remedy (drinking) and an explanation (constipation). In this way the response embodies an under-standing of Lanie's reported sensation as genuine and legitimate and suggests a potential course of action for remediating it.

Mum infers that Lanie's pain is a serious (though acute and solvable) condition. However it is produced in a manner that mediates the rights Mum has to assert a diagnostic explana-tion. The turn begins with 'Mm thi:nk.' which presents the turn as a perspective display. Like subjective-side assessments (Wiggins and Potter 2003), this diagnostic explanation is marked as the speaker's own, without indicating whether other speakers present do or should have the same perspective. In this way she softens her claim. In the pause she puts her napkin on the table and swallows, and then delivers a remedy 'need to have full day:, of getting you drink-ing' and the diagnostic explanation 'cause I think you're probly a bit (1.2) co:nstipay::ted.' Again the explanation includes the word 'think' and 'probably,' which hedges the certainty with which Mum makes her claim, possibly as a way of softening a concerning explanation or an objectionable course of action.

The nature of Lanie's experience has evolved, firstly in Lanie's initial report in which she claims primary rights to report on her sensation, and secondly in Mum's response which treats the sensation as genuine and makes (mediated) claims to diagnose the nature of the experience and propose a possible remedy. In the third position space that follows in lines 13 and 14, Lanie, after another delay, responds with disagreement, saying 'I ar:m't', which seems to be doing something along the lines of 'I am not'. In this way, Lanie disagrees with Mum's explanation, reporting the absence of Mum's proposed condition and by doing so re-asserts her privileged rights to access her own state. Lanie, the first pair part speaker, is here in third position, resisting the second pair part by asserting her competence. She is not aligning as an advice-recipient.

Mum then produces a form of increment to her previous turn and handles Lanie's resistance, 'Mm:, either that or you've got a tummy bug.' and continues her inference by adding a possible alternative. This reopens the second pair part, this time with no markers mediating her epistemic claim. Lanie, again in third position, rejects the second pair part in line 19 with 'I've got nothing', this time opening up her turn to address Dad in addition to Mum when she says 'you two'.

This sequence demonstrates that both parties claim opportunities to resist or defend their or the other party's formulation in third position. Lanie rejects Mum's explanation by appealing again to her own primary access to the experience. While the rejection is taken seriously enough for Mum to produce further second pair part to defend her explanation, it does not appear to be successful in terms of discrediting Mum's account: in the subsequent talk (not shown here) Mum produces further description of Lanie's stomach condition as serious (not 'quite right') over a recent time period.

Example 4: Child and parent negotiate the diagnostic explanation
In this final example, Haydn asserts that his tummy is feeling different, and over several turns he works to distinguish between being sick, ill and needing the toilet. During this sequence there is a conflict in the diagnoses produced by Haydn and his mum. The sequence demonstrates how rights to report on the sensation, and the nature of that sensation, are negotiated over several turns in a more complex sequence. This extract is 3 minutes into the recording in which the serving of food and drink has been discussed. There is then a lapse in talk where this extract picks up:

Extract 4: Jephcott 6: 3.00 My tummy's feeling different

```
04 Hay:    My tummy's feelin' bit diff'rent.
05         (.)
06 Mum:    Bit what sorry? ((Isabelle stands up on her chair))
07         (.)
08 Hay:    Different.
09 Mum:    Different. <Sit down plea:se Isa[belle. ]
10 Hay:                                   [I'm not ] sure
11         if I'm s:ick or not.
12         (0.6)
13 Hay:    N[ot sure if I'm s-      ]
14 Mum:     [I think if you were sick] you
15         wouldn't be eating.
16         (1.4)
17 Hay:    I'm not sure if I'm sick or i::ll:.
18         (6.0) ((Children are eating. Mum is serving food.))
19 Hay:    I'm not sure if I'm sick or il[l. ]
20 Mum:                                  [( ] ) ring
```

```
21          me.
22          (0.1)
23 Dad:     Yeah
```

Haydn declares on line 4 that his tummy is feeling a bit different, as in the previous examples, claiming unmediated access to his sensation. Mum responds on line 6 by producing an other-initiated repair, for which Haydn provides the repair solution in line 8, acknowledged by Mum in line 9. She then issues a directive telling Isabelle to sit down, turning her body away from the children and towards the kitchen area of the open plan room (not marked on the transcript). Haydn develops his first pair part in lines 10–11 to propose (cautiously) that he is unsure as to whether the 'different' feeling indicates that he is sick. Haydn uses terms which mediate the certainty with which he asserts a diagnostic explanation for the sensation (in contrast to simply reporting the sensation itself) prefacing his turn with 'I'm not sure'.

Following 0.6 seconds of silence Haydn begins to re-issue this turn on line 13 as Mum produces a response, asserting that if Haydn were sick he wouldn't be eating, mitigating her epistemic access with 'I think' which indicates that her assessment displays her own perspective rather than her experiential access. Mum is resisting Haydn's diagnostic explanation that he might be sick or ill, and she indexes observable information (Haydn eating) to strengthen the epistemic position of her disaffiliative claim. Mum resists Haydn's proposed diagnostic explanation of his sensation as being ill, on the basis that he wouldn't be eating if he was ill. Contesting Haydn's claim is oriented to as potentially problematic with the provision of evidence to support the assertion.

Haydn reasserts his proposed diagnostic explanation, reworking it to contain the options 'sick or ill' rather than 'sick or not,' presenting the possible diagnoses of tummy trouble or a more general illness. He designs his turn to more strongly prefer a response that suggests there is something the matter. After 6 seconds during which Haydn continues to eat and Mum does not respond, Haydn reissues his turn, again indicating that the response (or in this case, the silence) is deemed to be in some way deficient to the speaker's project (Antaki *et al*. 2007). Before Haydn completes his identical repeat in line 19 Mum launches something new which is partially inaudible but Dad responds to it.

In the talk that follows (shown in extract 5 below) Haydn goes on to reissue his puzzle, with a term of address, selecting Mum as recipient and pursuing a response (Stivers and Rossano 2010).

Extract 5: Jephcott 6: 3.00 My tummy's feeling different (*continued*)

```
24          (0.5)
25 Dad:     °(           [                )°]
26 Hay:                  [I'm not sure if] I'm sick or i:ll
27          mummy.
28          (2.0)
29 Hay:     I'm probably s- I'uh probably am I'm probably
30          i:ll cause it fee:ls like it.
31          (0.2)
32 Mum:     You >wou'n't< ea:t anything if you're i:ll.
33          (1.4)
34 Hay:     [(             )]
35 Isa:     [HE:::Y (      )][(          )]=
```

```
36 Mum:                              [(           )]
37 Isa:    =di[dnt ]  [(      ]  )=
38 Hay:       [I:( ]  [       )]
39 Dad:              [No.   ]
40 Hay:    [(          )]
41 Dad:    [(          )](       ) today.
42 Mum:    Oh right.
43 Dad:    Where [d'you want the gravy.]
44 Hay:          [ I need a poo       ] tha:t's why
45         [.h I didn't notice    ]
46 Mum:    [Go and have a poo. Out!]
47 Hay:    I didn't notice I needed a poo but now I
48         no:[tice.]
49 Isa:       [M:m. ]
50 Mum:    Right.
```

At this point reissuing the first pair part has proved relatively unsuccessful. Haydn, still not receiving uptake from the re-issued first pair part with the additional turn-end term of address on lines 26 and 27, produces a slightly different turn on line 29 following a gap. With some difficulty in delivery (several self-repairs) he says he is probably ill (retaining uncertainty) but this time indexing his access to his own feelings with an account 'cause it fee:ls like it..' This first pair part contains further evidence of his account based on the notion that he has primary access to the experience. This new assertion has more certainty than his first report (upgrading from 'not sure' to 'probably') and retains a single descriptor of his state ('ill') rather than proposing a second alternative candidate ('or sick').

This assertion is successful in gaining a response. Mum produces another second pair part in line 32, maintaining her position that Haydn is not ill. However this time she formulates it in more certain terms dropping the 'I think' and again indexes her access to more expert knowledge of evidence of sickness and draws on the observable information about Haydn's eating. Haydn's new formulation asserting that he is probably ill, appealing to his privileged access to his experience, is rejected by Mum.

A number of turns (lines 33–42) follow which are difficult to hear. It seems that Mum and Dad begin to engage in a topic unrelated to Haydn's announced experience. Then on line 44 Haydn again issues talk related to his experience, this time announcing that he needs 'a poo,' and produces it as a solution and explanation for his sensation by saying 'that's why'. This causal account for his tummy sensation is immediately resolvable, in contrast to his initial candidates of 'sick or ill' which are illness accounts potentially indicating a problem. It also contains no markers of mediated epistemic access or uncertainty. The delivery of the turn in overlap with Dad's turn on line 43 seems to orient to the contrast of his new interpretation as being different from anything he has previously suggested, indicating a suddenness to the realisation. After a short in-breath he produces another TCU 'I didn't notice' to account for why he (the owner of his experience) hadn't produced this explanation before.

In overlap with this TCU Mum responds in line 46 by directing Haydn to go to the toilet to alleviate the problem he has announced. In this way Mum accepts the explanation Haydn has proposed and the claims he makes to be able to diagnose his own experience. In line 47 Haydn reissues his explanation which was originally delivered in overlap, formulating his turn in a way that particularly emphasises the contrastive newness of his realisation that needing a poo was the cause of his tummy sensation ('I didn't notice … but now I no:tice'). Mum issues a receipt in line 50, acknowledging this diagnosis. In this way she explicitly aligns to and agrees with his new diagnosis. Unlike her responses (and lack of responses) to Haydn's previous 'sick or ill' account, Mum produces her agreement to this explanation non-problematically and with no delay. Within this sequence Haydn reissues his proposed diagnostic explanation in a way that rejects his Mum's 'not ill' diagnosis; however this is relatively unsuccessful in eliciting an alternative response from Mum, even when he emphasises the primacy of his access to the experience. Eventually Haydn produces an alternative explanation which is immediately accepted.

Each of the five examples discussed in this analysis have demonstrated ways in which children produce expressions of sensation which claim unmediated access to their own experience, and described how an adult's response makes claims about the nature of that experience, in terms of its authenticity, severity and possible explanations and remedies. A response may formulate the sensation as serious, easily resolvable or as exaggerated, and in the subsequent interaction children display rights to accept or resist these claims.

Discussion

By subjecting examples of children's expressions of bodily sensation in everyday family interaction to fine-grained analysis, I have pointed out the way in which children's expressions claim unmediated access to their experience and rights to report on their experience. In addition, the analysis demonstrates the negotiated character of physical sensations in interaction in terms of how they are shaped by contributions from both children and parents, and the way in which the authenticity and nature of a child's experience is produced, amended, resisted or accepted in the turns that follow, with varying degrees of success.

These findings provide clear evidence in support of the new sociology of childhood (Moran-Ellis 2010), demonstrating that children are active agents in constructing the nature of their experience. The analysis builds on this theory by showing that, specifically in regards to their health, children's pain and bodily sensation is something they themselves construct in talk. It is produced as an experience to which they maintain primary access. Yet, issuing these reports within the context of everyday family life, the child's experience is available to the recipients (parents) to be reformulated and reworked in subsequent turns.

By adopting a CA approach to everyday talk-in-interaction, this analysis has shown how the child is capable of producing descriptions of a sensation (such as a hurting tummy), and utilising resources by which to mediate (or not) their claims to access the experience. Further, an examination of the more extended sequences shows that while parents may rework the nature of this sensation in their responses, children display rights to deny or accept these formulations in the subsequent talk. In this way the analysis illustrates children's agency in terms of how they actively construct and negotiate the nature of their pain and physical experiences within family interaction. The child is not passively subject to their parents' versions of their illness experience, in a way that would support a traditional sociological framework which treats the child as victim of external influences. Rather, within the fabric of talk between parents and children about episodes of pain, the social study of childhood's notion that children assert agency and actively contribute to the construction of their experience is exemplified. Children not only produce assertions about their physical sensations; they can, and do, object to and rework parental descriptions and causal explanations of their experience. Intergenerational relationships have already been identified as a key site in which to observe agency in the sociology of children's health (Prout and James 1997, Mayall 2001a).

What this study adds is a thorough account of each turn as produced by children and adults, demonstrating the invaluable means by which CA can be used to describe, in concrete terms, the way in which inter-generational relationships between adults and children are produced and managed.

At the outset I indicated that the theoretical shift in understanding children as social actors has also been reflected in policy that promotes listening to children's views in institutional settings. Ordinary conversation has the potential to form the basis for comparative studies of institutional talk (Drew and Heritage 1992), and the patterns of mundane talk about the body and being unwell within families described in this study are relevant to the way in which children and adults interact in medical settings. For example, episodes in which children disclose a bodily sensation may precipitate entry into the medical setting. The findings in this study potentially represent the first occasion in which children can exert agency in medical decision-making. While this was not explicitly topicalised in the instances in this corpus, it is possible to see how issues to do with severity, authenticity and legitimacy become alive in these episodes. The description of resources (such as re-asserting a description or disagreeing with the other speaker's claim) by which children and parents negotiate these issues provides a foundation for future work that could examine interactions in which seeking medical help is discussed in everyday settings.

The findings in this study are also relevant to medical settings in terms of identifying similarities with patterns of talk presented in this chapter, and those described in existing studies of talk in institutional environments. For example, the current study describes the resources which children and parents use to make epistemic claims and exert agency in relation to the nature of their experience. These resources include the way in which children claim unmediated access to an experience by producing descriptions with no epistemic markers, or assert rights to confirm or resist a parent's description. Comparatively, previous research has shown that adult patients (who like the children in the current study are the 'experiencers') construct themselves as having superior knowledge of their illness experience (Heritage 2006, Heritage and Robinson 2006, Peräkylä 1998). Further work is needed to examine if and how the resources by which to handle these sorts of issues, developed in everyday talk, are available to be used by adults and children in institutional settings.

In conclusion, a CA approach represents an effective methodological technique for exploring topics within the framework of a new sociology of childhood. By closely examining what children and adults say, and how they say it, a CA study is able to bypass many of the problematic power relations inherent in alternative forms of research that ask children to describe or reflect on such interactions. A CA study is ideal for facilitating a detailed description of the child's role as a social actor, and the child's everyday participation in their health care.

Acknowledgements

The author would like to thank the members of the Discourse and Rhetoric Group (DARG) at Loughborough University, particularly Alexa Hepburn and also Derek Edwards, for their invaluable supervision of this project, and Jonathan Potter, Alexandra Kent and members of DARG for helpful discussions in data sessions. Thanks to Alison Pilnick for her comments on an earlier draft, and to the anonymous reviewers for their constructive observations. I would also like to thank the participants for giving up their time for the research. This work was supported by the Economic and Social Research Council (grant no. ES/ F020864/1, 2007).

Notes

1   Thanks to Sarah Crouch and Alexandra Kent for permission to use these data.
2   The expressions of bodily sensation in this study, while projecting a response (and therefore representing an initiating action), also display that there was a 'source' that preceded
it (see Schegloff's 2007 description of retro-sequences). This example, unlike the others,
appears more explicitly to contain a clear cause of the child's bodily expression – the
sound of the scraping saucepan. In other sequences the cause of the sensation is less
clear. The expressions themselves are what surface as the first effective component in
the interaction, signalling that the sequence is in progress. While it is interesting to note
that in this case the source is more explicit, any analytic distinction between sensations
with external or internal causes was analysed as a participants' concern, as part of the
ongoing issue of the degree to which information about the nature and severity of the
expressed sensation is revealed.

References

Alanen, L. (1988) Rethinking childhood, *Acta Sociologica*, 31, 1, 53–67.
Antaki, C., Finlay, W.M.L. and Walton, C. (2007) Conversational shaping: staff members' solicitation of talk from people with an intellectual impairment, *Qualitative Health Research*, 17, 10, 1403–14.
Clemente, I. (2009) Progressivity and participation: children's management of parental assistance in paediatric chronic pain encounters, *Sociology of Health & Illness*, 31, 6, 872–8.
Department of Health (1989) *Children Act*. London: Department of Health.
Drew, P. (2005) Conversation analysis. In Fitch, K.L. and Sanders, R.E. (eds) *Handbook of Language and Social Interaction*. Mahwah: Erlbaum.
Drew, P. and Heritage, J. (1992) Analyzing talk at work: an introduction. In Drew, P. and Heritage, J. (eds) *Talk at Work: Interaction in Institutional Settings*. Cambridge: Cambridge University Press.
Edwards, D. (1995) Two to tango: script formulations, dispositions, and rhetorical symmetry in relationship troubles talk, *Research on Language and Social Interaction*, 28, 4, 319–50.
Heath, C. (1989) Pain talk: the expression of suffering in the medical consultation, *Social Psychology Quarterly*, 52, 2, 113–25.
Hepburn, A. (2004) Crying: notes on description, transcription, and interaction, *Research on Language and Social Interaction*, 37, 3, 251–90.
Heritage, J. (1984) A Change-of-state token and aspects of its sequential placement. In Atkinson, J.M. and Heritage, J. (eds) *Structures of Social Action*. Cambridge: Cambridge University Press.
Heritage, J. (2006) Revisiting authority in physician-patient interaction. In Maxwell, M., Kovarsky, D. and Duchan, J. (eds) *Diagnosis as Cultural Practice*. New York: Mouton de Gruyter.
Heritage, J. (2012) The epistemic engine: sequence organization and territories of knowledge, *Research on Language and Social Interaction*, 45, 1, 30–52.
Heritage, J. and Raymond, G. (2005) The terms of agreement: indexing epistemic authority and subordination in assessment sequences, *Social Psychology Quarterly*, 68, 1, 15–38.
Heritage, J. and Robinson, J. (2006) Accounting for the visit: giving reasons for seeking medical care. In Heritage, J. and Maynard, D. (eds) *Communication in Medical Care: Interactions between Primary Care Physicians and Patients*. Cambridge: Cambridge University Press.
Jefferson, G. (2004) Glossary of transcript symbols with an introduction. In Lerner, G.H. (ed.) *Conversation Analysis: Studies from the First Generation*. Amsterdam and Philadelphia: John Benjamins.
Jenkins, L. (2013) Children's expressions of pain and bodily sensation in family mealtimes. PhD thesis. Loughborough. Loughborough University.
Lansdown, G. (2001) *Promoting Children's Participation in Democratic Decision-making*. Rome: United Nations Children's Fund Research Centre.

Mayall, B. (2001a) Towards a sociology of child health, *Sociology of Health & Illness*, 20, 3, 269–88.

Mayall, B. (2001b) Understanding childhoods: a London study. In Alanen, L. and Mayall, B. (eds) *Conceptualising Child-Adult Relations*. London: Routledge.

Maynard, D.W. (1997) The news delivery sequence: bad news and good news in conversational interaction, *Research on Language and Social Interaction*, 30, 2, 93–130.

Moran-Ellis, J. (2010) Reflections on the sociology of childhood in the UK, *Current Sociology*, 58, 2, 186–205.

Parry, R.H. (2004) The interactional management of patients' physical incompetence: a conversation analytic study of physiotherapy interactions, *Sociology of Health & Illness*, 26, 7, 976–1007.

Peräkylä, A. (1998) Authority and accountability: the delivery of diagnosis in primary health care, *Social Psychology Quarterly*, 61, 4, 301–20.

Pilnick, A. and Zayts, O. (2012) 'Let's have it tested first': choice and circumstances in decision-making following positive antenatal screening in Hong Kong, *Sociology of Health & Illness*, 34, 2, 266–82.

Pomerantz, A. (1984) Agreeing and disagreeing with assessments: some features of preferred/dispreferred turn shapes. In Atkinson, M. and Heritage, J. (eds) *Structures of Social Action*. New York: Cambridge University Press.

Prout, A. (2002) Researching children as social actors: an introduction to the children 5–16 programme, *Children and Society*, 16, 1, 67–76.

Prout, A. and James, A. (1997) A new paradigm for the sociology of childhood? Provenance, promise and problems. In James, A. and Prout, A. (eds) *Contemporary Issues in the Sociological Study of Childhood*. London: Falmer Press.

Raymond, G. and Heritage, J. (2006) The epistemics of owning grandchildren, *Language in Society*, 35, 5, 677–705.

Sacks, H. (1984) On doing 'being ordinary'. In Atkinson, J.M. and Heritage, J. (eds) *Structures of Social Action*. Cambridge: Cambridge University Press.

Sacks, H., Schegloff, E.A. and Jefferson, G. (1974) A simplest systematics for the organization of turn-taking in conversation, *Language*, 50, 4, 696–735.

Schegloff, E.A. (1992) In another context. In Duranti, A. and Goodwin, C. (eds) *Rethinking Context: Language as an Interactive Phenomenon*. Cambridge: Cambridge University Press.

Schegloff, E.A. (1995) Discourse as an interactional achievement iii: the omnirelevance of action, *Research on Language and Social Interaction*, 28, 3, 185–211.

Schegloff, E.A. (2005) On integrity in inquiry of the investigated, not the investigator, *Discourse Studies*, 7, 4–5, 455–80.

Schegloff, E.A. (2007) *Sequence Organization in Interaction: a Primer in Conversation Analysis I*. Cambridge: Cambridge University Press.

Stivers, T. and Rossano, F. (2010) Mobilizing response, *Research on Language and Social Interaction*, 43, 1, 3–31.

UN (1989) Convention on the Rights of the Child. Adopted and opened for signature, ratification and accession by General Assembly resolution 44/25 of 20 November 1989. Available online at http:// www.ohchr.org/en/professionalinterest/pages/crc.aspx (accessed 30 October 2014).

Wiggins, S. and Potter, J. (2003) Attitudes and evaluative practices: category vs. item and subjective vs. objective constructions in everyday food assessments, *British Journal of Social Psychology*, 42, 4, 513–31.

11

Understanding inter-generational relations: the case of health maintenance by children
Berry Mayall

Introduction: sociological approaches to childhood

It has convincingly been argued that key to sociological understanding of childhood is studying relational processes across the generations, since childhood has to be understood as a
social status (rather than an age-range): a minority status, defined in contra-distinction to
adulthood, and also essentially as occupying conceptual and physical space mapped out
through adult visions of childhood (Alanen 2009, Qvortrup 2009). Thus a central topic to be
considered in studying inter-generational relations is bodily relations between children and
adults; for it can be said that child-adult relations in the early years are constructed, partly,
through the character of adult attention or lack of attention to children's physical bodies; and
children's relations with adults are embodied. As children get older, we learn about how far
children and adults in our societies can and do take account of changes in children's bodies
(e.g. Prendergast 2000; Henderson *et al.* 2007). The paper aims to suggest that understanding
inter-generational relations between children and adults may be helped by consideration of
what concepts of the body come into play, the body understood as ontology and/or the body
as the object of knowledge, or the body within epistemological thought. Clearly, a central
topic for both children and adults is how best children's health may be maintained, promoted
and restored, through children's and adults' agency. Their beliefs and practices will be influenced by societal norms and prescriptions.

 This chapter will take account of (some of) the work on the sociology of the body and
of the emotions (Hochschild 1979, 1983; Shilling 1997, 2005; Bendelow and Williams 1998);
most of this work is about adults; but the paper will build on the work of a few scholars who
have considered children's bodies as constituent entities informing, determining and modifying children's relations with adults (e.g. Bendelow and Mayall 2000; Prout 2000; Alderson
et al. 2005). The argument is also influenced by feminist work on how women as embodied
people move within and across 'public' and 'private' domains, given that these domains are
structured by dominant male concerns (Martin 1987, Hochschild 1979), for children, adult
concerns structure children's experiences of their bodies and emotions. I build on previous
theoretical and empirical investigations into the social status of childhood, how children
negotiate their status and in particular how they negotiate and maintain their health and
well-being (Mayall 1994, 1996, 1998, 2002), to consider how the study of intergenerational
relational processes may be further developed by exploring how children's embodiment is
integrated into their social relations.

Children, Health and Well-being: Policy Debates and Lived Experience, First Edition. Edited by Geraldine Brady,
Pam Lowe and Sonja Olin Lauritzen. Chapters © 2015 The Authors. Book Compilation © 2015 Foundation
for the Sociology of Health & Illness/Blackwell Publishing Ltd.

I start from the position that children and adults constitute two social groups, and that in most if not all societies, children and childhood are subordinated to the authority and power of adults and of adulthood (Shamgar-Handelman 1994). While, therefore, children and adults may make common cause in some circumstances, nevertheless key to understanding how childhood is lived and what opportunities, challenges and difficulties children face (and adults face in their relations with children) are inter-generational processes whereby children's lives are constructed and reconstructed and whereby their contributions to social arenas (home, school, neighbourhood, health services) may be enabled and respected, or may be hindered and rejected. As a social group within minority world societies, children contribute to the division of labour, not just through school work (Qvortrup 1985, 2009) but also in the construction and maintenance of personal relations ('people work') (Stacey 1988). Even in our heavily industrialised and scholarised societies, children also contribute through household work and most, during their childhoods, do other work, paid and unpaid (e.g. Mizen *et al.* 2001).

In line with my central approach outlined above, I take it that institutional and ideological structures shape childhoods and child-adult relations (e.g. Mayall 1998; Bendelow and Mayall 2000). Long established traditions, policies and beliefs structure how childhoods are understood and how they are lived in specific societies. Notably, educational institutions and the whole edifice of schooling, its ideologies and its power to shape childhoods and children's relations with adults has to be a major focus in the study of childhoods. This is so in minority world societies, where children's major activity is deemed to be schooling, but in majority world societies too, where globalisation of 'western' ideas is leading to hard decisions for children and parents: whether schooling should take priority over productive work, and if so, why and how (e.g. André and Hilgers 2015; Morrow and Vennam 2015). The tension between schooling and productive work for children has implications for the well-being of children, since at stake are their understandings of their responsibilities to their families and communities. In this chapter I use some examples from research to explore how we are moving forward in our understandings of childhood and inter-generational processes; and in particular in our insights into the negotiations children and adults engage in relating to children's bodily health and emotions.

I assume in this chapter that inter-generational processes take place at both macro and micro levels, at institutional and personal levels and that these are interlinked (Alanen 2009; Mayall 2009). Under consideration here is how these processes shape and re-shape children's and adults' experience, and how they seek to re-assert the ascribed characteristics of each social group, but are challenged, especially by the less powerful negotiators in a relational exchange. The specific focus of the paper is on how children and adults negotiate the status of the child's body and emotions, in the daily give-and-take of relational processes; these negotiations have to be understood in the context of the large-scale factors structuring childhood bodies and emotions. Here it is relevant to consider how far children's emotions (like those of adults) are conditioned through social policies and social norms (e.g. Bendelow 2009); for, as discussed by Hochschild (1979, 1983) and Bendelow and Williams (1998), emotional health is closely linked to physical health.

Alongside others, I have worked to develop understandings of children and of childhood as fully social: children as agents in social worlds and childhood as a social group that contributes to the maintenance and progress of the social order. Here I aim to consider three intersecting themes in the sociological study of childhood: children as a minority social group, children as embodied social actors, and children as agents within the intergenerational division of labour. I aim to consider the sociology of childhood in relation to health maintenance, restoration and promotion; in particular I take up the above topics, which I outlined in an earlier paper (Mayall 1998). I aim, not to do a literature review, but to point to some important developments and studies that have emerged over the last 15 years.

Children as a minority social group

As suggested above, children are to be understood as both an active social group in society, and also as a social group subordinated to adult groups. Subordination may start from bodily weakness and inexperience, requiring childhood dependence on adulthood, but it is also powerfully sedimented in social norms and practices. While it is important to keep in mind distinctions between natural dependencies and socially constructed dependencies (Lansdown 1994), we must also respond to the power of the social throughout the span of childhoods. In particular, as discussed by Greene (1999), powerfully established concepts in minority world societies, while they are challenged by recent work within psychology, continue to link age to competence: young children are deemed to lack competence to make decisions affecting their lives, since biological maturing is linked to psychological capacity.

We can develop these points in relation to the main service sectors that children are or may be exposed to: education, welfare and health. As regards education, London children I have spoken with accepted their subordination at school, but they identified adult lack of respect for their human rights, for their moral competence, for their moral status as persons (Mayall 2002: chapter 6); indeed their best chance of being respected was at home, where they were more likely to be understood as complex, embodied, thinking and feeling persons. Their arguments are supported by evidence from two large-scale empirical studies (1967 and 2001) of UK children's experiential knowledge of the school system. Though these studies took place thirty years apart and though the UNCRC was ratified by the UK in 1991, children in both studies found that they were treated as morally incompetent, that teachers did not respect them (Blishen 1969; Burke and Grosvenor 2003). So what is at stake here is children's welfare and self-esteem in the long years they are required to go to school. Indeed we may add that the very choice of school tends to rest with parents, rather than with children, with profound impacts on children's experience (Knight 2013). A somewhat different set of pressures and factors accounts for the status of children in majority world countries; for evidence indicates not only that adults, by long-standing traditions, assume moral and social superiority over children, but that children's paid and unpaid work has allowed for children to be understood and respected as important contributors to household economic and social welfare (e.g. Panelli *et al.* 2007). However, the raised status of schooling in children's lives, promoted by international agencies, is challenging these well-established concepts. Singal and Muthukrishna (2014) discuss the consequent identification of the individual child as school achiever and the erosion of the social status of kinship and community networks in helping disabled children lead happy healthy lives.

These points about respect and its relations with children's self-esteem and well-being, and their experience of inter-generational relations have been studied in relation to welfare services in the UK. Thus Hallett *et al.* (2003) studied the well-being of children 'in care' of the local authority, focusing on how they deal with problems they encounter, whom they turn to, how far their voices are heard, and by whom. Similarly, Mullender and colleagues (2003) studied how far children were able to access sympathetic responses to their experiences of living with domestic violence. Winter (2015) found that social workers' knowledge about children, grounded in developmental models of normality, downgraded children's rights to participate in decision-making about their lives 'in care' of the local authority, since these adults deemed the children incompetent to participate. In all three cases, children found that many of those who were employed in the 'caring professions' failed to respect their partic-ipation rights. Studies have been conducted about mentoring services, where children are assigned a person whose job it is to work with the individual child, to help them cope with their family and school contexts (e.g. Colley 2003). Such services require practitioners to think about the individual child's circumstances and predicaments in the context of social policies and practices within the welfare state and specifically within the education service. It has been found, again, that crucial to success is to work on the basis of respect for the positive aspects of the child in his or her social relations, rather than on the assumption that the child has to be helped to behave better – or less anti-socially (Davison 2014).

Within the health care sector, Alderson *et al.* (2005) have pioneered work on the care of very young children – premature babies in special care units – and has studied the extent to which the staff work on the basis of conceptualising the children as persons deserving of respect and as needing respect if they are to achieve well-being. This work continues in the traditions mapped out by Bluebond-Langner (1978), who studied the social and psycholog-ical circumstances of children dying of cancer, and showed how the children, as competent social agents in relational processes, worked towards understanding of the journey they were engaged on and helped their parents come to terms with it.

Running through all these examples in education, welfare and health, is the point that children are dealing with systems, services, policies and practices established by adults, in many cases sedimented over time and aimed at outcomes that may give low priority to chil-dren's lived experiences. Children have to make what they can of the social worlds they are presented with. And, as I have suggested, a running, central theme in their own accounts is the crucial importance for them of adult respect for them as persons; for being respected is a critical factor affecting children's self-esteem. Thomas (2012) discusses these topics in relation to the implementation of children's participation rights, exploring Honneth's anal-ysis of respect (see also Fraser and Honneth 2003). For Honneth identifies three types of respect: emotional recognition at inter-personal levels, legal recognition – respect for per-sons as rights-holders, and social recognition – respect for persons as contributors to social welfare. This three-fold identification allows us to reflect on what is entailed in adult respect for children's engagement with social worlds: inter-personal responsiveness, understanding that children are rights-holders and understanding that children participate in structuring social worlds.

Embodied social actors

The second topic I explore here is understandings that children are social actors acting with, through and for their bodies. Here researchers have been concerned with how bodies shape self-image (and whether self-image shapes bodies); and how bodily changes alter self-image. Linked to these concerns is a focus on what it means to people to be culturally ascribed (or not) moral responsibility for their health; and how emotions mediate between bodies and minds (Hochschild 1979, 1983; Bendelow and Williams 1998). The approach here is simi-lar to that explored by Shilling (1997, 2005), using his concept of corporeal realism, which proposes that both body and society exist as real things, possessed of generative properties. Children present an important and interesting set of issues here, and one which is increas-ingly attracting research attention. Early UK work in the 1990s explored these issues (e.g. Mayall 1998; Prendergast and Forrest 1998; Prout 2000).

More recently, these topics have been explored in research programmes in mainland Europe, building on the earlier work. Thus Favretto and Zaltron (2013), focusing mainly on Italian children aged 7 to 10 years, have explored their competences in relation to health and illness and compared children's increasing competence over time with parents' and health professionals' poor recognition of this experiential and theoretical knowledge. The researchers found that many adults they studied relied on the idea of the child essentially as in need of adult attention and care, rather than as a contributor to the health care process.

Similarly, a French research programme, over four years, focused on children aged 9 to 14 and compared adult discourses (mainly parents, educators and health professionals) on childhood, 'pre-adolescence' and 'adolescence', with young people's own experiences of bodily, emotional and social changes.[1] The programme included over 30 studies of children's daily lives at home, in the neighbourhood, at school and in contacts with health services, and focused on intersections of social class, age, gender and ethnicity. Thus, for instance, Tersigni (2013) studied adult discourse on ethnicity in France and Italy, compared it with the experiences of 'migrant' children, and considered the 'fit' between the adult-defined 'otherness' of these children and their own accounts of their experiences. Beunardeau (2013) studied physical violence in a Parisian school, in relation to the social order of the school; she argues that asserting physical dominance in class and playground constitutes an aesthetic presentation of the physical self that challenges official school discourses (compare Prendergast and Forrest 1998). Julien (2013) studied the choices children make about what clothes to wear, and how these relate to their embodied sense of who they are, and changes in this sense as they get older, and also in relation to the varying norms and pressures affecting their choices (parents, school, friends, media). Nicoletta Diasio, one of the directors of the programme, has summarised the findings of this large programme (I quote with her permission):

> Our study has deconstructed the adult rhetoric about risk that propagates adult concerns, which have little relation to children's experience of growing up. Medical literature has constructed an ontology of pre-adolescence based on gender and the body that professionals in the sector do not necessarily subscribe to . . . The wide range of children's and adults' experiences questions the idea of children's development which places growth in a continuum of universal, objective phases. Rather, growing up means coming to terms with a multitude of norms, models and recommendations.

She notes too that adult discourses tend to focus on girls' growing up as problematic; and argues that boys' experience should be given more consideration.

If, as regards England, we consider intergenerational relations at individual levels and at levels of practice, we find that within child-adult negotiations there is an important embodied component both at home and in nurseries and schools. Parents, at home, during their interactions with children, have to take into account the physical entity of the child, as well as cognitive and emotional characteristics and wishes of the child. Children themselves advance their bodily feelings, wishes and troubles in their negotiations for adult response (e.g. Mayall 1994). Newson and Newson (1970: chapter 9) noted that while in the early morning four-year-old children's bodies may be subordinated to adult-related and nursery-related time-tabling demands, at bedtime children ask for, are granted and enjoy embodied rituals – fun and games around bathing, story-times while cuddled in parental arms, being comfortably settled with a goodnight kiss into blankets and pillows. Alderson (2013) gives many examples of the pro-active agency of babies and young children in embodied interaction with (mainly) their mother. These demands echo feminist work on how women's bodies are understood in social settings and how women negotiate their embodied selves, both at home and in workplaces (e.g. Martin 1987). At nursery, government guidelines require childcare staff to observe the children's physical, social and academic achievement; these observations may aim at normalisation and the 'docile body', but the requirement also raises the question how far it leaves space for responsiveness to children's embodied selves (e.g. Jones *et al.* 2010).

Indeed, in England, the concept of an equal balance between physical and mental education (traditionally part of the private school ethos) has never been fully endorsed for state-educated children; and in the last 20 years, political concern about academic attainment has reduced the space and time for school attention to children's bodies in nurseries and schools (James and James 2004: Chapter 4; Penn 2011). For instance, a teacher in one of my studies pointed to the double problem he faced. The school had been built in the 1970s in response to national policy dictating small class sizes, but now, in the 1990s, educational policy had changed, housing in the area had expanded, and more children were crammed into the class-room space; furthermore the national curriculum demanded that children spend most of their time in the classroom. He said children, especially boys, needed to be running about outside, not sitting at desks; but he had to keep them there (Mayall *et al.* 1996: 149).

It is important to take account here of the extent to which generational processes, whereby adults and children inter-relate, are sensitive not only to national policies but to children's embodied selves. I have long argued that parents at home are – or can be – more sensitive to the demands of children's bodies than schools are or can be (e.g. Mayall 1994). But the ideas promoted by the education system pervade parent-child negotiations at home. School takes priority. Thus in the morning a parent has to get a tired child to school on time; and, after the school day, a tired child still has to do school homework.

If we look at children's embodiment from children's own points of view, we may have to consider the concept of the alienated body. The complex relations between embodiment and social experience are complicated by ambiguity in how children experience adult responses to their bodies. So for instance a young child finds her body is loved by parents, and is respected, but her experience outside the home is sometimes of a body disrespected, indeed rejected from the social. For at school, bodies are managed, and often rejected and alienated. Children at school have to learn to subdue their bodies (Mayall 1994; 2015); and this subduing and subordinating includes controlling their emotions, in order to conform. On the other hand, ontological considerations recur; thus it has recently been argued that physical changes associated with puberty demand that teenagers go to sleep later in the evening than adults and need to sleep longer in the early morning; some schools in England are experimenting with starting the school day at 10 or even 11; and it is claimed that teenagers' behaviour and academic achievement is thereby improved (Weale 2014).

To put these points in more general terms, in child-adult relational processes we may see over the time of childhood a struggle between ontology and epistemology. Parents' respect for and love for their baby's physical body and physical activity may shift, as the child moves into school and later into puberty, towards a more epistemological stance – parents' understanding about the child's body in relation to its status and value in the school system may take precedence over valuing the child's embodied person. Yet, perhaps to the extent that schools bow to pressure from their students, they can develop into health-promoting institutions, which respect children's physical embodiment.

Inter-generational relations

In this third section, I focus directly on relations between the local and the large-scale. Sociologists of many kinds have emphasised the central task of sociology: to consider linkages between personal troubles and public issues – policies, practices, rhetoric (Wright Mills 1959;

Qvortrup 1994; Lemert 2012). I take up two sets of studies where these linkages have been explored in recent years in relation to the health and well-being of children: the Young Lives study and studies using Bourdieu's concepts.

Young Lives is a 15-year study of children growing up in poverty in Ethiopia, Andhra Pradesh in India, Peru and Vietnam, exploring links between poverty and the characteristics of children's lives; overall, the research aims to inform the development of better social policies for children. It is a collaborative project, where local teams of researchers in the four countries are linked together by a team working at Oxford University, who coordinate the international work. Data are collected from two cohorts of children in each country (2000 children born in 2000–1 and 1000 children born in 1994–5). Methods, repeated over time, include quantitative and qualitative data collection: questionnaires and individual interviews, household, community and school surveys. A consistent message from the on-going studies is that there are wide differences in the circumstances and opportunities experienced by children; and deprivations in one area of a child's life may influence outcomes in another. The study has provided, along the way, insights into appropriate methods for collecting data (Crivello *et al.* 2009).

Morrow and Pells (2012), using some aspects of this large study, have focused on qualitative data collected with 15–16-year-olds in rural Andhra Pradesh and Ethiopia. The data point to young people's understandings of how well-being is achieved. Young people in Andhra Pradesh found that work was hard, and difficult to combine with attending school; but it was essential for them to contribute to their family's economic survival; further, they said, work teaches you valuable skills and it is fundamental to relations with others in the community. Young people in Ethiopia, whose parents had died, noted that poverty underlay many of their concerns, for again it was necessary to work, in order to help the household they lived with. Morrow and Pells argue that the common assumptions held by agencies across both minority and majority worlds that these children are orphans and vulnerable victims do not reflect children's own experiences and perspectives, for they themselves stress the importance of their inter-generational responsibilities and relationships in households, shaped by the structures and processes of poverty within which they exercise agency and live out their childhoods.

These findings feed into the authors' wider discussion of how children's rights are understood by varying commentators. They challenge a narrowly legalistic interpretation of children's rights, which, they argue, fails to engage with the roots of children's circumstances: their experience of poverty. They follow Galant and Parlevliet (2005) who propose that it is appropriate to approach rights as not only rules, but as structures, relationships and processes; that is, to study how respect for rights plays out – or not – in the circumstances of people's lives. Thus it is not appropriate (as some economists do) to think about children as human capital who through education can lift themselves out of poverty. Instead attention should be focused on how economic deprivation affects children's experiences directly, how political and economic processes structure, encourage or reduce poverty. Nieuwenhuys (2005) contributes here a critique of the World Bank's and ILO's endorsement of children's rights to a protected, scholarised childhood; she offers a more nuanced view, as do Morrow and Pells, of the intergenerational reciprocities and responsibilities observable in majority – but also in minority world – societies.

Next I consider the usefulness of Bourdieu for understanding childhood. I argue that taking account of both embodiment and time as inter-related factors helps to explain generational relations at both institutional or structural levels and at inter-personal levels (Mayall 2015). While Bourdieu's concepts identify children mainly as objects of socialisation, a number of researchers have focused on childhood as social status for considering what Bourdieu calls game-playing, where adults and children negotiate concepts of childhood and the character and quality of lived childhoods (Alanen *et al.* 2015).

Bourdieu proposes that traditions, policies and beliefs are absorbed into people's understanding of who they are (habitus) and in interactions with others they bring both habitus and capital to bear (social, cultural and economic capital) (Bourdieu 1995a: 72–7). As Bourdieu says (1986: 483), his concept of habitus has been so constructed that we do not have to choose between 'objectivist' theories (as presented, for instance, by Durkheim) and 'subjectivist' theories (for instance in ethnomethodology); ontology and epistemology are interfused in his theory.

Bourdieu's concept of field where negotiations take place (Bourdieu and Wacquant 1992: 94–115; Bourdieu 1995a) recognises that homes (for instance) are not necessarily environments where harmony in loving relationships prevails. Instead the home is where negotiations and even battles are fought out, in relation to power and about how far ascribed characteristics are accepted by the players. This is helpful for considering child-adult relational negotiations, especially about children's social status. In these negotiations, children have some advantages as compared to adults but some disadvantages. Thus children may deploy cultural capital: they may have up-to-date knowledge about current social trends (including the media), and may draw on the knowledge displayed by a network of children, who are modifying how childhoods and teenage-hoods are lived. But, as compared to adults, children are likely to lack economic capital and some important aspects of social capital – contacts with influential adults, for instance.

Fields where negotiations and struggles take place have to be understood as arenas or spaces (in time) where certain ideas hold sway (Bourdieu 1995a). Defining the borders is tricky, and depends on the extent and boundaries of the influence of these ideas; but it seems arguable that in England, homes, as well as national policies, practices and institutions (such as schools) are implicated in the education system. In England, parents are enlisted in the education system, as influences on the child from birth, as providers and as collaborators; this point has also been demonstrated for France by Garnier (2015). At local levels, not just teachers, but parents too are involved in the education of children, and children themselves are involved in negotiations about their status in inter-generational relations, in the light of their objectification as objects of adult socialisation. So we have interpenetration of home and school, with parents expected to contribute to school agendas, as well as endorse and conform to them. Of crucial importance to children in these negotiations is the status of children's embodied selves and their well-being as persons acting in this complex field.

Thus we can identify home-school education as a field in which, at policy and ideological levels, childhood is seen as a time for socialisation in the interests of state agendas, and parents are seen essentially as agents in ensuring the conformity of childhood to these state agendas. At personal levels, children are faced with the double supervision and control of adults – both parents and teachers, acting in concert; for, while 'the home' has traditionally been for children a place of relative freedom – often described by children as where they experience 'free time', that free time is now sucked into the ideological education policy arena. So children have to negotiate their embodied status at home, at school and across the two and these negotiations change over time, as children get older, and so do parents. Thus while the embodied character of the child is recognised in early child-parent negotiations and indeed is central to them, as children grow older, school agendas encourage parents to downplay their child's bodily wishes and needs, in favour of socialising their children to conform with these agendas.

These individual activities in relational processes have to be seen against the wider forces structuring childhood's relations with adulthoods: the sedimented policies and practices impacting on childhoods, both those being lived in the present and those their parents and teachers lived as children. For one feature of present-day child-adult relations in England is the contrast, which can be experienced as a clash, between the generations – that is, how each experienced childhood; thus policies and practices that led to present-day parents' experiences of childhood are likely to differ from present-day children's experiences of childhood (as discussed by Mannheim 1952). For young people nowadays, being a teenager (wanting money for fashionable clothing and social life) clashes with the state requirement for longer schooling (currently to 18), as well as with parents' own experiences of their rather different teenage years (Bourdieu 1995b). We must again acknowledge the subordination of children to adults and of childhood to adulthood; this early biological dependency is endorsed and extended as socially constructed dependency through later childhood, via the policies that exclude or discourage children from active economic agency in later childhood.

Knowledge about how to parent can be seen as having two main components: what we learn both during our own early life and during our experience of parenting. Though ideas about childcare and about parenting are handed down the generations (and consolidated through policies and childcare books), parents learn while doing the job of parenting and, crucially, they learn in negotiations with their children. This means that we have to take account of time – time during which both adults and children learn what it means to do parenthood (parenting) and what it means to do childhood ('childing'?); also what it means to negotiate – as between children and parents – the character of childhood and parenthood.

Thus, I would argue, at the intersections of institutionally endorsed ideas and interpersonal negotiations, can be interposed the idea that people acquire theoretical and experiential knowledge, along the way, and notably through those interpersonal negotiations. In the case of child-adult interactions over time, the changing embodied character of the child, the developing expertise of both child and adult, the varying societal and especially school-related demands on both children and adults provide a complex set of factors to be taken into account.

Discussion

In this chapter I have drawn attention to some developments over the last 15 years or so in sociological work on child health, viewed, especially, from the point of view of children's contributions. In the examples chosen to illustrate these developments, inter-relations between the individual and the societal, the micro and the macro, are always under consideration. In research on child health and how it is achieved, maintained and restored, I argue, first, that it is essential to take account of the point that children are best understood as a minority social group, subordinated to, but in negotiation with, adult groups, notably parents, teachers and health and welfare staff. These powerful adults rely on well-established ideas about childhood, but we may identify parents as particularly well placed to negotiate with children, since they have learned over time to take account of the embodied character of their children and have a more complex, experiential and flexible repertoire of relations with their children, than service-providers do. Second, I develop this point in more detail, through consideration of children as embodied social actors, in a range of recent research studies. Third, I widen the discussion somewhat, in order to consider how inter-generational relations take place at all levels, from the individual interaction to the shaping of children's lives by large-scale forces. Bourdieu provides a useful tool-kit of concepts: field, habitus and capital, to explore the inter-relations of macro forces with micro negotiations.

As I have briefly noted, the last few years has seen the expansion of sociological approaches to childhood in terms of both language and geography. For instance, there are now research centres and groups working in French, Spanish and Portuguese and these are linking European investigators with those in the wider world, such as the Americas. Work within the so-called majority world has also been developed. Our horizons are broadening as we are required to widen our understandings about what constitutes child well-being. In particular we must welcome the information coming from studies in the majority world, where many children's lives are structured by the need and wish to do paid work and where understandings of inter-generational relations stress responsibilities both up and down the generations. Children's sense of well-being in, for instance, Ethiopia depends on what they can contribute to family and community welfare.

The globalisation of ideas about the proper activities of childhood has focused the attention of many in majority world countries on the importance of schooling, which has led to dilemmas for parents and children about how children should use their time. In minority world societies it goes almost unchallenged that school is where children should be – and for increasing numbers of years. As regards England, during the many policy interventions into the school system in the last quarter century, there has been little political attention to the well-being of children during their childhoods. Yet it seems clear, as I have suggested, that children in both minority and majority world societies put high value on respect for them as persons actively engaging in making and remaking social relations both within and across the generations. Well-being is associated with being a valued and respected person. And, crucially, such respect must include respect for a person as embodied. The social status of childhood is in need of reconsideration; and recognition of the embodied character of children's daily lives could help us raise children's status in appropriate ways.

Note

1   The French research programme referred to here was funded by the Agence Nationale de la Recherche. A special edition of the *Revue des Sciences Sociales* (2014, number 51), edited by Nicoletta Diasio and Virginie Vinel is entitled La préadolescence existe-t-elle? and includes 13 papers by researchers on the programme, based in France and Italy.

References

Alanen, L. (2009) Generational order. In Qvortrup, J., Corsaro, W. and Honig, M.-S. (eds) *Palgrave Handbook of Childhood Studies.* London: Palgrave Macmillan.
Alanen, L., Brooker, E. and Mayall, B. (eds) (2015) *Childhood with Bourdieu.* London: Palgrave Macmillan.
Alderson, P. (2013) *Childhoods Real and Imagined: Volume 1: An Introduction to Critical Realism and Childhood Studies.* London: Routledge.
Alderson, P., Hawthorne, J. and Killen, M. (2005) The participation rights of premature babies, *International Journal of Children's Rights,* 13, 1, 31–50.
André, G. and Hilgers, M. (2015) Childhood in Africa between local powers and global hierarchies. In Alanen, L., Brooker, E., and Mayall, B. (eds) *Childhood with Bourdieu.* London: Palgrave Macmillan.
Bendelow, G. (2009) *Health, Emotion and the Body.* London: Polity Press.
Bendelow, G. and Mayall, B. (2000) How children manage emotion in schools. In Fineman, S. (ed) *Emotions in Organizations.* London: Sage.
Bendelow, G. and Williams, S. (eds) (1998) *Emotions in Social Life.* London: Routledge.

Beunardeau, P. (2013) La violence physique dans la construction des rapports d'âge et de genre: Ethno-graphie scolaire en milieu populaire. Paper presented at conference : Sortir de l'enfance, entrer dans l'adolescence, Strasbourg, September 2013.

Blishen, E. (1969) *The School that I'd Like*. Harmondsworth: Penguin.

Bluebond-Langner, M. (1978) *The Private Worlds of Dying Children*. Princeton, NJ: Princeton University Press.

Bourdieu, P. (1986) *Distinction*. London: Routledge and Kegan Paul.

Bourdieu, P. (1995a) Some properties of fields. In Bourdieu, P. (ed) *Sociology in Question*. London: Sage.

Bourdieu, P. (1995b) 'Youth' is just a word. In Bourdieu, P. (ed) *Sociology in Question*. London: Sage.

Bourdieu, P. and Wacquant, L. (1992) *Invitation to Reflexive Sociology*. Cambridge: Polity Press.

Burke, K. and Grosvenor, I. (2003) *The School I'd Like*. London: RoutledgeFalmer.

Colley, H. (2003) *Mentoring for Social Inclusion*. London: RoutledgeFalmer.

Crivello, G., Camfield, L. and Woodhead, M. (2009) How can children tell us about their wellbeing? Exploring the potential of participatory research approaches within Young Lives, *Social Indicators Research*, 90, 1, 51–72.

Davison, C. (2014) Relational approaches to childhood and its status: Intergenerational exploration through theory, method and practice. MA dissertation, Institute of Education, University of London.

Favretto, A.R. and Zaltron, F. (2013) *Mamma, Non Mi Sento Tanto Bene: La salute et la malattia nei saperi e nelle pratiche infantili*. Rome: Donzelli Editore.

Fraser, N. and Honneth, A. (2003) *Redistribution or Recognition? A Political-philosophical Exchange*. London: Verso.

Galant, G. and Parlevliet, M. (2005) Using rights to address conflict: A valuable synergy. In Gready, P. and Ensor, J. (eds) *Reinventing Development: Translating Rights-based Approaches from Theory into Practice*. London: Zed Books.

Garnier, P. (2015) Between young children and adults: Practical logic in families' lives. In Alanen, L., Brooker, E., and Mayall, B. (eds) *Childhood with Bourdieu*. London: Palgrave Macmillan.

Greene, S. (1999) Child development: Old themes, new directions. In Woodhead, M., Faulkner, D., and Littleton, K. (eds) *Making Sense of Social Development*. London: Routledge.

Hallett, C., Murray, C. and Punch, S. (2003) Young people and welfare: negotiating pathways. In Hallett, C. and Prout, A. (eds) *Hearing the Voices of Children: Social Policy for a New Century*. London: RoutledgeFalmer.

Henderson, S., Holland, J., McGrellis, S., Sharpe, S. and Thomson, R. (2007) *Inventing Adulthoods: A Biographical Approach to Youth Transitions*. London: Sage.

Hochschild, A. (1979) Emotion work, feeling rules and social structure, *American Journal of Sociology*, 85, 3, 551–75.

Hochschild, A. (1983) *The Managed Heart: The Commercialisation of Human Feeling*. Berkeley CA: University of California Press.

James, A. and James, A.L. (2004) *Constructing Childhood: Theory, Policy and Social Practice*. London: Palgrave Macmillan.

Jones, L., Holmes, R., MacRae, C. and Maclure, M. (2010) 'Improper' children. In Yelland, N. (ed) *Contemporary Perspectives on Early Childhood Education*. Maidenhead: Open University Press.

Julien, M.-P. (2013) Choisir ses vêtements et ouvrir la boîte noire des habitus. Paper presented at conference : Sortir de l'enfance, entrer dans l'adolescence. Strasbourg, September 2013.

Knight, A. (2013) Young people travelling to school: social lives and local possibilities; constraints or opportunities? PhD thesis. Institute of Education, University of London.

Lansdown, G. (1994) Children's rights. In Mayall, B. (ed) *Children's Childhoods: Observed and Experienced*. London: Falmer Press.

Lemert, C. (2012) *Social Things: An Introduction to the Sociological Life*. 5th edition. Lanham, MD: Rowman and Littlefield.

Mannheim, K. (1952) The problem of generations. In Mannheim, K. (ed) *Essays on the Sociology of Knowledge*. First published 1928. London: Routledge and Kegan Paul.

Martin, E. (1987) *The Woman in the Body*. Buckingham: Open University Press.

Mayall, B. (1994) *Negotiating Health: Children at Home and Primary School*. London: Cassell.

Mayall, B. (1996) *Children, Health and the Social Order*. Buckingham: Open University Press.

Mayall, B. (1998) Towards a sociology of child health, *Sociology of Health and Illness*, 20, 3, 269–88.

Mayall, B. (2002) *Towards a Sociology for Childhood*. Buckingham: Open University Press.

Mayall, B. (2009) Generational relations at family level. In Qvortrup, J., Corsaro, W., and Honig, M.-S. (eds) *Palgrave Handbook of Childhood Studies*. London: Palgrave Macmillan.

Mayall, B. (2015) Intergenerational relations: Embodiment over time. In Alanen, L., Brooker, E., and Mayall, B. (eds) *Childhood with Bourdieu*. London: Palgrave Macmillan.

Mayall, B., Bendelow, G., Barker, S., Storey, P. and Veltman, M. (1996) *Children's Health in Primary Schools*. London: Falmer Press.

Mizen, P., Pole, C. and Bolton, A. (eds) (2001) *Hidden Hands: International Perspectives on Children's Work*. London: RoutledgeFalmer.

Morrow, V. (2001) Young people's explanations and experiences of social exclusion: retrieving Bourdieu's concept of social capital, *International journal of Sociology and Social Policy*, 21, 4–6, 37–63.

Morrow, V. and Pells, K. (2012) Integrating children's human rights and child poverty debates: examples from *Young Lives* in Ethiopia and India, *Sociology* 46, 5, 906–20.

Morrow, V. and Vennam, U. (2015) 'Those who are good to us, we call them friends': Social support and social networks for children growing up in poverty in rural Andhra Pradesh, India. In Alanen, L., Brooker, E., and Mayall, B. (eds) *Childhood with Bourdieu*. London: Palgrave Macmillan.

Mullender, A., Hague, G., Imam, U.F., Kelly, L., Malos, E. and Regan, L. (2003) 'Could have helped but they didn't': the formal and informal support systems experienced by children living with domestic violence. In Hallett, C. and Prout, A. (eds) *Hearing the Voices of Children: Social policy for a new century*. London: RoutledgeFalmer.

Newson, J. and Newson, E. (1970) *Four Years Old in an Urban Community*. Harmondsworth: Penguin.

Nieuwenhuys, O. (2005) The wealth of children. In Qvortup, J. (ed) *Studies in Modern Childhood: Society, Agency, Culture*. London: Palgrave Macmillan.

Panelli, R., Punch, S. and Robson, E. (2007) From difference to dialogue: conceptualising global perspectives on rural childhood and youth. In Panelli, R., Punch, S., and Robson, E (eds) *Global Perspectives on Rural Childhood and Youth: Young rural lives*. London: Routledge.

Penn, H. (2011) *Quality in Early Childhood Services*. Maidenhead: Open University Press.

Prendergast, S. (2000) 'To become dizzy in our turning': girls, body maps and gender as childhood ends. In Prout, A. (ed) *The Body, Childhood and Society*. London: Palgrave Macmillan.

Prendergast, S. and Forrest, S. (1998) 'Shorties, low-lifers, hardnuts and kings': boys, emotions and embodiment in school. In Bendelow, G. and Williams, S. J. (eds) *Emotions in Social Life: Critical Themes and Contemporary Issues*. London: Routledge.

Prout, A. (ed) (2000) *The Body, Childhood and Society*. London: Palgrave Macmillan.

Qvortrup, J. (1985) Placing children in the division of labour. In Close, P. and Collins, R. (eds) *Family and Economy in Modern Society*. London: Macmillan.

Qvortrup, J. (1994) Childhood matters: an introduction. In Qvortrup, J., Bardy, M., Sgritta, G. and Wintersberger, H. (eds) *Childhood Matters: Social Theory, Practice and Politics*. Aldershot: Avebury.

Qvortrup, J. (2009) Childhood as a structural form. In Qvortrup, J., Corsaro, W. and Honig, M.-S. (eds) *The Palgrave Handbook of Childhood Studies*. London: Palgrave Macmillan.

Shamgar-Handelman, L. (1994) To whom does childhood belong? In Qvortrup, J., Bardy, M., Sgritta, G. and Wintersberger, H. (eds) *Childhood Matters: Social Theory, Practice and Politics*. Aldershot: Avebury.

Shilling, C. (1997) The undersocialised conception of the embodied agent in modern sociology, *Sociology*, 31, 4, 737–54.

Shilling, C. (2005) Introduction. In Shilling, C. (ed) *The Body in Culture, Technology and Society*. London: Sage.

Singal, N. and Muthukrishna, N. (2014) Introduction: education, childhood and disability in countries of the South – re-positioning the debates, *Childhood*, 21, 3, 293–307.

Stacey, M. (1988) *The Sociology of Health and Healing*. London: Routledge.

Tersigni, S. (2013) Grandir au prisme de l'ethnicisation. Une comparaison sur la sortie de l'enfance entre 'descendant-e-s de migrant-e-s' d'Alsace, Lorraine et Vénétie. Paper presented at conference : Sortir de l'enfance, entrer dans l'adolescence, Strasbourg September 2013.

Thomas, N. (2012) Love, rights and solidarity: Studying children's participation using Honneth's theory of recognition, *Childhood*, 19, 4, 453–66.

Weale, S. (2014) Major study of teenage sleep patterns aims to assess impact on learning. *The Guardian*, 9 October.

Winter, K. (2015) Decision-making processes in review meetings for children in care: A bourdieusian analysis. In Alanen, L., Brooker, E. and Mayall, B. (eds) *Childhood with Bourdieu*. London: Palgrave Macmillan.

Wright Mills, C. (1959) *The Sociological Imagination*. Oxford: Oxford University Press.

Index

Children, Health and Well-being: Policy Debates and Lived Experience, First Edition. Edited by Geraldine Brady, Pam Lowe and Sonja Olin Lauritzen. Chapters © 2015 The Authors. Book Compilation © 2015 Foundation for the Sociology of Health & Illness/Blackwell Publishing Ltd.